Rick's Café

Rick's Café

Bringing the Film Legend to Life in Casablanca

KATHY KRIGER

LYONS PRESS

Guilford, Connecticut

An imprint of Globe Pequot Press

Lyons Press is an imprint of Globe Pequot Press.

Project editor: Meredith Dias
Text design: Sheryl P. Kober
Layout: Melissa Evarts

Library of Congress Cataloging-in-Publication Data

Kriger, Kathy.
Rick's Cafe : bringing the legend to life in Casablanca / Kathy Kriger.
p. cm.
ISBN 978-0-7627-7289-6
1. Rick's Cafe (Casablanca, Morocco) 2. Nightclubs—Morocco—Casablanca.
3. Casablanca (Morocco)—Social life and customs—21st century. 4. Kriger, Kathy.
5. Businesswomen—Morocco—Casablanca—Biography. I. Title.
PN1968.M67K75 2012
792.70964'38—dc23

2012027900

Printed in the United States of America

10 9 8 7 6 5 4 3 2 1

To Kyle—for allowing your mother to grow up at her own pace

and to Charles, Thomas, and Sami—may the legend continue.

Only the tent pitched by your own hands will stand.
—ARAB PROVERB

Contents

ACT I: BRINGING THE LEGEND TO LIFE

ACT II: THE LEGEND CONTINUES

Starring

KATHY KRIGER
ISSAM CHABÂA
DRISS BENHIMA
BILL WILLIS

Yasmina Baddou
Aicha Ghattas
Hakim Benjelloun
The Usual Suspects
Houssein
Chef Rachid
Abdallah Ghattas

with
Kyle Ewing and Sarah Aberg
Mehdi El Attar
Pacha

EXECUTIVE PRODUCER
Kathy Kriger

DIRECTOR
Issam Chabâa

PROLOGUE

Setting the Scene

Full of action and intrigue, *Casablanca* opens as the camera scans roof-tops, a clock tower, a mosque, and finally settles on the frenzied activity in the traditional Arab quarter, the Ancienne Medina.

The police, alerted to the murder of a German courier and the theft of letters of transit that he was carrying, are rounding up the usual suspects. As the bus unloads the shady characters at the Palais de Justice, an English couple observes the action from a lattice-trimmed sidewalk café, drawn into conversation by a man who explains the scene across the street. The man drapes his arm around the Englishman's shoulder and alerts the couple to thieves and pick-pockets working the area. Mere seconds after the man dashes off, the Englishman discovers his wallet missing.

The scene quickly shifts. A landing plane passes over a sign that reads RICK'S CAFÉ AMÉRICAIN. At the airport, local officials, including Captain Renault, the préfet of police, meet Major Heinrich Strasser of the German Reich. They discuss the murder of the courier, and Renault assures the German that his men have collared twice the number of suspects as a precaution—even though they already know the identity of the murderer. Renault plans a public arrest at Rick's Café, the gathering place for everyone in Casablanca.

Another scene change. The camera again pans over the sign and down to the elaborate carved front doors of Rick's Café. Faint sounds of music and laughter drift from inside. The doors open to another world. A piano player is singing, voices hum, and glasses clatter. Arches divide the space, and hanging lamps and stenciled lanterns cast dramatic shadows on white walls. Inlaid wooden screens and clusters of palms give tables privacy as customers plot their strategies for escaping Casablanca. A door opens to a gaming room where a tuxedo-clad croupier presides over the roulette table and a cosmopolitan crowd of Europeans and Arabs dressed in their elegant evening finery.

The scene perfectly represents Casablanca in the 1940s—except the place never really existed. Workmen had constructed the iconic gin joint on a set on the back lot of Warner Bros. Studios.

"Bonjour, Madame Rick," said two older men, nodding as they passed me on the street, and I had to smile.

Over the three years of watching the film and trying to make a "real" Rick's Café in Casablanca that went beyond what appeared onscreen, a bond had formed between me and the tough saloonkeeper with a soft heart, Monsieur Rick. Somehow his spirit hovered over me as I navigated a maze of roadblocks and challenges. If I'm honest, I always thought that I'd find a man while following my dream. Instead, with Rick looking over my shoulder, I found myself. The simple yet courtly bow and greeting, *"Bonjour* Madame Rick," made me realize that I'd stepped into a role that I'd been waiting to play all my life—but not on a movie set.

After March 1, 2004, Rick's Café finally existed.

ACT I

Bringing the Legend to Life

ONE

Ancienne Medina

I was sitting in my office at the US Consulate in Casablanca, eight years after I had entered the Foreign Service as a commercial attaché. "I don't know anyone less suited to government work than you," a friend said at the time, but it was a deliberate choice in order to provide for my son, Kyle, then thirteen years old.

My assignment was to help American exporters and companies bidding on public sector infrastructure projects, and—during an earlier posting in Prague and now in Morocco—it had become evident that my friend was right. My entrepreneurial talents languished, my passion unencouraged and underappreciated by the bureaucrats in Washington. Decisions were made always "for the good of the Service," and "follow orders" became a mantra. But I was at my best when there were no orders, challenged to find my own solutions. Yet I was on the verge of accepting a third posting, more out of inertia than interest.

An unexpected visit from an engineer at the National Water Office in Rabat interrupted my crisis of conscience and the memo I was writing for a US-Africa Business Summit scheduled in Philadelphia at month's end. Even though my portfolio covered commercial matters, people often asked me to put in a good word for someone trying to get a visa. Some things never change in Casablanca.

The man—mid-fifties, graying hair, dressed simply in slacks and sports coat—shyly expressed his embarrassment about bothering me. But concern for his son, who had flown for the Moroccan military and was a finalist to be hired for a Moroccan domestic carrier, overcame

3

his reticence. He needed only to get his commercial pilot's license. A flight training school in Florida had accepted the young man, and all his credentials were in order—except his visa application had been rejected. While my visitor waited, I called the Consular Section for a fuller explanation.

"The rejection came in with no details," the officer told me. "We suggest he reapply in six months."

Strange. Morocco and America had, and still have, excellent bilateral cooperation in both military and civil aviation sectors, and the young man had a job waiting for him, which meant there was no doubt that he would return to Morocco at the end of his training. I didn't let on that I was puzzled. It was difficult enough to convey the response. Shoulders bent and clearly dejected, the man thanked me for my efforts on his behalf as I walked him outside.

Back at my desk, the phone rang—another interruption.

I may never finish this memo, I thought.

"Turn on your TV," said Magda, the press officer in Rabat.

It was September 11, 2001—and the world changed forever.

As the terrible events of the appalling tragedy unfolded, I thought about the engineer from the water utility on his lonely drive back to Rabat. He, too, would be hearing the news now. A small detail in the larger picture, it was still sad to think that his son would never get his visa.

I experienced the aftermath of that day through the eyes of an expatriate American living in an Arab country. The atmosphere in Casablanca and indeed in all of Morocco subtly changed. Even the ambience of Marrakech, long a haven for foreign tourists, shifted. The Friday after 9/11, I took the train to my weekend home in the Marrakech Medina. The Place Jamaa el Fna, outside the souk, usually a crowded scene of food stalls, acrobats, snake charmers, storytellers, and dancing transvestites had grown surprisingly quiet. I got out of the taxi at 11:30 p.m. and began the ten-minute walk through the souk to my house as I had done almost every Friday night for the last two years, kids on the street describing me as "the American lady who comes only on the weekends and who carries her purse like this," mimicking me hugging it tightly to my side.

But no sooner had the taxi door closed than the old man who sold religious books from a little stall came running at me, djellaba flying. Rage contorted his wizened face as he screamed at me in Arabic. Even without knowing the language, I got the message—and, shocked, quickened my pace. But then the group of men who always hung around the little convenience kiosk on the corner protectively surrounded me. They were a motley lot. A birthmark covered half the face of one large man in a djellaba. Another, smaller man had slick hair and wore tight jeans. Without any hesitation, they escorted me through the dark, tunnel-like passageways all the way to my door and refused to accept the tip I gratefully offered.

Slipping into my house that night, I mused on the kindness of the men who walked me home. Anyone who didn't know Morocco as well as I did would no doubt focus on the screaming bookseller as proof of the country's religious fundamentalism—a false characterization.

Morocco is a moderate Muslim country, situated at the tip of North Africa, only nine miles from Spain across the Strait of Gibraltar. It is not only hospitable but tolerant, qualities no doubt engendered by its multicultural history. In describing his country, the late King Hassan II once said, "Morocco seems like a tree whose nourishing roots reach deep into African soil and whose leaves breathe in the wind blowing from Europe." In addition to Berber, Portuguese, and Spanish influences, Morocco was a French protectorate for forty-four years, and French is still the lingua franca of business.

Marrakech Dinner Alfresco under the Stars

Preparation time: 30 minutes
Serves many

Entering my lovely Marrakech *riad* late on Friday nights was like stepping into another world. I shook off all the worries of the week and reveled in the ambience. I used this recipe, or a variation of it, for a solitary late-night snack or when friends came for predinner drinks on the terrace. More than once my guests and I canceled our dinner reservations at some nearby restaurant as we enjoyed a simple feast looking over the rooftops of the Marrakech Medina.

1 lovely restored riad with central courtyard open to the sky

1 orange tree, perpetually in bloom, perfuming the air

1 fountain providing calming background music

10 candlelit lanterns, complementing natural moonlight

1 cushioned alcove, with painted wood ceiling, set into the courtyard

1 rooftop terrace with sweeping views of the Medina and the Atlas Mountains

Maria Callas arias to taste

With the above ingredients, you could eat anything and feel that you were having a sumptuous feast. Usually I had a light snack of provisions from the Jamaa el Fna and the souk: rotisserie chicken, nicely brined and roasted, from a stall near the Jamaa el Fna; sliced tomatoes with olive oil/balsamic vinaigrette (three to one ratio, salt and pepper to taste); mixed peanuts and almonds; *harissa*-spiced red, green, and tan olives, all from the neighborhood; dates stuffed with cumin-spiced Gouda cheese; dried figs stuffed with prosciutto; a glass of Ksar Bahia Syrah.

Note: Even a tin of Moroccan sardines tastes fantastic in this dramatic setting.

A traveler's smorgasbord, Morocco has deserts, mountains, and coastlines along the Mediterranean and the Atlantic. Colors range from the paprika sands of the Sahara and the blinding blue of a Casablanca sky to the mint green of rooftops in Fes to the ocher-colored walls of Marrakech. Heaps of spices spilling from burlap bags in souks perfectly represent the country itself: lush, fragrant, colorful, diverse.

With five million residents, Casablanca is Morocco's largest city. When the French established the Protectorate in 1912, Casablanca was designated the economic hub of the country and the region. Like any big city, it has some rough edges—noise, pollution, poverty. Traffic is frightening whether you are a driver or a pedestrian. Shanty towns called *bidonvilles* exist in the middle of upscale districts, and the urban sprawl of housing tracts lines the motorways.

As the commercial center, Casablanca has for decades absorbed masses of rural poor who flee the countryside, leaving their families to find work. In the city, they lead solitary, impersonal lives and easily fall prey to employers who exploit their naiveté and country ways. The absence of family structure and discipline; an overwhelming, competitive, and corrupt urban environment; and the difficulties of finding work take their toll on these struggling youths. Resentment inevitably builds and often flashes after soccer matches, when rampaging gangs of young men tip over garbage cans, hurl stones at buses, and generally wreak havoc, regardless of whether their team has won or lost.

Shadowy elements, promising them the glories of paradise in the hereafter, even entice some of these lost souls into sacrificing their lives.

Nevertheless, Casablanca leaves a lasting impression on anyone curious and adventuresome enough to explore. The city's charms, however secret and subtle, remain. At sidewalk cafés, time stands still as men smoke and chat over a glass of dark coffee in a ritual that hasn't changed in over a century. But a growing young middle class is striking out in new directions. Women may dress as they wish, with Western fashion often prevailing. Though they must work harder and break through barriers of chauvinism, women have seized opportunities in business and politics. My women friends in Casablanca include a lawyer who ran successfully for public office and became a government minister, a pilot for Royal Air Maroc, and the president of a firm producing and distributing natural mineral water.

The idea of creating Rick's Café in Casablanca had crossed my mind before, but the events of September 11 clarified my thinking and gave me the impetus I needed. Watching *Casablanca* again on September 12, I realized once more that we live in a crazy world. A fear gripped me that Americans—frightened and unsure of the future like the refugees in the celluloid café—would fall back on intolerance and xenophobia and that an anti-Arab backlash would engulf my beloved city.

Continuing to serve as a commercial attaché wouldn't do much to change that, I realized as the credits rolled, but opening a Rick's Café might remind Americans of the values we exhibited during World War II: sacrifice for the greater good, sympathy for the underdog, the willingness to take a stand. Americans would clearly see something unique about Morocco if an American woman on her own could create the iconic gin joint in today's Casablanca.

A fantasy now became an obsession. Within a week I had decided to resign from the Foreign Service. Creating a "real" Rick's had become a case of do or die.

When it struck me to stay in Casablanca and create Rick's Café, Driss Benhima was the first person I went to see. We had developed a special relationship both as friends and colleagues.

Within days of my arrival in Morocco, we met at a welcome reception held at a beautiful villa in the hills of Casablanca. At that time, he served as chief executive officer of Morocco's Office National de l'Électricité (ONE), and his energy and opinionated point of view drew me to him. The per-

Driss Benhima, one of my leading men, encouraged me to find a place for Rick's in the Ancienne Medina.

sonification of a man comfortable with authority, Driss has a sensitive side and a perceptive sense of humor often masked by his abrupt and intense managerial persona. He is also tall and handsome with gray hair and a ready smile.

Close to King Hassan II, Driss's father served as minister of the interior, minister of agriculture, and prime minister. At that time, the 1960s, the king chose all his ministers and consolidated power among his closest confidants. In 1997, he put technocrats in charge of the government prior to the first election of representatives to take place the following year. Then it was Driss's turn to lead three ministries— tourism, energy and mines, and transportation—while retaining the directorship of ONE.

When a commercial project derailed, Driss often knew the behind-the-scenes reasons. He taught me a lot about how business is done—and not done—in Morocco. More often than not, family rivalries or jealousy play a bigger role in the failure of projects than a lack of merit. I realized I was catching on to the subtleties of Moroccan business when I found myself nodding in comprehension as he explained why a major American company was being excluded from a big tourism development.

"The problem is with one of the companies in their consortium," Driss said. "The wife of the CEO is a first cousin to someone who is on the outs with the palace. The palace didn't interfere, but the Ministry is afraid to offend anyone."

The palace has business interests including banking, mining, and agriculture, as well as stakes in a major holding company. Political and economic pressure from European and Arab countries historically weighed on the upper echelons of the monarchy. Reforms initiated by King Hassan II in the early '90s—partly attributable to the state of emergency in neighboring Algeria*—brought incremental improvements in education, civil society, government, and economic development. The king's initiatives culminated in the first real democratically elected government in March 1998. Even though the king continued to name key ministers and kept his trusted allies close, the new government focused on economic reform and development, emphasizing transparency in procurement, with projects judged on their merits and the best commercial bid.

---

* Algeria plunged into a decade of turmoil when the government canceled runoff elections in January 1992, knowing extreme Islamists would win. A military-led government crackdown ensued against hard-line Islamists, nationalist Berbers, and all forms of dissent.

"You'll be half-happy," said the director of the National Telecom Agency to Edward Gabriel, the American ambassador, on July 3, 1999, when he said the winner of the Second Mobile Phone License would be announced the next morning in Rabat. Very high profile, the tender, even before the announcement, was garnering international attention. The ambassador kept pressing the importance of the process appearing transparent, as much as he might have wished for an American company to win.

My colleague from the Economic Section, Richard Johnson, and I, plus our counterparts from the French Embassy, were the only diplomatic representatives present. We felt optimistic for Motorola, on the France Telecom team, but our optimism lived a short life when the National Telecom Agency announced the winner as the Spanish-Portuguese bid led by Telefónica. True, it pleased us that the process had been open and transparent, but that didn't exactly make us "half-happy." We spent a good part of July Fourth nursing our wounds.

The announcement of the renewal contract for Royal Air Maroc's fleet—with bids from French Airbus and American Boeing—crowned a process lasting more than two years that had mobilized not just me and the economic counselor but the ambassador and the entire Embassy Country Team. King Hassan II had a soft spot in his heart for Boeing, it was believed, because he was forever grateful for the skillful maneuvering of the pilot of the Royal B-727 during the failed coup attempt in 1972. But Hassan II had died in July 1999. We focused our lobbying efforts on the government, carefully avoiding any perceived attempt to draw King Mohammed VI into the process. The palace kept its distance, but the French exerted pressure on all fronts. Royal Air Maroc judged the two bids on their commercial merits and announced their decision in the spring of 2001 to award the contract to Boeing. This time we were totally happy.

Driss shared my appreciation for Casablanca and dismay at what seemed a lack of bureaucratic will to solve the city's problems. A realist, he accepted that a bloated municipal government kept in that state by pervasive corruption offered a seemingly insurmountable obstacle. Although he clearly despised these practices, he knew that the system by its very nature resisted change.

Drinking espresso in his well-appointed office at ONE in the late spring of 2001, having one of our wide-ranging conversations about the city's plight, I suddenly blurted out, "Driss, you have so many good ideas. Why don't you run for mayor of Casablanca? It would be great for the city."

"That will never be possible," he responded, gesturing with his cigar. "I don't belong to a political party and wouldn't want to join one."

He was admitting that he couldn't be effective in the collegial yet shortsighted and risk-averse political arena. A city council governs Casablanca, made up of politically elected representatives from various parties. To designate a mayor when no clear majority emerges—which is invariably the case due to the number of parties and distribution of the vote—the parties negotiate and trade anticipated favor for favor so that the mayor arrives at his post already overwhelmed with enough IOUs to ensure highly limited progress. Casablanca exists, even today, in a constant state of gridlock, both literally and figuratively. The bold action plan so urgently needed could never survive negotiation among the eight prefectures and sixteen communes or *arrondissements*—administrative districts, as in Paris—to reach workable consensus.

Then, three months after that discussion, Mohammed VI announced his decision to reorient local government. He installed new regional governors, or *walis,** outside the structure of the Ministry of Interior in order to give them autonomy. The king named Driss Benhima the wali of Casablanca. I immediately called to offer my congratulations.

"I just said to my deputy, 'Perhaps Kathy got me nominated!'" he joked.

To say the jest flattered me would be an understatement. I thought back to our conversations over the last three years about what he thought he could do if . . . Now his chance had appeared, and I felt like part of his inner circle. I set to work on an agenda memo, derived from our past conversations, and delivered it to him when he was cleaning out his office at ONE. It included developing the Corniche, a waterfront commercial strip, for tourism; traffic control and mass-transit planning; and, most urgent of all, tackling Casablanca's garbage problem—specifically the city's open landfill populated by scavengers who lived in huts atop the waste and combed through the garbage in the company of goats.

"You're the first person who has brought me ideas of what to do for the city, rather than wanting to line your pockets," he said, excited about his nomination and touched by my enthusiasm.

Driss had been wali for just two months when I walked into his office in the Wilaya (City Hall) in late September to tell him my decision. Outwardly calm and breathing deeply to keep my emotions in check, I was shaking inside. Much was at stake, and Driss's response wouldn't be subtle. Either he would totally support it or completely oppose it. While I was passionate about my idea and knew in my heart that it was the right move, it wasn't a conventional project by any

---

* Arabic for custodian or protector, referring to someone who has walayah, which means authority or guardianship over somebody else.

means, and I was starting from absolute scratch. His approval would not only affirm our friendship but it would also give me a sense of security. If favorable to the idea, he would express his feelings in a way to remove any doubts that I might have about plunging into such uncharted waters.

"Where do you want to put your restaurant?" he asked, his reaction at once positive and enthusiastic.

I thought that upgrading and redeveloping the Corniche—the anarchic strip that runs along the Atlantic coast—would be a priority and offered that view. He scoffed, knowing the Corniche was too mired in corrupt land deals to offer good prospects.

"You're going to put your restaurant in the Ancienne Medina," he said. "It will bring other investors, and we'll have more of a chance to clean the place up."

"I've never been in the Medina," I admitted.

My visit a year earlier, when a friend from Washington, DC, insisted that I come with him to look for a leather aviator jacket, didn't count. A good number of sleazy people and street hawkers filled the new outer area across the street from the Hyatt Hotel. The shops sold counterfeit handbags, watches, CDs, and those aviator jackets. Surely not the Medina.

Driss cut short my arguments. "No, no, no. You just haven't seen the interesting part, the original, interior section overlooking the Atlantic."

I gulped but trusted Driss. When he called a few weeks later inviting me to meet him and his chief of staff, Driss Slaoui, on Sunday morning for a walk in the Medina, I jumped at the chance. A well-connected figure in Casablanca's bureaucracy, Slaoui had grown up in the Ancienne Medina. His parents still lived there. He had watched his childhood neighborhood decline, the old families dying off or moving out, replaced by the influx from the countryside. He, too, wanted to revive the area and had asked his parents about houses for sale.

On November 18, 2001, the first day of Ramadan that year, Driss Benhima and Driss Slaoui were waiting for me at the clock tower adjacent to the main arcade entrance to the Medina—not unlike the minaret pictured in the opening scenes of the film, looming above a frenzied street scene of merchants, trained monkeys, jugglers, parrots, and shifty-looking characters. Today's clock tower overlooks a twenty-first-century version of money changers, contraband, cheap souvenirs, and similar shifty-looking characters. The only visible animals, the ubiquitous scrawny street cats, prowled the area as usual.

Like the film's minaret, the clock tower of Casablanca looks out on a frenzied scene of shady activities and shifty characters in today's medina.

Originally called Anfa, meaning "hill," Berbers settled Casablanca in the seventh century BC, trading first with Phoenicians and Carthaginians and later the Portuguese and Spanish. When it became a safe haven for Barbary pirates pillaging European ships in the fifteenth century, the Portuguese retaliated by destroying the city, building a military fortress on its ruins some decades later. The new settlement that grew up around the fortress became known as Casa Branca, Portuguese for "white house." The Great Lisbon Earthquake of 1755—its epicenter lying equidistant between the two cities—destroyed Casablanca a second time. Sultan Mohammed ben Abdellah—in 1777 the first foreign ruler to recognize the independence of America—rebuilt the city again.

Joining the Berber tribes inhabiting the Medina came tradesmen and craftsmen from Fes and Marrakech in the early 1800s, and decades later, European traders: Portuguese, Spanish, French, and English. The town that Sultan Ben Abdellah had named Dar el Beida—Arabic for "white house"—formally adopted the Spanish rendering, Casablanca, during this era. While some French stubbornly referred to their town as Maison Blanche, it didn't stick, and they lost this round.

When the French expanded the harbor into a working port in 1907, the Ancienne Medina became the center of all of Casablanca's commercial activities. It was the first area settled by the French when they established the Protectorate in 1912. Town planning began, and new districts sprang up, including an area near the Sultan's Palace that came to be called the New Medina.* It became the center for the souk, the main market, drawing merchants and residents away from the old city.

---

* From its founding in 1666, the Alaouite Dynasty was headed by a sultan. After independence in 1956, Sultan Mohammed V, the father of Hassan II, became King Mohammed V.

Over the years, the grand mansions previously inhabited by the bourgeoisie had lapsed into a state of extreme disrepair, and with the passage of time they had become packed with tenants. The Jewish *mellah* on the south side—a lively quarter with commercial and residential areas flourishing around synagogues and schools—shrunk in size beginning in 1949 with Jewish emigration to Israel, Europe, and America. Today it has disappeared almost completely except for a few shops that still sell gold jewelry.

During the years of the Protectorate, the Medina, a rough and tumble area, teemed with rowdy cafés and bars, plus a quarter notorious for licensed prostitution. Cabarets of international renown, like the Coq d'Or (Golden Rooster) where entertainers such as Josephine Baker performed, interspersed themselves among tawdrier establishments.

After independence, the Medina remained a shady, dangerous place, drawing its inhabitants mainly from the port, but it also became home to growing numbers of transients, destitute widows and divorcées, and families overcome by poverty, bereft of hope. Today's Medina, despite its historic and cultural significance, microcosmically reflects the economic and social suffering of the sprawling Casablanca metropolis.

I'd often driven along the Boulevard des Almohades, the avenue that separates the Medina from the Atlantic. From a distance, the white houses and domes sprouted like mushrooms over the clay Medina walls, but this was the first time I'd actually stepped inside the gates. The urban decay only partly caused the shadiness of its atmosphere. Its dark, narrow, mazelike streets hid drug trafficking, prostitution, petty crime, and the illegal sale of today's version of letters of transit: clandestine passage inside a truck or ship bound for Europe. I didn't need letters of transit, but I, too, was looking for a new beginning.

Driss Benhima, of course, had his own agenda. Always ready to throw himself into any project that could improve the lives of Casablanca's people, he understood that tourism could catalyze economic and social development, and restoring the Ancienne Medina made both for a great strategic and a great symbolic place to start. Certainly the Old City had never received much attention from previous walis, who wouldn't have walked the streets without local officials clearing the way first and then accompanying them. Driss preferred surprise and improvisation.

Curiosity about the old Arab quarter filled me, and secretly I was happy to have this time with Driss, to witness his personal interest in me and in my project.* Driss always moved fast. Someone once said that when he walked through a crowd, it looked as if his clothes were falling off. Today was no exception. He took off—coattails flying—while his chief of staff and I struggled to keep up. There weren't many shops in this inner section, and the cafés were closed because of Ramadan, but the area wasn't exactly deserted. Kids dressed in sweatshirts, jeans, and sneakers stopped their impromptu game of soccer to watch us.

Word quickly spread: *The wali is in the Medina!* People with something to hide scattered; those who saw hope in his accessibility followed us and vied for his attention. Others peeked from windows as he sped past. He chased panhandling street urchins and other unsavory characters hanging around with too much idle time on their hands while giving notes to Driss Slaoui on what needed fixing or improvement.

—————

* I confess that, mixed in with my respect for him, was a small fantasy of romance, although I kept those feelings to myself. Life had taught me that the fantasy usually was more enjoyable than the reality.

We approached the Place Sidi Bousmara with its clustered palms and fabled fig tree, planted by the saint who gave his name to the square.* Legend has it that immigrants from other towns in Morocco hammered nails into the tree as a way to connect to the roots of their new home. You can still see the nails today. Since I was also considering tying my future to Casablanca, I made a mental note to return another day, maybe during construction when I was more confident, sneaking a hammer and nail from the building site to join others who'd cast their lot with the city.

Unwashed, unkempt juveniles with runny noses lurked in the corners of the plaza. Seeing them gave me the shivers. Driss mentioned that it was here that he'd heard of attempts to sell children, perhaps kidnapped or bought from families too poor to raise them. Charming, fabled fig tree aside, my memory of Sidi Bousmara that day shows a sinister, shadowy place—despite the sunshine.

As we continued our walk, the buildings with their arches, verandas, latticework, and domed roofs started to win me over. We came to a picturesque square, bordered on one side by the rundown Hotel Central and on the other by the Bab-al-Marsa, "Gate to the Port," built in the 1700s, the only remaining Portuguese stone-arched entrance to the Medina, which Sultan Mohammed ben Abdellah restored in the eighteenth century.

A sign on a distinctive building in the Place Belgique identified it as the former German Consulate. Further along, we came to a shoddy-looking game parlor framed by picturesque latticework arches that brought to mind the film's pickpocket scene in the outdoor café. My mind was already racing with impressions and ideas.

---

* Sidi is an Arabic honorific for a man, similar to "sir."

Down the street from the game parlor lay the neighborhood mosque, the Jamaa Ould el Hamra. Larger than it seemed from where we had been standing, the mosque had an entrance for male worshipers—an unobtrusive, narrow doorway in the Medina—that led to the generous prayer room for men. Down on Boulevard des Almohades, a grand carved wood entrance for women led to their tiny prayer space. During Friday prayers, when the mosque fills to capacity, men worship on the sidewalk, their prayer rugs stretching for blocks.

Everything fascinated me now. Caught up in the architecture and the rough-edged charm of the Medina, I barely noticed the garbage-strewn streets, cardboard-box kiosks selling cigarettes, feral cats scattering as we approached. Driss pointed out a huge gated Mauresque Art Deco villa with tall palms and other immense old trees rising high above its whitewashed walls. Originally Hubert Lyautey, marshal of France, lived here, the first French colonial administrator of Morocco, who served from 1912 to 1925. As a protectorate, Morocco technically retained its sovereignty, although the sultan's power was reduced to that of a figurehead.

"Marshall Lyautey was instrumental, in a way, for my parents meeting," Driss said, as we walked past.

Originally from the town of Nancy, France, Lyautey and his wife had loved their years in Morocco, his last post before retiring. Twenty years later, in the mid-'40s, Driss's father was preparing for medical school when King Mohammed V established grants for a small group of young men to attend graduate school in France. When Mme. Lyautey—by then a widow—heard the news, she requested that one of the young Moroccans be sent to Nancy for his studies. That was Mohamed Benhima. He met his future wife, Marie Thérèse, at the university in Nancy, they married, and he brought her to Morocco on the eve of the country's independence.

In a famous anecdote, the great French marshal Lyautey once asked his gardener to plant a tree. The gardener objected that the tree was slow growing and would not reach maturity for one hundred years. The Marshall replied, "In that case, there is no time to lose. Plant it this afternoon!" Lyautey's trees have almost come of age.

We passed a public school, not in session on Sunday, and a couple of ateliers of furniture makers and woodworkers. The neighborhood *hammam*, the public bath, stood next to the communal wood-fired baking oven. The women bringing their loaves of dough for baking captivated me. It took all of ten seconds to wonder whether I could ever work a deal for pizzas.*

By the time Driss Slaoui led us into a narrow dead-end street, a crowd was trailing behind. We knocked on a heavy, dark, wooden door. No one answered, so we walked back down the alley and turned the corner. The Medina ends here, at the Boulevard Sour Jdid. Driss Slaoui pointed to another house with a smaller façade, a distinctive balcony, and stunning stained-glass windows. It looked Portuguese or Spanish. He said he thought it, too, was for sale. The front faced the Boulevard Sour Jdid, the Atlantic, and the Mosque Hassan II, but because the back stood in the Old City it was considered part of the Medina.**

---

* Communal ovens, primarily used for baking bread, are becoming a rarity in Casablanca, with all its bakeries and grocery stores. On the other hand, the *hammams* remain plentiful, especially in the densely populated Ancienne Medina where they function like neighborhood social centers.
** Rising from the rocks along the Atlantic's edge, the Mosque Hassan II was built to mark the king's sixtieth birthday, opening in 1993. The third largest in the world after those in Mecca and Medina, it is known for its elaborate decoration, for which more than six thousand artisans worked with the very highest quality wood, plaster, tile, and marble to showcase exquisite traditional Moroccan craftsmanship. It also has the tallest minaret in the world.

Across the street lay the tear-shaped Jardin Zerktouni, where women had hung their laundry on the cast-iron fence that rimmed the space, creating a colorful montage, a contradiction to the littered, messy space that was the park itself. Suddenly a man appeared, dressed formally in a business suit similar to my companions', and approached Driss Benhima. He seemed a bit agitated. He was the *caid*, the local official in charge of the Ancienne Medina. He had come to pay his respects to the wali but was clearly put out that he hadn't been forewarned of the visit. Driss Slaoui jotted down the names and phone numbers of people in the crowd who had issues with which they needed the wali's help while, speaking in Arabic (the language of officialdom in Morocco), the wali himself gave instructions to the caid noting the various infractions we'd encountered during our morning stroll.

While the men conducted their business, I looked at the house and back at the Medina. It had been an intense morning, but it had exhilarated and inspired me.

"You're right," I said to Driss, after he had dismissed the caid. "The Ancienne Medina is the only place for Rick's Café. The atmosphere is perfect. Now I just have to find the right house."

Somewhere in those labyrinthine streets, Rick's was waiting, but it would be a while before I was ready to start looking seriously. I needed an idea of my financing options, and I had to be discreet while still working at the Consulate. Meanwhile, I couldn't wait until my son, Kyle, came to visit in December. He was studying at the University of Chicago, and it would be our first time together since 9/11. I'd called Kyle when the Rick's Café idea came to mind and asked what he thought.

"It must be right for you, Mom," he said. "You sound so happy."

When Kyle arrived in Casablanca for the Christmas holidays, we had a day before taking the train to Marrakech. I couldn't stop talking about the project and wanted him to see the part of the Medina I'd been describing. The absence of Morocco's usual bright blue sky cast a gray pall over the sights on the cold, misty December day when my son and I took the same walk. It was depressing without Driss's imposing presence and energy, and the weather only made it worse. But I was going to have to pull this off by myself, rain or shine, following an old Arab proverb that says, "Four things come not back—the spoken word, the sped arrow, the past life, and the neglected opportunity." I remained upbeat, but Kyle, I could see, was cautious, more accustomed to the developed Medina and my pretty riad in sunny Marrakech.

By January I had a prospective investor, and so it was time to resume the search. Driss assigned Mahir Tammam, a member of his staff, to help me. Mahir, in turn, found a local middleman, Idriss Bousfiha, who knew what was for sale and could arrange access. He wasn't a fully fledged real estate agent, more a neighborhood gadfly with a track record that accorded him semiofficial status. He worked out of a small cubicle on a narrow side street.

A short, gray-haired man with a round face, Bousfiha always wore a nappy brown djellaba. Even though the style and color of his robe reminded me of a Franciscan monk, he was a strict Muslim, which meant he wouldn't shake my hand. I'd first encountered this custom not in Morocco but at a diplomatic reception in Prague. The Iranian ambassador reeled backward in horror as I held out my hand.

Mr. Bousfiha led our party of three through the Medina: Mahir Tammam, my prospective investor—a prominent Moroccan businessman—and me. It didn't go well. The investor, who ran his wife's family's company, had probably never set foot in the Medina in his life, and he panicked when he and I were separated from Mahir and Idriss, fearful no doubt that he would never find his way out of the labyrinth and back to his BMW. The confusing lattice-like maze of the Medina's interior was intimidating enough in the daytime. I couldn't imagine the *Casablancais,* let alone tourists, finding their way through these streets at night.

The house-search itself was disappointing, too. Other intermediaries had tried to cut in and "psst psst" at Mahir about a hot prospect, but our pious Muslim agent sent them scrambling with a few choice words and a wave of his hand reminiscent of Signor Ferrari swatting flies in *Casablanca.* Not that his list of properties impressed much. No one came to the door in some places. Others didn't make the cut either because they were too small, too far into the winding interior of the Medina and hard to find, or too unattractive architecturally.

As we came to the end of our walk, I told Mahir that I wanted to see places similar to the houses I remembered seeing two months ago with the wali. "Tell Monsieur Bousfiha that I want something bigger, with better access, and closer to the water," I said in my basic French. He translated my words into Arabic for the middleman, and we agreed to meet the following Sunday.

A week later we again set off to find Rick's Café. The investor opted to stay behind—probably a good idea. His moneyed looks might give a homeowner the wrong idea of my own financial situation. He was still financing the purchase of the house, but maybe I could get a better deal if the seller thought I was just a woman on her own.

Hoping that the third time would be the charm, I was optimistic starting out. This time we took another route into the Medina. We passed the clock tower and the chintzy shops and the scenes of our earlier visit, turning in at the Taverne du Dauphin, one of my favorite restaurants. Once again the sun shone, the sky gleamed blue, and, as we came to the Place Sidi Bousmara, some changes had been made as a result of the wali's to-do list for the caid back in November. The square and surrounding streets looked cleaner, and fewer suspicious characters were lurking about.

We soon picked up the same interior street that paralleled the walls and walked past the old Portuguese Gate again. The first place to which Mr. Bousfiha led us lay at the end of a small, mysterious, dead-end passage. My heart skipped a beat. Driss Slaoui had shown us the house months earlier, but no one had answered the bell. We tapped the iron knocker.

The ornate wooden door opened, and Zoubida Ghattas introduced herself as the owner's daughter, ushering us inside. We walked through a narrow, dingy corridor lit by a single bulb hanging from the ceiling. Colored ceramic tiles, cracked and dull, covered the lowest three feet of the walls, reaching waist high. Above the tile, gray plaster was crumbling from the walls, a first impression of the house's poor condition. As we picked our way carefully through the dim passageway and climbed the stairs, Zoubida said that her mother and the rest of the Ghattas heirs in the sale had designated her to represent their interests.

At the top of the stairs we passed a small toilet with a sink out in the hallway. This wasn't an impressive introduction, and I didn't know what to expect. Zoubida opened a door to the living area and introduced us to Aicha Ghattas. Stunned by what I saw, I could barely concentrate on the formalities. A central atrium with an octagonal cupola directly above it dominated a grand space beyond anything I could have imagined. Columns supported elaborately carved arches, and balustrades framed a gallery. Already visualizing the possibilities, I couldn't contain my excitement. Walking around the second floor, we peeked into long salons partitioned with makeshift flimsy plywood walls and doors, jerry-rigged as bedrooms.

The street-side facade of the house before construction. Earlier we thought this a separate, small house.

With Zoubida in the lead, we made our way past a gallery, along the balustrades of the open courtyard. We passed under intricate arches to another gallery and finally through doors decorated with colored glass to a large salon. At the opposite end of the floor now, someone said, "You have to see the balcony."

It was difficult to open the warped and splintered doors—but worth the effort. When we stepped out, we could see the Mosque Hassan II, the Atlantic, and palm trees everywhere. As I looked at the view, I realized that I was standing on the balcony of the little house with the stained-glass windows from our first visit to the Medina. The two houses I saw that day with Driss Benhima and Driss Slaoui were, in fact, one grand mansion, L-shaped and with three façades: one that looked to the sea and fishing port, the main entrance in the small dead-end street, and another facing the Boulevard Sour Jdid, the ocean, and the mosque.

Back inside, rickety steps led up to a terrace. Beyond hanging laundry lay a panoramic view of the port, the Medina walls and ramparts, and downtown Casablanca. Zoubida led me back downstairs to the kitchen, directly below the terrace. It was dark and dilapidated, the stunning view masked by windows covered with yellowed newspapers and tape.

Our tour culminated with a visit to the ground floor—in even worse condition than the rest of the house. Yet the space was striking. The broken base of a marble fountain occupied the center of a courtyard covered by marble squares, beautiful despite their cracks and missing pieces. A small rectangular opening in the roof of the cupola allowed for TV cables and provided the only natural light to the ground floor. It also allowed rain to pour in. Even though very little had been done to maintain the house—it was in terrible shape—I saw it with the eyes of someone falling in love at first sight.

I returned to the second floor and looked over the balustrade to the courtyard. I imagined the arches smooth and white, touched by shadows from soft lighting. I heard glasses clinking over dinner conversation and piano music. For a moment, I saw myself as Rick looking down on the Germans singing "Die Wacht am Rhein," and giving Laszlo the nod to strike up the band and sing "La Marseillaise."

My spirit soared. It was clear that a force other than Idriss Bousfiha had led me here. Finding the house was a sign that the project was destined to succeed. I knew I could turn it into a magnificent, real-life interpretation of Rick's cinematic gin joint. The malaise of the last eight years of my life disappeared. My creative juices were flowing once again. That night I e-mailed friends, called Kyle with the exciting news, fixed myself a great dinner, settled in with my glass of wine, and put the video of *Casablanca* in the VCR.

As the screen filled with the familiar story, my mind drifted back to a séance I had had with a psychic named Manfred in the summer of 1993, just before leaving Tokyo. Every prediction had come exactly true except the last. "You'll leave Japan and never come back to live," Manfred told me. "You're going back to the US. You'll buy a house there and live in it for a short while before moving to another continent." He was right: I left Tokyo and moved to Washington, DC, while I prepared for my first posting in Prague. He continued: "You'll sell that house from overseas, but you'll also move on to another destination, a different continent." Also true. I sold the house while in Prague and moved to Morocco. Then he said, "You'll be settled there in a place you'll never leave. I see palm trees. I see water." Again, true. I planned to retire in Marrakech, but Marrakech lies in the desert. Palm trees, yes, but no water. It had always puzzled me because Manfred had been so right about everything else. Now his last prediction was coming true. As the film ended and the credits played, I was transported back to the house in the Medina, with its sweeping view from the balcony.

Destiny had taken a hand. I saw palm trees. I saw water. My own Casablanca story had begun.

TWO
The Usual Suspects

Even before finding the house, I had begun to put financing in place. I needed help purchasing the building itself as well as with a construction loan. Driss was willing to make any introductions I needed. After our first visit to the Medina, he asked with which financial or investment banking group I wanted to work, rightly assuming that I wasn't going to go at it singlehandedly. Here, individual entrepreneurship is rare. Most banks give preference to friends and family clients. If a project doesn't have a sponsoring friend inside the bank, you might as well forget it.

From my very first visit to the Medina back in November, I had set out to find that sponsoring friend. I'd worked up a nicely bound proposal with pictures of the house paired with photos from the film and financial projections calling for a total initial investment of $450,000. Of that, $250,000 had to come from a bank and the remaining $200,000 from one or more investors. That dossier accompanied me everywhere as I made the rounds.

I expected that money men would jump at the chance, supporting me almost as a civic duty. Hah! It didn't take long to see how wrong that expectation was. Driss first introduced me to a major holding company with palace interests then headed by his brother-in-law, who found the project too small and at the same time too complicated. Another investment banker said his company would only consider the loan if I worked with an operator, someone with clout, someone with a background in this sort of business, someone, not incidentally, who was a client of the bank.

He suggested a consortium that owned—among other properties—a major hotel on the outskirts of the Medina. I feared that group would limit my personal involvement and squelch my intention to replicate the drama and ambience of the film. The man's body language indicated that he didn't see anything wrong with his suggestion. He could only relate as a banker. Clearly my idea left him cold.

Any Moroccan group might be risky. What about an outsider? Maybe media mogul Ted Turner—the last owner of the film before Turner Classic Movies merged into Time-Warner—would want in. I took pains to find a private contact for Mr. Turner in Atlanta and drafted a letter for Driss's signature, expounding on the project and inviting him to Casablanca. His reply came back wishing Driss well with the plans but apologizing that his schedule didn't permit a visit—and sending me back to the drawing board.

Diplomatic channels had introduced me to a number of well-established local businessmen over the years. One of them and I had met when I was stationed in Prague. The Moroccan ambassador to the Czech Republic introduced us. As we chatted, Ahmed's friendliness and his sophistication impressed me. The elites of Ahmed's generation—born in the years after the war—grew up in families who had worked alongside the French for decades and felt comfortable in both societies. They carried that comfort in the way they dressed, their manners, and their quiet self-confidence.

In Morocco I had occasion to see Ahmed frequently. In fact, on my second night in Casablanca, it was at his mother-in-law's hillside villa that the Embassy threw a lavish reception to welcome its new officers. It was there that I first met Driss Benhima and many others who became friends and contacts in the ensuing years. Very comfortable with Americans, Ahmed worked closely on projects both with the Embassy and Consulate. As commercial attaché, I had helped him and an American joint-venture partner with a telecommunications project, and he had put in a good word with a bank when I needed a mortgage to buy my riad in Marrakech.

Well respected in the business community, with a solid reputation, Ahmed would give the project weight and status. Driss liked the idea. Ahmed's involvement wouldn't trigger any of the rivalries and resentments that, more than a lack of merit, caused a project to fail. He wouldn't draw any critics.

"He's clean," Driss said.

Ahmed headed his wife's family company, big clients of the bank with which I had already spoken about a construction loan. Driss called Ahmed first on my behalf, and Ahmed expressed sincere interest. We met at his house for lunch, a nice, comfortable, modest place compared to the sprawling mansion of his mother-in-law in the Anfa Hills, Casablanca's exclusive residential enclave above the Corniche. Ahmed had given up an academic career to direct the holding company and was no doubt exercising some independence by agreeing to back my idea. Excited about investing, he agreed to provide the majority of the capital needed to buy a property that could become Rick's. It seemed almost too good to be true.

In the end, it was.

Ahmed's interest began to subside mere days after seeing the house in the Medina. He had brimmed with enthusiasm when he first made the commitment, when I believed the investment would come from his wife's family business. Perhaps he'd expected that, too, but it seemed no longer to be the case. No matter whose money he was using, I needed him desperately, so when he insisted that I meet his wife's cousin, who was, as he put it, an "accomplished decorator" and would be a "great addition to the project," I warily agreed.

"You have to meet her," he said. "She has experience running a hotel, and she has impeccable taste. Plus, she can put some money into Rick's."

In Marrakech, my friend Bill Willis—then my aesthetic advisor, but who eventually designed all the decorative and architectural details that comprise the look and feel of Rick's—gave me the dirt on the woman. He had designed the hotel she supposedly had experience "running."

"My dear, she has no taste," he said. "It was her husband who had the business sense, and he gave me free reign with the design of the hotel. After he died, she had to sell it. She'll be of no use to you."

Armed with this insight and aware of the proverb that says "If a camel once gets his nose in the tent, his body will soon follow," I nevertheless rushed back from Marrakech. She did lack taste—a taste for my project. She hated it from the moment she emerged from her Lexus. Wearing tight beige twill jodhpurs with brown boots and designer sunglasses, she frowned as she beheld the façade before her.

"What could Driss Benhima have been thinking?" she sniffed. "No *Casablancaise* will ever come here."

"Well, there's easy access from the Boulevard des Almohades," I said, "and plenty of parking right here on the street."

She continued to demean the property and the neighborhood, clearly not sharing any of my enthusiasm. Her domineering personality quickly and completely demoralized me and made me doubt my vision. Aicha wasn't home, so we didn't see the inside—for which I was thankful. I could only imagine how this arrogant woman would have scorned the petite, proud widow.

Back at her immaculate villa, Ahmed and his wife joined us for tea. Nothing sat out of place, everything beautifully, if impersonally, appointed. The "decorator" trashed the site to them, and Ahmed's face revealed that, even though (I thought) he shared my dream, he was inclined—out of family politeness, practicality, or his more conservative inner feelings—to agree with her. Fortunately he held his tongue.

Then she proceeded to describe *our* menu.

"Of course we'll have Moroccan food," she said.

"Well, actually I was contemplating something different," I countered. "Rick was an American; the movie café was filled with refugees. Frankly I had more of an international menu in mind."

She ignored me and continued to speak as if already running the project. This woman had been in my presence for less than two hours, and already my self-esteem had fallen about as low as Rick's when Ilsa jilted him at the train station in Paris.

She and I agreed to meet two days later to see the inside of the house, and Ahmed drove me home. He tried to calm me by saying that she would appreciate the house more after she saw the interior, that I would warm to her later, that she really was well-meaning, although admittedly she came across a little strong.

Reeling, I e-mailed Driss, describing the meeting and telling him that I was afraid that control was slipping out of my hands already. I hardly slept that night. I didn't know what to do. Should I alienate my investor or follow my instincts and dump this woman?

The answer was clear by morning. This was *not* going to be the beginning of a beautiful friendship. I called Ahmed and told him that I couldn't work with her. "It's better to be honest now before things go any further."

He didn't argue; he must have seen the truth, too.

My driver, Salah, was waiting downstairs before our weekly trip to Rabat and the Country Team meeting at the Embassy. A huge weight had lifted from my shoulders, and I called Driss's secretary, Fatima, to tell him that he could ignore my e-mail of the night before, that I had solved the problem. He called back immediately and asked how.

"I told Ahmed that she couldn't be involved, period," I said.

"Good. There's only room for one woman in this project, and that's you," Driss replied.

I laughed as I hung up.

"What did he say?" Salah asked, chuckling, too, when I told him.

Salah and I had traveled many a bumpy road in the three years he'd been shuttling me around, and we didn't have many secrets. Tall and lanky with salt-and-pepper hair, he had twinkling eyes and a smile that revealed wide gaps between coffee-stained teeth. He spoke perfect English with just a trace of a British accent from the couple of years he had spent in London as a waiter. I regarded him as my cultural advisor, and he always slipped me gossip from the motor pool or explained a passing scene.

Once during Ramadan, in my first year in Morocco, a group of men gathered in heated argument just an hour or two before the end of the day's fasting. It looked like fisticuffs were about to break out, but Salah was nonchalant.

"It's never serious until someone takes off his shirt," he said.

That afternoon, on the way back to Casablanca, we discussed corruption, the police, and how the traffic actually seemed to be worsening. He hated that bribes controlled the traffic. "The honking of horns is the only thing that is free in Morocco," he once said.

"Watch the bus in front of us," he said. "The driver is going to throw something out the window."

Sure enough a white sack, lobbed from the driver's window, fell onto the median just before two motorcycle policemen. Salah had a knowing look in his eye.

"There's money in that bag," he said. "The bus was speeding and didn't want to be stopped."

Obviously I still had a lot to learn.

⁓

My solitary evenings passed in screenings of the film and soaking up ideas for decoration and ambience. I also wracked my brain for ways to raise money. I had to have a fallback position in case Ahmed didn't come through, and it still wasn't clear how much he was willing to invest. I needed my own plan. First I thought of selling my house in Marrakech as a time-share to friends. It might have been a good alternative . . . if I actually owned the house, but I was still paying the mortgage. Plus, my friends' excitement centered more on Rick's Café than on having a share in a riad.

That's when it hit me. I'd invite my friends to become investors, to share my dream. I designed a flyer that played on lines from the film, the last one saying: "Of all the gin joints in all the towns in all the world, I'd like you to buy into mine." Asking for an investment of $5,000, I decided to name the company The Usual Suspects so that the notice of our annual board meeting would say: "Round Up The Usual Suspects." The idea—so light, so fun, so funny, and so blindly optimistic—masked the desperation and fear that gripped me.

The response proved overwhelming. Suddenly wire transfers from all over the world were coming in to The Usual Suspects in Morocco. In the post-9/11 world, eyebrows were raised at a few banks and at the Treasury Department—and, in the case of one American investor,

35

resulted in a visit from the FBI. But by the end of July 2002, over twenty investors had sent money from Algeria, America, Australia, the Czech Republic, Great Britain, Italy, Japan, and of course Morocco.

But a revelation nearly derailed the entire project.

When I went to register the name "Rick's Café" with OMPIC (Office Marocaine de la Proprieté Industrielle et Commerciale), they informed me that the name had already been taken.

What?

As a stopgap, I registered "Vic's Café"—after the Resistance hero Victor Laszlo—but the prospect of settling for less than the real deal didn't thrill me. For weeks I hesitated about having to approach someone who might demand an exorbitant amount of money for a name that, I suspected, he had registered for that very purpose. Then a potential Usual Suspect promised that, if I got the name, he'd invest. I started my research.

An intern in our real estate lawyer's office offered to help and reported that the man wasn't a big-name industrialist or civic hot shot, the type to slip into deals by connections or through favors. He seemed interested in me and in my story.

At 10:00 a.m. on a Saturday I arrived at the address in one of the older, established commercial areas. He was younger than I'd expected, probably in his mid-thirties. His interest in the movie had developed during his years at Northeastern University in Boston.

"It was so depressing that, whenever I was introduced to people who learned I was from Casablanca, the first thing they would ask is, 'Oh, do you hang out at Rick's Café?' I had to tell them there was no such place. So I registered the name when I came back to Casablanca after graduation. It was my dream one day to create a Rick's Café. But my father, a distributor of heavy industrial equipment, needed help with his business. I stepped in . . . and I'm still here."

I held my breath. Where was the conversation going next? Maybe he wanted to hold onto his dream—and if he did I couldn't blame him. It was a powerful dream, I knew.

"Over the years other people have approached me to buy the name, but I never felt they had the right motivation. You're the first person I've met who seems capable of making the dream come true."

I almost hugged him. He promised to sell me the name for 100,000 dirhams (around $10,000 then). I suggested that he become an investor, one of The Usual Suspects, for 50,000 dirhams, and I would pay the additional 50,000 dirhams.

"That way you can share the dream," I said.

It was the perfect solution for us both.

⌐

Driss couldn't overtly champion the project, but he continued to support me behind the scenes by allowing members of his staff to help. Yasmina Baddou, who had a law practice in Casablanca, served as Driss's legal advisor, and prominent architect Rachid El Andaloussi his urban affairs advisor. When Driss became wali, he knew the only way to break through the closed system was to involve his own people, not to have to depend on entrenched bureaucrats. Most of his outside advisors—community activists like Yasmina and Rachid—donated their time pro bono, but he also brought with him from ONE his two secretaries, Fatima and Leila, as well as his longtime driver, Bouchaib.

The senior secretary, close to retirement, Fatima had worked at ONE for decades and knew all the local bigwigs and power brokers. Her formidable presence at a large desk dominated their office. Junior to Fatima, Leila was a cheerful, enthusiastic, willing worker, proficient in written and spoken Arabic. Bouchaib had been about to retire when Driss became wali, but he faithfully stayed at the wheel, driving Driss and guarding his privacy. People often joked that when the time came for Driss to pen his memoirs, Bouchaib would write them.

Mahir Tammam, whom Driss had enlisted in the house search, now helped arrange a second meeting with Aicha and her family. Yasmina and Rachid joined Ahmed and me, and together we would get an idea of the price that the Ghattases wanted and the conditions for paying off their renters. Ideally my bargaining skills honed at the souks and markets should have come in handy in negotiating for the building, but I lose any kind of poker face when I really want something. Fortunately Yasmina was going to handle the financial negotiations and the conversations would be in Arabic, so I wouldn't tip my hand in any way.

The existing arches, balustrade-enclosed central courtyard, and views of the port and the Mosque Hassan II stunned my three colleagues as much as they had me when we all entered the house. We sat around banquettes in one of the galleries, drinking mint tea and chatting. Aicha recounted how she was the first of Bouchaib Ghattas's three wives and the only one still living. A diver, her husband had worked at the port repairing boats. It was serendipity perhaps that his surname, Ghattas, means "diver" in Arabic. Everyone referred to him as Hadj, though, because he had made the *hadj*, meaning "pilgrimage," to Mecca.

A dashing photograph taken at the time of his marriage to Aicha showed him in a keffiyeh. A more comical painting depicted him, underwater in his diver's suit with its bubble-shaped top, entangled in the tentacles of a giant octopus, his distinctive face showing through the helmet's tiny glass window. That painting now hangs between the two restrooms downstairs, the most subterranean space in the restaurant.

Mint Tea

Preparation time: 5 minutes
Cooking time: 5 minutes
Serves 6

Mint tea plays a supporting role in all social and business occasions in Morocco. A meeting can't begin until tea has been served. At dinner, the service is more dramatic with the teapot raised high, allowing the fragrant stream to perfume the air as it finds its way not into a cup but a lovely glass.

It didn't surprise me when Aicha offered me mint tea during my visits to the old house. What did surprise me was the more simplified version served later at the construction site, the famous *thé du chantier*. Though served in a plain glass filled from a dented teapot—and with my diet requiring the standing order of no sugar—the tea that Houssein served me during my visits seemed to taste the best of all.

Rick's Café's tea service follows the traditional raised-teapot routine described above, with the server effortlessly balancing a tray of glasses while pouring the aromatic brew for appreciative guests.

4¹/₂ cups boiling water

1 tablespoon loose Chinese gunpowder green tea

¹/₄ cup sugar

1 cup fresh mint leaves

In a teapot combine ¹/₂ cup of the boiling water and the tea. Swirl gently for a few seconds. Strain liquid, reserving the tea leaves. Return tea leaves to the pot, and discard the water.

Add remaining 4 cups of boiling water to the teapot. Let steep 2 minutes, then add sugar and mint. Let steep 2 minutes more.

Note: It's best to practice the serving technique described above a few times backstage before performing for your guests.

Photos of Aicha Ghattas and Bouchaib, her husband, commemorating their marriage.

Looking from Aicha to Yasmina highlighted the contrast between a woman's role then and now. Changes have come slowly but surely, with great strides made under the present king. Mohammed VI has one wife, Princess Lalla Salma. Everyone knows who she is, and she participates in events and travels on behalf of the monarchy. King Hassan's wives, on the other hand, had no public role. It wasn't until he died that any mention was made of the woman who had borne his son and heir. When I wondered aloud why no one had ever heard of her before, Salah, my driver, went right to the point.

"She was never important until she became the mother of the king," he said.

But now women were becoming important politically, and Yasmina had announced that she was running for Parliament in national elections scheduled for September 2002. Speculation was already rampant that she and other women candidates would do well. She and her husband, Ali Fassi Fihri, director of the National Water Office in Rabat, fell in love and married when Yasmina was seventeen and hadn't yet finished her *baccalaureate*, the French equivalent of high school diploma. Her father, whom she revered, made Ali promise that Yasmina would finish her *bac* and continue her studies, so they spent their university years in France, where she eventually earned a law degree.

Striking and vivacious, with straight black hair pulled back, long-lashed dark eyes, and an expressive mouth, she has real presence. One evening at dinner in Marrakech at the home of former ambassador Frederick Vreeland, Yasmina nonchalantly navigated three levels of an uneven staircase in excruciatingly high heels that she had just brought back from Paris. Ambassador Margaret Tutwiler said with her characteristic Alabama accent, "How can you possibly walk, let alone climb stairs, in shoes like that?"

Yasmina did love Parisian designer shoes for fun, but at work she wore simple suits and shoes practical for driving and walking. When we visited the Medina, she dressed casually, sometimes even wearing jeans to avoid intimidating the people we were seeing. She could have worn *babouche*, the quintessential Moroccan slipper, and she still would have commanded my respect and admiration. No other lawyer in Casablanca could have put up with me as a client. I didn't know the first thing about the Moroccan legal system—arcane, at best—and the various legal roadblocks that we encountered had me in a near-constant state of outrage. Undaunted, Yasmina was always pulling miracles, or at least quick fixes, out of the hat with her deft ability to respond to changing situations.

Aicha Ghattas had also been beautiful when she was young. A photo showed her with raven hair, large dark eyes, and a Berber tattoo

Aicha Ghattas greeted us with mint tea and entertaining stories of the Ancienne Medina from earlier days.

from her bottom lip to the edge of her chin. The tattoo remained but had faded over the years, and her dark eyes had sunk deeper into her face as sun, time, and raising ten children had etched their lines into her once satiny skin. The Moroccan djellaba that she wore seemed too full for her small frame.

Still, she appeared more animated than on my first visit. In fact, she was quite entertaining. She described in Arabic (translated into French for me) how the Ancienne Medina had looked in the decades long before she and her husband acquired the house. "The waves of the Atlantic had lapped up to the thick brown stone walls until Allah pushed back the sea," she said, gesturing dramatically. In reality, the authorities extended the land to expand the port and build a seafront boulevard through to the Corniche. She also reminisced about the Allied Embarkation, which started in Casablanca with Operation Torch on November 8, 1942.

She was referring to a key event of World War II. In the early morning hours that day, America and Great Britain launched an air and naval attack on sites in Morocco, Algeria, and Tunisia. Blockading Casablanca's port was key to Allied strategy, as German warships considered it a safe harbor. The success of Operation Torch forced the Germans to refocus on North Africa, relieving pressure on Russia and buying the United States valuable time to prepare for eventual landings in northern France.

Warner Bros. pulled forward the world premiere of *Casablanca* to November 26, 1942, a scant eighteen days after the start of Operation Torch. They also capitalized on the Casablanca Conference of January 1943, where meetings between President Roosevelt, Prime Minister Churchill, and their commanders in the field set in motion America's involvement in the European Theater. The film went into general distribution just as the Casablanca Conference was announced publicly, and "Rick's Place" even became the military code name for Casablanca during the war.

Although she hadn't been living in the house then, Aicha recounted how American planes had accidentally dropped a bomb on the old city, damaging the house. Shocked and embarrassed, I later asked a local historian if this was true. He assured me that it was not. Occasionally metal pieces had fallen off planes during some of the air action of Operation Torch, but they had caused no injuries or damage as a result. Clearly Aicha had a flair for the dramatic and a knack for storytelling—or maybe she just enjoyed having a new audience.

Getting down to business, she told us that we would have to deal with two sets of tenants: a family in the front apartment and Mme. Zerktounia, who lived downstairs, the elderly sister of Mohamed Zerktouni, Morocco's most famous resistance fighter. Born in the Ancienne Medina, he had known all the back alleys and used some of the houses to hide both weapons and other resistance fighters from the police. His suicide in 1954—swallowing cyanide rather than revealing the names of his fellow revolutionaries—made him both a martyr and a hero to the independence movement. Most Moroccan cities have a Boulevard Zerktouni. Casablanca's starts at the ocean and the Mosque Hassan II and forms the main thoroughfare through town.

Years later it surprised me to discover that Mme. Zerktounia had been a heroine in her own right during the resistance and a militant for women's rights afterward. With her brother when he committed suicide, she herself went to jail where authorities tortured her. After her release, she carried on fighting, even selling her house to support the resistance. After independence, local authorities gave her the right to rent the ground floor of the house as a reward for her heroism.

Now, however, Mme. Zerktounia—about seventy, a large woman, with sad, watery eyes—appeared tired and distracted. She always seemed agreeable to moving, but we suspected she was under family pressure. She had lived in her apartment for over forty years, with an out-of-work son and his family, paying a pittance, the equivalent of $40 per month. What we were willing to pay her would buy her a nice apartment—but not one big enough for the freeloading son and his family as well.

We agreed to tie the compensation for each renter into the sales agreement. In other words, the sale couldn't take place until both tenants were paid off and out. It proved to be the major stumbling block to buying the house. Zoubida Ghattas, Aicha's daughter and spokesperson for the heirs, negotiated with the family in the front apartment. We thought Yasmina—given her position as a member of the Istiqlal party, the party of the independence movement—the best person to negotiate with Zerktounia.

Souad Hamzaoui, a *notaire* (real estate lawyer) and Yasmina's sister-in-law, was going to handle the purchase of the house, including drawing up the sales agreement and the final sale documents. It was good that Souad and Yasmina were related. Here I came, a blundering American with no understanding of Moroccan law or the real estate process, along with a raft of small investors, most of them foreign; renters reluctant to move; plus the slow process of assembling the money. Anyone not obliged by family ties would have thrown up her hands at the very idea.

When the sales agreement was finalized early in February, I had to make the equivalent of an escrow payment, but I had no bank account. Funds from The Usual Suspects were frozen until I filed corporation papers. Luckily Ahmed, my investor, stepped in and wrote a personal check to Souad for 277,000 dirhams, about $27,000 then.

Once the sales agreement had been signed, Driss publicly could visit the house, and on a sunny Sunday in early spring 2002, he and his wife, Selma; Yasmina; and her husband, Ali, joined me for a tour. I'd never seen Driss at a loss for words until he climbed the stairs and took in the expanse of the second floor. On the terrace we looked out at the port and the green space along the walls toward downtown Casablanca. He said that in five years the Ancienne Medina would thrive with new investment. When his wife, Selma, said she thought the neighboring ex-bordello/hotel would be good follow-on development, he said, "We'll make that four years."

In July 2002, at the urging of my supervisor, I took a one-year leave of absence without pay to ensure that I would have benefits and could return to the service if the restaurant didn't succeed. I had vacation pay until September, but otherwise I was on my own. I stored most of my belongings and moved into a four-month furnished sublet, foolishly thinking that my apartment atop the restaurant could be built first. I also foolishly thought that construction would begin fairly quickly.

We never knew when Zerktounia would agree to move, but as soon as she did we had to follow the sales agreement and buy the house.

Most of the money from my investors was languishing in the account for "The Usual Suspects, a company in the process of being formed." We had to form the company to get the money. Yasmina and Souad tore out their hair over how to structure the statutes with investors flung all over the world. Somehow they managed the details so that only those investors physically in Morocco had to sign the statutes.

When the time came to sign the papers creating The Usual Suspects, I was sitting in Yasmina's office, frantically trying to call Ahmed, the only investor I hadn't reached. He had become somewhat reclusive and isolated, but surprisingly he answered my call. When I asked him what time he'd be available that day to sign the papers, he said he was in Paris.

I was seething. He hadn't bothered to tell me, even though he knew we were rushing to ready the papers for filing. I said I'd discuss with Yasmina if it was safe to wait until he returned and that I'd call him back. Maybe his absence offered a way to ease him out—even though I still needed more investors to come up with the sale price. When I asked Yasmina if I should say that we needed to sign the statutes without him, she said he'd never accept such a blow to his pride. As she and I talked, I had second thoughts, so I called him back to say that we would wait five days for him to return. He graciously told me to go ahead and sign the papers without him, effectively removing himself and his financing from the project completely.

"I'd never be able to face Driss Benhima if the house sale failed because I wasn't there," he said.

His exit meant more financing work for me, and six months down the road I'd have to pay the escrow back with interest, but suddenly I felt truly liberated. Then, as if on cue, Moroccan friends approached, wondering "Why haven't you asked us to invest?" With a few more Moroccan Suspects, we had enough to buy the house.

Meanwhile, the tenants in the front apartment moved and were compensated. Zerktounia and family, however, stayed on.

And on.

And on.

"She shows a real *resistance* to moving," someone joked.

But actually her recalcitrance proved a blessing in disguise, as Yasmina reminded me. "It's just as well since we haven't yet collected enough from The Usual Suspects to buy the house."

She had a point.

～

I'd been having discussions with my bank about a construction loan. They had agreed to lend me the equivalent of $250,000. I worked on a daily basis with Mouna, an officer at the branch conveniently located across the street from bank headquarters. There my friend Nabil, the investment officer, acted as point of contact. At least he had been my friend when I was at the Consulate. As soon as I was on my own, any notions of friendship disappeared from his side of the equation.

In August, still with no movement from Zerktounia, I made my last trip back to the States as a government employee, turned in my diplomatic passport, and returned to Casablanca as a private citizen. Driss's secretary, Fatima, held power of attorney for me in case the sale had to close while I was away, but nothing had changed.

The Widow Ghattas now spent nights with her family but returned to the house each day with a variety of children and grandchildren to wait out Zerktounia. When I came to visit, it became something of a social event. One of the grandkids cranked up the radio full blast, reminding me of the methods that US forces employed to dislodge Panamanian dictator Manuel Noriega from his refuge in the Vatican

Embassy in December 1989. After Aicha cut the electricity and water to the house, Zerktounia and her family finally moved.

Finally, nine months after I first saw the house, came the day for documents to be signed and money to be distributed. While we were waiting for everyone to arrive, Idriss Bousfiha, the neighborhood gadfly middleman showed up. He whined and tried to wheedle a commission from me, even though Aicha had already paid him an amount to which he had earlier agreed. He showed up at Souad's office nearly every day so he wouldn't miss the day of the sale.

I refused his demand, but after the closing he pestered me, Mahir, and even Driss at the Wilaya. Then I had an idea. I asked Mahir to tell Monsieur Bousfiha that I wanted him to start looking for another property that I could develop into a hotel. The fear of doing another project with the crazy American woman proved too much for him. None of us ever heard from him again.

The Ghattas heirs met at Souad's office. Two of Mr. Ghattas's children (not Aicha's) sat in a separate room. Old family animosities still boiled between the children of different wives. Bad feelings and resentment aren't uncommon in societies where men take multiple wives and their children must compete with each other and the wives for property, family rights, and position. One of Aicha's sons arrived at the midday closing after too much to drink and loudly chastised his siblings for agreeing to sell.

Despite his shouting, everyone signed the papers—mine just a paragraph making a statement of ownership; theirs a long, elaborate document listing the fourteen heirs and heiresses and specifying unfortunately but not unexpectedly that the men received a larger percentage.

When the mayhem ended, I left with the keys. It was the middle of September 2002. I didn't cry for joy. Indeed, no overwhelming emotion ran through me at all when the keys touched my hand. You see, the house had been mine from the day I first saw it.

I did, however, have the locks changed immediately . . . just in case Mme. Zerktounia had second thoughts. As I soon found out, though, it wasn't Mme. Zerktounia who was having second thoughts.

THREE
Destiny Takes a Hand

The first sign of trouble came in October 2002. I was in Marrakech attending a conference of airport executives, a project initiated two years earlier while at the Consulate. Whether in Portland, Tokyo, Prague, or Casablanca, my work has always given me self-validation and a basis for meeting people and forming a social life. Suddenly isolated, I was floating in limbo. Yasmina took her seat in Parliament, and Driss was dealing with all the impending crises of Casablanca. The house was mine—just—so all I needed was for the loan to come through from the bank.

It became clear from the moment that she arrived that my successor at the Consulate and I would have zero rapport. In fact, she snubbed me from day one, not inviting me to her welcome reception at Villa Mirador, the residence of the consul general in Casablanca. Mail that continued to trickle in for me was returned "addressee unknown."

I was "addressee unknown" as long as she was at the Consulate, but the Marrakech conference invitation had come from the organizers in Washington who appreciated my efforts on their behalf. A luxury hotel on the city outskirts hosted the event—a hotel at which I'd stayed numerous times during Embassy functions or as the control officer of a congressional delegation. This night, however, I wasn't in charge, and that was a relief.

These events follow a set protocol and pattern: cocktail reception to meet and greet, then the official opening ceremony the next day with a speech by the ambassador. That was the important part, but I just wanted to see friends and people from Washington, not to mention local contacts, many of whom hadn't heard from me in months. My successor surely wasn't telling people that I was even still in Casablanca, even though my total immersion in the restaurant project presented no conflict to her. She had nothing to fear, safe in her four-year assignment. I'd burned so many bridges in Washington that if the project failed and I were to return to the Foreign Service at the end of my year's leave of absence, the bidding panels would have a field day with my assignment.

The reception took place outdoors in a setting lit by traditional lanterns and encircled by tall, stately palms. The soft percussion of Gnaoua musicians heightened the atmosphere. White-jacketed, fez-topped waiters smoothly circulated through the crowd of around a hundred American executives and bureaucrats and their Moroccan counterparts from the public and private sector, proffering trays of Moroccan wines, fresh fruit juices, and Moroccan-style lamb-stuffed filo triangles called *briouates*, marinated olives, and other spicy canapés.

I greeted my successor politely, trying to maintain a low profile. When some Moroccan contacts asked me to introduce them to her, I couldn't refuse, but I excused myself from the conversation immediately after the introduction. Doing the same several more times was proving onerous, so I thanked the hosts for the invitation, said goodnight, and returned to the welcome solitude of my riad. The reception that was supposed to raise my spirits only lowered them, painfully reminding me that I no longer belonged in the cocoon of the Embassy's inner circle.

The next morning, while I was getting ready to head to the hotel for the ambassador's speech, a member of the delegation called. My successor had complained that my presence at the speech would make it "difficult" for her. I was being uninvited.

At first the slight stunned and hurt me, but on reflection—as I poured myself another glass of orange juice on my sunny terrace—this was exactly the sort of small-minded pettiness I had endured for almost ten years in the Foreign Service. It spared me a thirty-minute taxi ride to the hotel, which meant I could have a rare relaxing day puttering around in the Marrakech souk. I set out on my course, checking in at Mr. Karimi's in the carpet souk and on to one of my favorite shops, Mustapha Blaoui's Trésor des Nomades. I'd just settled in at Mustapha's with a glass of mint tea when my phone rang. It was Mouna at the bank. Mouna means "gift" in Arabic—which the call was not.

"There is a problem," she said. "Take the first train back to Casablanca, and come here in the morning."

Usually we chatted informally, and she had provided good insights on people at the bank's headquarters and background on some of the less than friendly people at the branch. She spoke perfect English, so I talked with her more as a friend than a client, but a tone in Mouna's voice that I hadn't heard before indicated that something was gravely wrong.

On the train back to Casablanca that afternoon, the blazing sun, blue skies, and cactus-dotted desert-red hillsides blurred together, my stomach in a knot. All during the trip I tried to imagine what could be wrong. Now that I had bought the house, I needed the funds from the promised construction loan. The bank had seemed totally positive in our earlier discussions. I slept fitfully that night and in the morning went directly to the branch at 9:00 a.m.

"Before the credit committee approves the loan," Mouna said seriously, "the bank will need personal guarantees from each investor."

I was totally unfamiliar with the fine print of Moroccan banking regulations, but banks do give preference to grand families, friends, and favorite companies, I knew. I couldn't imagine asking each of my

Moroccan investors to sign a personal guarantee for the bank loan! It was the first time that Mouna had heard of such a request, too.

Had my disgruntled investor pushed this tactic? His wife's family's companies had accounts with the bank, and, if they wanted to delay or derail a project, they could, but I didn't believe they wanted me to fail. Maybe the bank was acting on its own. After hearing that Ahmed had dropped out, perhaps they no longer had any reason to support me. Mouna confirmed that companies related to Ahmed and his in-laws didn't have any personal guarantees, and my friend and Usual Suspect Miriem assured me that she had never heard of minority shareholders in a company having to provide personal guarantees. When faced with these facts, the bank backed down, requiring only a personal guarantee from me.

They backed down, but no doubt this unorthodox move presaged further problems. I had to steel myself to handle their surprises. I came to hate the phrase "credit committee." I never met any of these nameless men, but surely they sat around a table in a bare, windowless room, smoking, drinking mint tea, and dreaming up ways to foil me. Paranoid, perhaps, but it did seem that way time and again.

Days later they threw another curve ball.

"The credit committee thinks the house is a landmark and therefore cannot be altered," Mouna said. "That means it wouldn't qualify as a guarantee for a loan."

"What should I do?" I asked.

"Send proof right away that the house is not a landmark."

I called Driss. As the wali of Casablanca, he could put things straight. He immediately sent a letter stating that only the Medina walls couldn't be altered. My house itself was not a landmark, but, although it did abut the walls, renovation would in no way threaten them.

An 0-2 count, but the bank was still pitching. They were looking for any reason they could find to deny me a loan. Mouna reported that people on the dreaded credit committee just didn't like preservation projects because they were "too messy." She advised that I go over their heads to the head of the bank. So I did.

The deputy director general didn't appear enthusiastic after seeing my booklet and hearing my presentation. Even though he commended me on the idea and the intent, he wasn't reassuring. As he escorted me to the elevator, another man emerged from a large corner office.

"Kathy, have you met the president of our bank?" the deputy asked.

I had not.

President El Alami asked his deputy about our meeting, and Ali showed him my presentation booklet. Mr. El Alami took the dossier and stared at it intently.

"Do you have thirty minutes to spend telling me about your project?" he asked.

I had all the time in the world for him, so he ushered me into his office.

The wraparound windows looked out at the grassy expanse of the Arab League Park and its rows of tall palm trees. Rising above the treetops were the spires of the Sacred Heart Cathedral. Ceded back to Morocco by the Vatican after Morocco's independence, the stunning building had turned gray with neglect and teemed with squatters. Countless plans to restore it never materialized. Hopefully Mr. El Alami would understand that, in my own small way, I was trying to ensure that a similar fate didn't befall the Ancienne Medina.

Distinguished looking, probably around sixty-five, Mr. El Alami listened with rapt attention to my description of the project as he leafed through the booklet. When I'd finished, he leaned forward in his chair, wistful.

"Some of my fondest memories I owe to the Ancienne Medina and the film *Casablanca*," he said.

He had first watched the movie in the late '50s, and, although he knew it was made in Hollywood, he couldn't help feeling that he had lived at one time in similar surroundings.

"My mother was still living then," he said. "I told her about seeing the film, and I asked her if we had ever lived in the Ancienne Medina. She said 'We didn't live there as a family, but there was a time, when you were around six years old, that your father and I took a trip one summer, and I left you with a friend who had a beautiful mansion in the Medina.'"

The friend had died, but his mother described the house and remembered the name of the street. Immediately he had set off to find it.

"As soon as I stepped into the Medina the sights and smells all came back to me," he said. "The narrow streets with bourgeois houses and grand mansions and the bustling activity related to the port—all were as I recalled, and the smells—the sea, fish, beignets and coffee—the smells were still the same."

After his emotional reverie, he asked why I'd been to see his deputy. I told him that the bank had suddenly raised objections to loaning me the money to restore the beautiful courtyard mansion that I had bought for the restaurant. A look of incredulity crossed his face, and he asked how much I had requested.

"That should be no problem. We must save the Ancienne Medina. Not one building should be demolished," he declared.

I don't know what he said to the credit committee, but it worked. Two days later the deputy director general called with the good news. They had approved the loan.

Now that the loan was back in play, I had to repay Ahmed for the escrow money and pay out preconstruction engineering fees as well as advances to the architect and my aesthetic advisor, Bill Willis. Between October and March, there would be subcontractors to select and more advances to pay, and equipment, including: porcelain, silverware, glassware, chairs, telephones, lamps, other decorative items—and a very small salary for me. With money in the bank and checkbook in hand, we were rolling.

There was just one more thing.

"By the way," I told Mouna, "now that I have a better idea of costs, I'll very likely need to increase the loan."

"Don't worry," she said. "Now you're with the bank; they'll support you."

Foolishly (perhaps) I believed her.

Just after construction began on March 3, 2003, the bank finally began formalizing the loan—even though they had agreed to it back in October after my meeting with Mr. El Alami. Since then I'd been operating on an overdraft basis with a year's deferral on the first payment. Suddenly headquarters, which had been letting Mouna at the branch office handle everything, paid attention to my account and saw that I had already drawn 70 percent of the entire loan amount.

She called on Friday at 5:30 p.m. asking me to make copies of all the invoices I'd paid thus far and deliver them to the bank on Monday morning. The branch was getting the file in order for a meeting with the investment officer at headquarters. It was a typical last-minute request, made in a panic and making for my own frantic Friday night sorting piles of paperwork. It also meant a few very intense hours at the copy center on Saturday morning before they closed at noon.

First thing Monday morning, I delivered the invoices, expecting that was that. But of course it wasn't. It never was.

"Don't write any more checks until we get all your invoices sorted out," Mouna said.

"Okay, but I have a deposit to pay on the apartment I'm taking on Boulevard Mohammed V." It was my third move in less than a year. The first apartment was perfect, but Driss had arranged only a four-month sublet. The real tenant was willing to let me stay, but Driss wouldn't allow it.

"A deel iz a deel," he said in his charming French accent.

Would that more Moroccans had his point of view!

The second was a sixth-floor walk up—which helped with my weight loss regime—but the landlord's leering attentions as I slimmed down made me uncomfortable. Once more Driss came to the rescue with an apartment that his family owned on Boulevard Mohammed V, near the Marché Central. For five years it had been a dentist's office, and, although I wouldn't be moving in until April, it needed some basic work, like painting, kitchen cabinets . . . and a bathroom.

"Don't worry," Mouna said. "It won't be long. A couple of days at the most."

It seemed like the bank was using, or perhaps even writing, a different rule book at each stage of the project. Her reassurances were increasingly less reassuring.

The following Wednesday, I called Mouna from a taxi in front of the property manager's office to tell her that I had to pay the deposit on my apartment that moment or lose it. It wasn't strictly true because Driss's family would give me some leeway, but it was time to force the issue with the bank. I was expecting her to say, grudgingly, that I could go ahead and pay the deposit. But that wasn't her response.

Goat Cheese Salad with Fresh Figs

Preparation time: 20 minutes
Serves 4

Fascinated with fresh figs, which I'd never tasted, I developed this recipe for Rick's most popular dish while living a block from the Marché Central.

- **½ pound soft, log-shape goat cheese**

- **8 fresh figs**

- **2 handfuls arugula**

- **4 leaves red leaf lettuce**

- **16 fresh basil leaves, cut in ribbons**

DRESSING

½ cup olive oil

1 tablespoon balsamic vinegar

2 teaspoons lemon juice

2 teaspoons honey

2 pinches salt

1 pinch pepper

Divide the goat-cheese log into 12 slices. Cut the figs lengthwise into quarters. Prepare the dressing, whisking together all ingredients. Wash and dry the arugula and lettuce and tear into pieces. Plate the salad greens, red lettuce first then the arugula over top. Around the lettuce, alternate the goat cheese medallions with the figs, then drizzle the dressing over all. Top with basil ribbons.

Note: If you can't find fresh figs, you can soften dried figs by simmering them for 30 minutes in a marinade of 4 parts water, 2 parts balsamic vinegar, and 1 part honey.

"You can't write that check or any check," she said. "I just got instructions from the investment officer at headquarters that you're not permitted to write checks until you find another bank to loan you more money!"

Breaking down, I began crying hysterically. The taxi was double-parked on Boulevard Mohammed V, and I'm sure both motorists and pedestrians gave me curious stares. If they did, I didn't notice. It felt like I'd been hit in the stomach. This couldn't be happening. Between sobs I speed-dialed friends for help. First Driss. Once, twice, no response. Finally his chief of staff, Driss Slaoui, answered.

"I need—to talk—to the wali," I sobbed. "The bank—the bank . . ." was all I could manage. Driss Slaoui said he'd forward the message and the wali would call when he could.

Next, for moral support, I called Yasmina's Parliament office, leaving a sobbing voicemail. Yasmina had worked at one time in the legal department of the bank, and she had her own bad memories. When I reached a well-placed friend in Rabat, who was on good terms with the directors of the bank, he couldn't believe what had happened. Clearly I was in no state to articulate the intricacies of the problem—or even breathe properly—so he asked me to fax an explanation of the situation. After I did, my friend called me later that day to say he was going to arrange a meeting for me with Mohamed El Kettani, the director in charge of investment.

When Driss Benhima finally called, I was sitting in my tiny sixth-floor walk-up, exhausted and depressed.

"Well you may just have to sell it to someone else," he said.

He had a talent for using the right words to get me back in the fight and I shrugged off my self-pity with renewed persistence.

"Never," I said. "I'll find a way out of this. I have to."

I had a financial emergency and few options. The reserves of capital from The Usual Suspects after the house sale were dwindling away, and although I had been living frugally I was still working through my savings from the government salary that ended six months earlier. It was clear I wouldn't be spending a lot of time in my Marrakech riad, let alone supporting the mortgage, so I'd put it on the market as soon as the Ghattas house sale went through. Potential buyers, still timid after 9/11, were few and far between. I couldn't expect it to sell or even close overnight. My own source of capital—the money in my USG Thrift Savings Plan (similar to a 401k) and my personal contributions to a Federal pension that I would never get—were tied up in Washington and wouldn't be available until the end of my one-year leave of absence, when I officially resigned. That was six months down the road.

Meanwhile, Jean Michel Vitalis, an excitable piano instructor, was hounding me daily for the $6,000 balance I owed him for the beautiful Pleyel piano that he was selling me.

"The bank has cut off all my money for two months," I told him.

After a few choice French comments about bankers, he sympathetically said that he'd await my call when I could pay, but he was anxious to move it out of his house. It took up most of the space in a room that it shared with an upright.

My meeting with Mohamed El Kettani coincided with the US military's March 20 "Shock and Awe" assault on Baghdad. Images of the destruction ran through my mind as I took my morning walk before going to the bank. Clearly tough times lay ahead for many, and an American woman's symbolic investment in Casablanca seemed ever more politically unpopular. Returning to my apartment, I mounted the six flights of stairs and suddenly felt dizzy. My heart was pounding, and I thought I was having a heart attack. I called Driss's secretary, Fatima, and asked her for the number of a cardiologist.

"I think you're just having an anxiety attack," she said. "Go to your regular doctor, and see what he says."

Luckily the doctor's office was close to the bank. He confirmed it was stress and gave me a prescription for something to calm my nerves. I took the first pill and headed for my meeting.

I'd visited bank headquarters on Boulevard Moulay Youssef so often that the security guards in the lobby greeted me by name. Low-key and understated as bank headquarters go in Casablanca, that exterior—just like the wall surrounding a Moroccan palace—belied the wealth inside. Linked to Morocco's largest holding company, the bank had ties to the palace, and lush carpet covered the executive floor, beautifully furnished, that displayed the best of the bank's extensive collection of Moroccan art.

Short, intense, and resembling Nicolas Sarkozy, Nabil, the investment officer, was sitting in Mr. El Kettani's office. Although (I thought) we had been friends when I worked at the Consulate, the young hotshot was trying to run up the "success-calator" as fast as he could. My project meant nothing to him now that I was no longer a US diplomat. Nor was I connected to the palace, a prominent family, or even a major company. I was a lone American woman. He hadn't paid any attention to my file from the outset, and at the sign of the slightest difficulty he tried to pull the plug. The call from Rabat had convinced the bank to try a little harder to help me out of my financial predicament, though, which is why we all were in Mr. El Kettani's office.

As I detailed the history of my six-month relationship with the bank—including a reminder that I had tried to tell them costs were exceeding the original estimates—Nabil cut me off.

"We're going to help you find a second bank to give you an additional construction loan," he said. "But you'll also need to find additional capital. The house itself isn't enough to guarantee another loan. You'll need to raise around 2 million dirhams," around $200,000 then.

The statement stunned me. They had loaned me 2.5 million dirhams, and, with what I'd raised already, was expecting in commitments, and my own contributions, I'd have another 2.6 million dirhams. Finding 2 million more in capital presented an almost impossible task. There were no more Usual Suspects to round up.

Then again those famous words: "Don't worry," Nabil said.

They would introduce the project to capital risk firms—as he clumsily put it "capital riskers"—and institutional investors on my behalf. With the bank's tacit approval, it would be a lot easier to raise the money.

"I'm going to assign someone from my team to help put a financing proposal together in French," he said, doubtless trying to look good in front of his boss. "In the meantime, I will have to approve every check to ensure it is strictly for construction. No decoration expenses, no equipment expenses, no living expenses."

It was no use arguing. I left the meeting grumbling under my breath and returned to my apartment. I climbed the stairs with no ill effects except residual anger, fixed my lunch, and took another pill. Sitting in front of the TV watching the bombing of Baghdad, I suddenly felt very tired and fell asleep. Dealing with the bank may have taken an emotionally exhausting toll, but I didn't usually nap in the middle of the day.

Comparing notes with Saad Berrechid, a friend and Usual Suspect, we determined that the doctor hadn't given me antianxiety medication at all. He had prescribed sleeping pills! I certainly didn't have time to snooze, so I never took another pill.

Now that my course leading out of the financial crisis seemed clear, I called Driss and asked to see him. He invited me to breakfast that Sunday at his official residence. He had been busy recently, and I didn't want to worry him with my own troubles when clearly he had his own weighing on his mind.

"Why didn't you tell me before now?" he asked.

"I didn't want to tell you when it was just a problem. I decided to wait until I'd figured out how I was going to get out of it. I didn't want you telling me to sell it to someone else again!"

A week later, Driss was named director of the Agency for the Development of the North. Had he tried to bring change too soon, or had his opinionated and outspoken comments disturbed the status quo in Casablanca? Now he would direct an agency whose role was advisory, consultative, and in the background. Not a place to use a man with energy, decisiveness, and a proactive nature. It wasn't good news for either of us. There would be a new wali, someone from the ranks of the Ministry of Interior. In one day he was gone, along with Driss Slaoui, Rachid El Andaloussi, Fatima, Leila, and Bouchaib. My whole support group. All at once, in every aspect of the work that lay ahead—supervising construction, wrestling with the banks, working with the Wilaya and city bureaucrats—I was totally alone.

~

Nabil had talked a good game in front of Mr. El Kettani, but our next meeting alone didn't go as well. I had a preference for the second bank, and I needed a meeting with their president. I asked Nabil if he could set it up.

"Your contacts are better than mine," he said. "You can do it."

So much for help.

A good friend interceded and made the introduction. When I finally connected with the president's secretary, she told me that he was heavily scheduled and traveling. He could see me May 6 at the earliest. When Nabil heard the news, his face fell. Clearly he wanted another financial institution to share the burden of supporting my project sooner rather than later.

"Can't we start with finding the additional capital?" I asked. "Could you begin to pitch the project to capital risk firms and institutional investors as you promised?"

"There's no sense going after capital before you have the second loan," he said. "Once you have the other bank on board, the capital will fall into place."

"I can't just spend six weeks spinning my wheels. I want to be proactive."

"I'll set up a meeting for you with one of my team who'll prepare the financial presentation."

He introduced me to Mlle. Benjelloun, a perky young woman from the investment department dressed for success in a snug-fitting expensive suit. She spoke English and probably wondered why she had to devote her precious time to my lunatic project. It wasn't what the bank normally did. I gave her my three-year projection tables, cost-of-sales calculations, records of expenditures, and forecasts. In retrospect, they were overly optimistic, but there was sound logic to the calculations. She was supposed to use my figures, calculate five-year projections, and add the French narrative.

It took her two weeks to give me the presentation. I made corrections on the hard copy and brought them to her. At which point, she gave me the disk and told me to make the corrections myself. Opening her files at home, I saw the disk didn't contain the financial projections beyond the first year, so it was left to me to finish the French presentation.

Two weeks later, preparing for the meeting with the president of the second bank, I realized in horror that she had vastly understated sales, profit, and cash flow in her projections. Not understanding the basis of her assumptions, I phoned and asked for a meeting to discuss the numbers. Irritated, she said she'd based her projections on my figures and, even more annoyed, said we would meet with the investment officer later that day to sort it out.

I reviewed the figures again and discovered her error. She had used only beverage sales to account for *all sales!*

Mlle. Benjelloun walked into Nabil's office visibly hostile. I calmly explained her error, and she screamed that she had never seen that page of my figures.

"Well, here's a note in your handwriting in the margin," I fired back.

She shrugged her shoulders, sniffed, and glared at me. "Well, at least there's positive cash flow. If you want something different, you're going to have to do it yourself," she said, before standing up to leave. On her way out she screamed hysterically, "*You're the worst, most ungrateful client I've ever had!*"

And you're nothing but an aspiring starlet who's muffed her lines, I thought.

Nabil sat totally immobile, no doubt ruing for the thousandth time that he had ever met me. I made the revisions myself. This was customer service.

I later delivered a chart of checks that I needed to write, marked URGENT. He ignored it. Meanwhile, on my daily visits to the construction site, all of my subcontractors were complaining about waiting to be paid for work completed on their contracts. It was getting harder and harder to put off the professional firms whose work was competent and on time.

Days went by with phone calls and faxes to Nabil unanswered. Taking a page from Idriss Bousfiha's book, I took to going directly to bank headquarters and waiting in the reception area to catch him coming out of the elevator. One time, he got word that I was waiting for him, and he fled out a back door—like a criminal! His lack of professionalism and client service outraged me, but I was determined to get my project done, and I would take on every last petty villain who kept trying to change the script.

In a way, though, Nabil's behavior made a perverse sort of sense. That I was here in Casablanca, fighting for my project, not going away, made me quite unusual. Well-intentioned Americans, coming to Morocco in hopes of doing business, arrived full of energy and enthusiasm, and their potential Moroccan partners treated them royally. The deal was close, an American executive would say on his exit interview, and he would return to Morocco in another six months to get started. In the meantime all the negotiation and paperwork would continue by phone, fax, and e-mail.

Six months later he would come back, surprised there had been no communication, perturbed to have to start all over again. More dinners, generous hospitality, and promises. The signing ceremony was being scheduled for his next visit. That signing ceremony would never take place, though. These executives couldn't understand why deals always fell through, but my colleagues in Rabat and Casablanca had a phrase for it: They'd been "couscoused." Nabil and the others didn't know what to do about me as they realized, much to their horror, that I wasn't going anywhere.

I wasn't about to be couscoused.

When the time came for my meeting with the president of the prospective second bank, his director for project investment joined us. I presented the project in French using the proposal that Mlle. Benjelloun had "helped" prepare.

"We'd be interested in providing the second line of financing," the president said, "if your main bank shares the real estate lien with us. But first you need to add capital." He had the exact same figures that Mr. El Kettani and Nabil had mentioned—between 1.5 and 2 million dirhams—but Nabil clearly had been wrong to tell me to wait until after the May meeting to look for more capital.

It perplexed the two bankers that my first bank hadn't already moved to help me. To them, it was a sign that the first bank didn't take me or my project seriously, so why should a second bank stick its neck out?

Next steps included following up with the (Moroccan) investment director, but he hadn't expressed the same enthusiasm as his (French) president. It was clear that, at least in principle, the French bank executive had the capacity to accept a complex and significant project headed by a woman. His Moroccan colleague didn't share the same attitude.

I was crestfallen. In six weeks of anticipation, I had built up expectations that the result would be immediate participation—but that wasn't the case. I went directly to see Nabil, himself anxious to get a report. I knew he was counting on good news because his secretary ushered me right into his office.

"*Merde*," he said when he heard the result.

I was none too happy myself, reminding Nabil that I'd asked him weeks ago if I should start trying to find capital. He'd told me to wait.

"Now we need to work fast to line up meetings with capital risk firms and institutional investors," I said.

Again he dragged his feet, but he said he was willing to talk with their own institutional investment arm, Attijari Finance. As for other firms: "You have all the contacts you made when you were a diplomat. Go ahead and see what you can come up with."

Truth is, he didn't know how to help an ordinary investor like me. He had no idea how to source capital cold. He worked with "relationships," and for his career the closer those relationships were to the palace or the wealthy elite, the better. He never would have told one of his Moroccan clients to go ahead and find backing on his own because he had connections with the palace. No, in that case, Nabil would stand right by his side.

But there was nothing to be done about it. My more immediate problem was that my cash was running out. Just as I'd feared, I was having to use funds from the US for urgent project payments that the bank wouldn't approve. But meanwhile, I had living expenses. I implored Nabil to help me and proposed a personal loan of 100,000 dirhams against my house in Marrakech, which had sold but not closed, and another 100,000 dirham loan to tide me over while I made the rounds of capital risk firms. He grudgingly agreed.

Then began a tedious and discouraging three-month process of meeting with capital risk firms. Venture capital firms in the States might have had more appreciation and understanding of what I was trying to do, but not only did I not need enough money to interest them but the international politics complicated the situation. The Bush administration's post- 9/11 rhetoric and now the Iraq War were feeding an already legendary American xenophobia. I didn't stand a chance. Anti-American sentiment doubtless fueled some of the chilly receptions that I received from a number of Casablanca firms—or at least it gave them a convenient excuse for their lack of interest.

I made the appointment with Attijari Finance myself, and the meeting further confirmed that Nabil had no idea what he was talking about: They didn't invest in small private projects. So I generated a list of names on my own and schlepped from one firm to another. One contact, who couldn't help, recommended another, who might. It came to feel like a ploy just to get rid of me, passing me off like a hot potato.

My ability to size up anyone even a bit serious about the prospect sharpened. Most of the men with whom I met wouldn't take even a small risk or even try to convince their superiors to consider my project. Almost uniformly condescending, they clearly found my idea frivolous, the product of an emotional reaction to 9/11. So when the facetious question—"Do you have any experience in the restaurant business?"—arose, I answered with a big smile, "No, but I really love to cook!"

A few capital risk managers said frankly that restaurants had a bad reputation in financial circles as money laundering fronts or as tokens of wealthy fathers indulging spoiled sons. One manager, warming to the subject, asked me, "Have you ever heard the Arab proverb, 'The son of a duck is a floater'? That really does describe some of these rich youngsters." I appreciated his insight but pointed out that I wasn't young, rich, male, or Moroccan. Still no dice. Another potential investor told me that my project was too risky because, in a city of 5 million, "only 5,000 people go out to restaurants."

If, on the other hand, I spotted a chance to convince a firm to consider investing, I told them about my twenty years as an entrepreneur in the service industry, first with a travel agency that I founded and later a real estate project that I helmed, renting out serviced executive offices in Tokyo. I made the distinction that Rick's wasn't just a restaurant; it was a total experience, a tourist escape, a romantic throwback to a bygone era. Then I told them that I loved to cook. Eyes invariably glazed over.

I'd barely started this exhausting odyssey when, on a balmy Friday night, as I was listening to Ella Fitzgerald singing Cole Porter, an explosion blasted through the city. *Probably something collapsing down at the port or a truck blowing a tire*, I thought. Then my phone rang.

"I'm having drinks with some guys from the Sheraton, and they just got a call that the Hotel Farah was attacked by suicide bombers," said a friend, his voice shaking. "That's not all. They got inside La Casa de España and set off a bomb, and there was another attack at the Belgian Consulate."

"The Positano is right across that narrow street from the Consulate," I said, reeling. "Flavio, their chef, is helping me with kitchen design and recruitment. I'll call him and call you back."

Flavio revealed that Jewish-owned Positano had been the real target. "Our restaurant was full of clients," he said. "One of the police guards from the Belgian Consulate stopped the bomber and was killed. Others were injured, and we're waiting for the ambulances."

The terrorists targeted five sites: the Hotel Farah, La Casa de España, the restaurant Positano, the Jewish Cemetery, and the Jewish Circle, a social club. In all, forty-five people died—a double tragedy for the country. Moroccans had targeted and killed their fellow Moroccans. The king visited Casablanca several days later to tour the sites, visit the wounded in the hospital, and meet with government officials.

The *New York Times* published an article criticizing the king for waiting so long to visit. The entire country was in shock, and the attacks followed the birth of his son by eight days. My letter to the *Times*, "Morocco Is in Mourning," related some of those details—and included a line to the effect that it said a lot about a country when an American woman, alone, could be working on a project like Rick's Café.

I never for a second considered packing my bags and abandoning Casablanca, but investment firms were even more skittish after

May 16. Meeting well over a dozen of what I now called capital risk-averse firms alternately left me discouraged, insulted, or defiant. The Canadian head of one of the firms looked at my investment figures and projections and offered some advice. "It's clear why you're having a hard time," he said. "Why in the world have you been paying your workers? Why don't you behave like Moroccan women? Don't pay. Just wring your hands and cry."

He was serious.

And I was seriously running out of money. At the end of May I had $800 and work that still needed to be paid. Nabil wouldn't approve checks for equipment, but the telephones, sound system, and the two cash registers all needed internal cabling. No suppliers would do any work until they had an advance. Construction had reached a critical point: Cables had to be strung internally before the plaster contractor could plaster the walls. Nabil refused to approve checks for any of it.

Meanwhile, Mr. El Alami had retired from the bank, and Mouna indicated that the new president was reading every letter he received to get a clear picture of the bank's ongoing projects. Apparently people had been receiving quick responses to those letters. I immediately wrote him and explained all my difficulties. I asked for a personal loan, which of course Nabil had failed to secure, and 500,000 dirhams more on the 2.5 million they'd already lent me—which they had promised to add once the second bank coughed up the next 2 million.

I explained my problems finding capital and while there were prospects it was taking time to convince a firm even to undertake an evaluation. I also asked him to assign my file to someone in the investment department—other than Nabil—not so overextended, who could work with me on a more day-to-day basis. Two days after I delivered the letter, the new president's secretary confirmed a meeting for May 30.

My friends in high places in Rabat raved about Khalid Oudghiri—
but that didn't quell my apprehension. This was a make-or-break
moment. If he didn't understand, it would put me at an impasse, a
dead-end. My meeting with Mr. El Alami, his predecessor, had offered
a lucky turn of fate. Dare I pray for lightning to strike twice?

We met in Oudghiri's office—modern, businesslike, starkly elegant. Unfortunately Nabil was also there, but as it turned out that
hardly mattered. He faded into the furniture almost immediately.
Later, when he "forgot" key details of the meeting, I wondered if he
really had been there at all.

Khalid Oudghiri represented an unusual choice to lead the bank.
Young and independent, not tied to any family or clique, Oudghiri
exuded self-confidence. He probably intimidated most of the other
bank directors, who were settled into static routines. The old guard
feared the changes that he might bring to their comfortable little
world—changes he *did* bring by introducing projects much more high
profile than mine, so that ultimately he was cast aside. But he was
there for me when I needed him, just like so many moments when the
planets aligned in my favor.

Focused, decisive, and pragmatic, Oudghiri listened closely,
actively assessing what I was saying. He understood the project, both
for its symbolic importance to Casablanca and its relevance to the
bank. He later said that the bank had to change its image from supporting projects linked only to elites from business, high flyers with
connections to the palace, family groups, or personal friends. Rick's
Café represented an important marker in the bank's evolution.

It was immediately clear that he wasn't going to let the project
fail. What's more, he didn't talk down to me. We reviewed the list of
outstanding bills that needed paying.

"We'll authorize this, this, this, this, and this," he said.

I couldn't believe what I was hearing. He was still strict, but he approved the final piano payment as well as advances for the telephones, sound system, cash registers, and other equipment. Still no respite for my personal and operational expenses, however. But he did commit to a personal loan to The Usual Suspects for my non-construction expenses and a bridge loan to keep construction going while I looked for capital. When the second bank materialized as a second financier, they'd work it out between the banks.

"The main urgency is not to let the project shut down," he said.

Is this love? I wondered as I left his office.

But of course, nothing happened quickly. By mid-June I could write checks for construction payments, but still no movement on the personal loan. I was down to $40. I hadn't been this poor since the early days of starting my travel agency in 1974 in Portland.

In early July, someone recommended that I see a capital risk firm that belonged to the largest banking group in Morocco. I called Moucine Bakkali, their deputy director, for an appointment. They didn't provide capital for restaurants. I tried to explain to him that it wasn't just any restaurant, but he politely declined a meeting. I called the contact who had given me the introduction, and he called Mr. Bakkali, who called me back and confirmed an appointment. It was my sixteenth meeting in the desperate search for a capital investor.

Their address placed them in an impressive modern metal edifice that contained the banking group's commercial headquarters and also a shopping complex. The lobby directory didn't have a listing for the capital risk firm, though.

"Oh, you want to go around to the back of the building," the security guard said. "Turn at the coffee shop on the corner, and go to the end of the block."

Even though Casablanca has a temperate climate exactly like San Diego's, it was still a hot July day. I tried to keep cool as I made my way down the street, past dogs barking loudly and incessantly. I'd driven past the racing track across the street many times but had never heard the yelping. They didn't stop the whole time I was inside. How could anyone work in this environment? It also made me wonder how prominent a member of the banking group this firm really was.

In his early fifties, Mr. Bakkali dressed sensibly in short sleeves and slacks. The laptop and files on his desk indicated a hands-on approach. *Good.* I gave him the sixteenth iteration of the presentation packet that described my inspiration to build Rick's, why it was important for Casablanca, and how it could help attract positive publicity for Morocco during these troubled times.

"Although I told you on the phone that we don't invest in restaurants, I can see this is much more," he said. "I'm going to help you. I don't know if I can convince the director general, and we have shareholders—the European Investment Bank and the Spanish and French investment agencies—who might not be keen, but I'm going to try to get them interested."

Mr. El Alami, Khalid Oudghiri, and Mr. Bakkali were the only finance people in the entire city sincerely interested. I burst into tears of relief. It was the first time I actually cried in front of a potential collaborator. I'd cried on the phone to friends asking for their help, cried alone when the situation soured, cried at the end of *Casablanca*—but I'd managed to maintain a stoic appearance in all these critical meetings. I adamantly refused to play along with the Canadian businessman's suggestion, which would allow detractors to claim I was using feminine wiles to achieve my objectives unfairly. But now I couldn't help it. Thankfully Mr. Bakkali didn't mind.

He asked for a week or two to sound out the various entities involved to see where the challenges were going to lie. But that still left me in limbo for the month of August, when the whole country goes on vacation. Nothing would move until September.

By mid-July I was literally down to loose change, still waiting for the proceeds from the sale of the Marrakech house. Nabil continued to be useless and even laughed at my predicament. He claimed that the president had never agreed to the personal loan and that they hadn't unblocked any money for construction or equipment. Mouna and the deputy branch manager finally advanced me 50,000 dirhams to keep me going until everyone returned from vacation.

After months of grief, Nabil left me a message on a Thursday relating that a meeting had been set up for the following Monday with my old friend the deputy director general, my original contact at the bank. There would be some sort of closure in this meeting, I knew, but I couldn't make it.

Midway through my humiliating tour of capital risk firms, I'd recalled the old Hollywood saying, "If you want to have a friend in this town, get a dog." Feeling friendless, I needed a source of unconditional love. My Internet research indicated that a Coton de Tulear would make for a compatible match. A kennel just outside Toulouse sent me an adorable photo of one, and I arranged to pick up Pacha that Saturday, returning to Casablanca on the Monday of the meeting. I wasn't about to deprive Pacha or myself of proper companionship, so Nabil moved the meeting to the Tuesday after my return.

I didn't know what to expect. In some ways, it was déjà vu all over again. I'd met with these two gentlemen in 2002 when the bank first tried to derail the project. Our relationship during the intervening months hadn't exactly been cordial, but they were meeting with me at the direction of the new president.

Ali attempted to clear the air and asked me to explain the situation. As I itemized the list of mistakes, affronts, and general lack of concern and interest, Nabil tried to deny or defend himself. Ali snapped at him in Arabic, after which he said nothing.

Then Ali indicated that the bank would loan me an additional 3 million dirhams—which meant I wouldn't need a second bank loan—but I was still obliged to source additional capital. They acknowledged that we all were counting on the capital risk firm of which they were well aware—with the caveat that approval would come in October at the earliest. Until then, they were adhering to the restriction that checks from the company account pay only construction, nothing else. They'd made a commitment to lend me the additional money, but the restriction to pay only construction costs finally broke me.

Ali had none of it, though. "Mme. Kriger, this is no cause for tears. This is finance!"

By the end of October, the capital risk firm agreed to back the project, the bank released the funds, and Rick's Café could finally become a reality.

~

I never thought twice about it but probably few in my place would have bought fifty lamps, lanterns, and beaded chandeliers prior to construction and before the bank started to pay attention. Little did I know that I was following an Arab proverb: "Spend what is in your pocket; you will get more from the unknown."

It wasn't that I was deliberately skirting their rules. A blundering American with no guidelines, I had a rather liberal interpretation of the word "construction." Call it an example of my canny naïveté. If I had waited to buy those beautiful lamps—which make the most stunning, dramatic impression—until the bank had approved, our customers might be dining in the dark!

Today, those glamorous brass-beaded lamps—so similar to the film that they immediately transport diners into the movie—heighten the ambience of Rick's Café. But the iconic design of the restaurant in my grand and dilapidated mansion was the work of someone else.

FOUR
Designing the Set

Now someone had to take the basic structure and add details to transcend the film. Only one person came to mind: William Henri Willis.

In a Prague bookstore shortly after I learned of my posting to Casablanca, I found a large illustrated book called *Moroccan Interiors*—a beautiful work with photographs and narratives of stunning homes throughout Morocco, their owners, for the most part, mentioned but not pictured. Not so with Bill. In the book, wearing red lounging pajamas and leather babouche slippers, he sits in a sculpted wood Moroccan armchair, a crystal water glass resting on a side table. Only the cognoscenti knew the glass held Jack Daniel's.

As soon as I arrived in Morocco in 1998, sunny Marrakech drew me toward it—the Place Jamaa el Fna, the souk, the palm trees, and the particular style that blended Western architecture with Moroccan craftsmanship. I didn't know that Bill Willis had had anything to do with this until I had dinner at Dar Yacout, a sprawling palace of pools, palms, fireplaces, and dramatic lighting. Gnaoua musicians played in the background while diners, seated on low banquettes, enjoyed a Moroccan feast. Bill had done the interiors when it was a private house and then again after Mohamed Zkhiri converted it into a restaurant. Zkhiri had lived in New Orleans and Munich before returning home to Marrakech with the energy and imagination to create a tourist's dream.

I was dying to meet Bill, and then—First Lady Hillary Clinton made it happen. She didn't do it personally, mind you, but the opportunity arose at the end of a reception given in her honor by then–Crown

Prince Mohammed in the Grand Ballroom of the Hotel Mamounia at the end of her visit to Morocco in March 1999.

Given my flair for logistics and my nickname as "the maven of Marrakech," I was appointed control officer in charge of the first lady's Marrakech schedule. That meant coordinating all events, including a speech on tolerance, a visit to an orphanage for abandoned infants, and a women's roundtable. I practically lived in Marrakech that February and March preparing for her visit.

The agenda included one unusual activity: a hike in the Atlas Mountains since she would arrive in Marrakech on the day of the Aid Al Kebir, one of the holiest days of the Muslim calendar. The holiday honors Abraham's willingness to sacrifice his son in obedience to God's command. While Jews and Christians identify the son as Isaac, Muslims believe it was Ismail. Whichever son, an angel of God appeared at the last minute to spare the boy and direct Abraham to sacrifice a ram instead.

Days before the holiday, loaded onto all forms of transportation— motorbikes, donkey carts, pickup trucks, ordinary cars, once even a school bus—live sheep are kept in garages or yards, on balconies or terraces, in sidewalk sheds or corrals . . . and probably in a few kitchens. On the morning of the Aid, they are slaughtered by the head of the family. The streets run with blood, bleating fills the air, then smoke and the pungent odor of burnt hair as the head (of the sheep, not the family) is put on the fire and families share the feast.

My colleague Paul Malik and I did the advance work to select the site, hearing of a mountain guide from Imlil, a village at the base of Mt. Toubkal in the High Atlas. It was an hour's nail-biting ride from Marrakech to Asni, thanks to the winding roads that had witnessed many a bus accident, but we knew that the police would control the route for the first lady. Eager to meet us, show us his family home, and suggest some possible short hikes, the guide, Mohamed, met us at the turnoff to Imlil and took us in his van along the narrow road that bordered a shallow running stream dotted with rocks. We passed the luxurious Kasbah Tamasloht—now a deluxe hotel owned by Richard Branson—and came to a stop at the small cluster of buildings that was Imlil.

Mohamed pointed across the stream and up the sloping, rocky foothill to his house. I looked for a bridge.

"There isn't one," Mohamed said. "But it's easy to cross on the rocks."

Easy for Mohamed maybe.

"Of course they'll build some sort of bridge for the first lady," I said. Hillary Clinton wasn't going to leap over rocks like a mountain goat—but that's exactly what I had to do. I clung gratefully to Mohamed's arm as we forded the stream.

On the other side, we climbed the fairly steep, gravely path, Mohamed again aiding me at various points where the rocks shifted loosely underfoot. The ten-minute climb left me a bit winded when we finally reached the house, a typical Berber mountain dwelling, built of handmade brick with two floors and a rooftop terrace.

We walked in the main entrance on ground level, passed the room where the donkey lived, and climbed cement stairs, covered with a Berber carpet, to the living quarters on the second floor. Mohamed's mother was preparing tea, and, although there was a nice salon with banquettes, Mohamed said we'd have tea on the terrace. We ascended a narrower stairway, and the stunning sight of snow-capped Mt. Toubkal—the highest in North Africa—came into view, dominating the mountainous panorama. It took away what little breath I had left. Apparently Martin Scorsese had shot the Tibetan mountain scenes in *Kundun* on location here. Serving tea to the first lady on the terrace of this simple home would nicely showcase Moroccan hospitality and the diversity of the country's natural beauty.

As we sipped our mint tea and marveled at the view, Mohamed pointed down to a path that followed the stream—the first lady's route. We climbed back down the hill, and he led us along a picturesque course where women were grinding wheat in a communal mill and we encountered smiling children in colorful attire—very natural and friendly. It was perfect. Well, almost.

Downstream, where we had to cross back, it was a bit wider. Paul hopped across, and I felt like a wimp crossing tentatively from rock to rock. I heard something behind me, turned, and saw a woman carrying a large, covered tagine scampering across the stones. She passed me with a look of pity, and Paul roared with laughter. In his cable to Washington reporting on the hike, the overall control officer for the visit, Economic Counselor Richard Johnson, wrote something like: "It's a ten-minute climb to the house, judged as 'fairly steep' by Commercial Attaché Kathy Kriger, fifty-three, and a 'city girl.'"

On the day the first lady arrived, I sat in the airport VIP tent waiting with the wali of Marrakech, who had already attended three slaughters, and it was only noon. After checking into the Mamounia Hotel and having a quick lunch, Mrs. Clinton and her entourage, including a Peace Corps volunteer who lived in a nearby village, set out for Imlil. Chelsea wasn't feeling well, so she stayed behind.

The night before, the Moroccan just-in-time logistics system sprang into action with supplies and workers flown in by helicopter. Footbridges instantly covered both crossings, and the path up to Mohamed's house gained some carved-out foot grips and a series of handrails. The first lady was thrilled but lamented that Chelsea wasn't there.

Once the hike was over, the gendarmes dismantled the bridges and removed the handrails. Squeezed in a *grand taxi*, Mohamed set out on the four-hour drive to Ouarzazate the next day to meet a group. Gendarmes waved it to the side of the road. An officer stuck his head in the window and asked if any of the passengers was named Mohamed. Mohamed nodded, a bit worried.

"You're wanted back in Imlil," the officer said. "Chelsea Clinton wants to take the hike."

Once again to the rescue, Moroccan logistics put back all the bridges and handrails.

Those thrilling, exhausting five days culminated in a who's-who reception at the Mamounia Hotel. Afterward, several of us repaired to the bar, where Paul nudged me and said, "Isn't that Bill Willis?"

"Yes, it is," I said, "and he's talking to Mohamed Zkhiri, the owner of Dar Yacout."

Bill's route to Morocco was even more circuitous than mine. Born in Memphis and raised in Mississippi, he was orphaned as a teenager and found his way to Paris, where he enrolled in the École des Beaux Arts in 1956. He returned to New York and worked as an interior designer, but Europe drew him back to Rome, where he set up an interior design practice and antiques shop. During the early '60s he lived *la dolce vita*, establishing a lifelong friendship with J. Paul Getty Jr. In 1966, he moved to Morocco and, like me, fell in love with the country and the culture.

Nor was his notoriety confined just to Morocco. Over the years, he'd established an international reputation for blending western architecture and design with Moroccan artisanal crafts. That he was a real character only enhanced his celebrity. He spoke with an accent

Lamb Tagine

Preparation time: 45 minutes
Cooking time: 2 hours
Serves 4

While the sound of braying sheep isn't jarring in the countryside, it's quite another thing in Casablanca. Bleating sheep, sold out of impromptu street markets in the week leading up to the great feast, increase the normal noise and congestion. Families originally hailing from the *bled*—rural Morocco—tend to maintain the tradition of the live sheep sacrifice. The *Casablancais,* however, have adapted to changing tastes and times by preparing a slow cooked stew with a nice cut of lamb in the same spirit.

1³/₄ tablespoons olive oil

4 meaty 1-pound lamb shanks

2 medium white onions, chopped

2 teaspoons minced garlic

2 teaspoons minced fresh ginger

pinch of saffron

cold water

1 teaspoon salt

1 teaspoon ground black pepper

1 tablespoon chopped fresh parsley

¹/₃ cup chopped fresh cilantro

1 tablespoon sugar

1½ cinnamon sticks

18 pitted prunes

¼ cup toasted sliced almonds

Heat 1 tablespoon oil over medium heat in the Dutch oven. Brown lamb shanks in batches in a Dutch oven. Remove and set aside. Add ½ tablespoon more of olive oil, onions, and garlic and cook on high heat, stirring frequently, until onions are translucent, around 5–10 minutes. Add meat, ginger, and saffron to the Dutch oven and then enough cold water almost to cover the meat. Add salt, pepper, parsley, and 1 tablespoon cilantro. Stir to blend, bring to a boil, and cook for 10 minutes. Reduce heat, cover, and simmer for 1 hour 15 minutes or until meat is fork tender. Remove meat and set aside, covered. Simmer the sauce uncovered for about 15 minutes until it slightly thickens.

To prepare the prunes, combine remaining oil, sugar, and cinnamon in a 1-quart saucepan. Cook over medium heat until sugar begins to caramelize, around 3 minutes. Reduce heat, add prunes and ½ cup water, stirring to blend. Simmer for 5–10 minutes until prunes soften. Set aside.

To serve, spoon thickened sauce over the shanks and garnish with prunes, almonds, and the rest of the cilantro.

Note: In Morocco this dish is commonly cooked in a flameproof ceramic dish with a conical vented top called a "tagine." A heavy Dutch oven can accomplish this same task.

of pure Mississippi. With his Jack Daniel's, cigarettes, southern drawl, and rakish courtliness, he seemed to have stepped right out of a Tennessee Williams play.

Paul and I introduced ourselves and apologized to Mohamed for keeping Dar Yacout on hold for two months while the first lady's advance team—who insisted she and her entourage had to eat there—went back and forth with the Secret Service, who insisted that the narrow winding streets made access and exit too risky. In the end, the Secret Service prevailed.

Just then, Mohamed's phone rang, and he excused himself, leaving Bill all to us. He was delightfully engaging, full of commentary on the reception and the people, recounted with acerbic humor. We gleefully shared anecdotes of the visit, including the story about the hike in the Atlas Mountains, which he loved. Bill told us how he accompanied J. Paul Getty Jr. and his wife, Talitha, on their honeymoon in 1966. Invited to their wedding in Rome, Bill demurred, having just settled in Tangier. He offered instead to guide them around Morocco.

The couple fell in love with Marrakech and on the spot decided to buy the eighteenth-century Palais de la Zahia around the corner from the Mamounia. They hired Bill for the renovation that launched his career. The two owners of the Palais who followed the Gettys—actor Alain Delon and current owner philosopher Bernard-Henri Lévy—also asked Bill to undertake renovations, providing him with a good source of income. A fan, I confessed to loving his eclectic style and said that my own decorating sense could be defined as "Bill Willis wannabe." He was very gracious and invited me to call or visit.

We learned later that Mohamed Zkhiri's phone call had come from the royal palace. The first lady had gone from the Mamounia reception to the palace for her audience with King Hassan II. At the end of their meeting, the King announced, "This evening, Mme.

Clinton, my daughters would like to invite you and your staff to join them for dinner at DarYacout." Suddenly those roads and access problems didn't seem so insurmountable.

Bill took vicarious pleasure in the popularity of Dar Yacout and loved to recount the old days there. Once, I mentioned I was having dinner with friends in the glassed-in room with just one round table and its own fireplace.

"Oh I do love that room," Bill said. "It was always Mick Jagger's favorite."

—

As soon as I saw the Ghattas house, I wanted to get Bill involved. We were friends, but I certainly didn't consider myself part of his inner circle, and it was obvious that I wasn't rolling in money. When I called and asked if I could talk to him about a project, he invited me to his house for drinks on a Saturday afternoon.

Bill's home lay at the end of a narrow winding route through the Medina, past the donkey orphanage and rows of iron workers' stalls. Just steps from the tomb of Sidi Bel Abbes, the patron saint of Marrakech, a simple, unadorned wood door gave entry to the twenty-two-room harem wing of an eighteenth-century palace that belonged to a distant relative of the royal family.

"It's been decades since the place was frequented by ladies," Bill once quipped, smiling and raising an eyebrow.

Traditionally the most beautifully painted and decorated spaces in homes and palaces, the harem wing in Bill's house had the addition of fireplaces, *tadelakt* walls, and decorative fixtures on the brilliantly ornate ceilings. He received guests in his bright, sunlit sitting room, seated in a straight-back Spanish chair with carved wooden arms. Behind the chair stood an antique floor lamp with an ivory silk shade, and to the side a marble-topped pedestal table with a crystal ashtray and a designated space for his glass of Jack Daniel's. An ice machine, placed discreetly and conveniently around a corner, hummed faintly.

Like Driss Benhima months earlier, Bill was nothing but positive. In fact, he was wildly enthusiastic about the project as soon as the words came out of my mouth.

"Well, I absolutely love that movie," he said. "I've always wondered why no one ever tried to create Rick's Café in Casablanca, but what luck that nobody ever did."

He agreed to join the project as my aesthetic advisor but said I'd have to get a local architect to draw up the official plans and handle all the permits. He gave me two names. The first—who just happened to be my investor Ahmed's brother-in-law's brother—had a reputation for being an "artist," but Bill had never met him. The second was doing some work in Marrakech and had expressed interest in collaborating with Bill.

I didn't know either man. I chose the comfort factor of the family connection with Ahmed. The man's wife had an office downtown, so he worked at home. He spoke no English, so we communicated in French. He wasn't nearly as enthusiastic about recreating Rick's Café as he was about restoring a mansion in the Ancienne Medina. I showed him the house later in the week. Still focused on restoration of the house as it had been during the '40s, he didn't have much of a feel for *Casablanca*—which frankly annoyed me. How could he miss the obvious value in linking our project to the movie?

More and more people were calling him an "artist," and I finally understood that as code to say that he had an artist's creative sense, loved restoration for restoration's sake, and had little interest in helping a client realize the commercial potential of an investment.

He dodged my question about how he anticipated collaborating with Bill, turning the conversation back to his own talents. Other architects had told me that I should expect problems with any architect having to work with Bill, given Bill's eclectic design sense, disdain for regulations, time, or budgets—not to mention his strong personality and reputation for high fees.

The first architect and I had one or two additional meetings, each at his home, but they were difficult to arrange because he was entering a competition and spending time at the offices of his bidding partner. I went to see him in July right after The Usual Suspects formed. By then Ahmed was out, and the purchase of the house could have happened at any time.

"Will you be ready to get to work in the coming weeks?" I asked.

"I'll be up north for the month of August, of course, so I suppose I could start sometime in September," he said. "That is, if we don't win this competition."

Bill had to take a larger role. He just had to.

Before I talked to him, I called Mohamed Zkhiri, owner of Dar Yacout, and asked his advice. Good friends, he and Bill had worked together for thirteen years, even though their forceful personalities made for some turbulent dustups.

Mohamed didn't hesitate. "It will be difficult from time to time, but you'll never regret it."

Relieved, I called Bill and told him the architect-"artist" was impossible and asked him to take a larger role.

"I'll be glad to do more," he said. "I've got plenty of ideas. We're lucky this guy didn't work out. But you still need a local architect. Why don't you call Hakim Benjelloun? He speaks English and has already said he wants to work with me."

Benjelloun sounded friendly and eager. We met in his office—already an improvement—that afternoon. He dressed like an American architect in a corduroy jacket with suede elbow patches. An exquisite vintage 1930s map of Casablanca dominated his office, a good sign, and his background immediately put me at ease. He studied architecture at the University of California at Berkeley and worked in New York before returning to Casablanca to start his own firm. He was excited about working with Bill on the project, had seen the film, and thought it was a great idea. He promised to have staff in his office in August in case the sale went through.

Shortly after Hakim agreed to work with us, Bill invited me to a "client lunch" one Saturday in his home, starting with Bloody Marys in the sitting room.

Drinking our delicious cocktails, we talked about the menu for Rick's.

"You have to have a good hamburger," Bill said, recalling the burgers that the AAA Club served across the street from the Wilaya.*

Then we moved on to lunch. It was summer, but Bill's house—apart from the glassed-in sitting room which overlooked a courtyard—felt cool and somber. The central sitting area had a domed, dark-wood painted ceiling dominated by a giant hanging brass lantern with clear glass panes and walls with a terra-cotta tint. We sat at a low round table in front of a fireplace. The dramatic dragon's head andirons caught my eye.

"I bought them from J. Paul Getty Jr. in 1973 at the auction he held to raise the ransom to free his son Paolo, who had been kidnapped by Italian gangsters," Bill said.

---

* Yes, the American Automobile Association. From the '60s until the mid-'70s, there were so many Americans attached to the military bases in Morocco that the AAA maintained a thriving restaurant, bar, and social club.

Bill Willis's Bloody Mary

Preparation time: 5 minutes
Serves 2

Bill's Bloody Marys made our lunch even more productive—Cheers!

3 ounces vodka

1 cup tomato juice

juice of $\frac{1}{2}$ lemon

$\frac{1}{4}$ teaspoon Worcestershire sauce

Tabasco sauce to taste

$\frac{1}{2}$ teaspoon Coleman's mustard powder, or more to taste

1 teaspoon horseradish, or more to taste

ice

1 celery stalk

pinch of celery salt

In a pitcher, mix vodka, tomato juice, lemon juice, Worcestershire sauce, Tabasco, mustard powder, and horseradish. Stir vigorously so that mustard and horseradish blend well. Pour into glasses half filled with ice. Cut celery stalk in half, widthwise, and add to glasses as garnish. Top with celery salt.

We had a delicious mushroom soup followed by pasta and chocolate cake for dessert. I bubbled with superlatives over the food, but I also gushed over the Ourika stone bowls and plates. In the mountains outside Marrakech, Ourika is known for its rocks and clay, and the dishes reminded me of the beautifully austere Japanese pottery I'd bought when I lived in Tokyo.

"Oh, I'd love to have plates like this for the restaurant," I said.

"That's not practical, my dear," Bill said wisely. "They're heavy and fragile."

Still, the terra cotta color captivated me. Bill eventually chose handmade terra-cotta tiles from Marrakech for the restaurant's floors and Ourika stone slabs for our front steps.

Back in the sitting room with our coffees, Bill and I approached our pet subject, the beaded table lamps on each table in the film. What we both wanted to do—in all aspects—was to take the basics from the film and go one better, making the props more elegant, more deluxe. Those table lamps were of dire importance.

"I think I've got just the thing," Bill said, bouncing out of his chair and rustling around on the floor behind the oversized, overstuffed armchair where I was sprawled. He emerged with an amazing brass lamp that looked part Moroccan, part Chinese that he'd brought from Rome.

"I carried it with me when I crossed from Spain by ferry in 1966," he said. The lamp had a brass base covered by painted enamel, and colored glass pieces set into a brass dome formed the shade. A single remaining strand indicated that the shade at one time had been beaded. It was perfect. Bill made a scale drawing that I gave to an artisan in the souk, who made a prototype. Bill approved, and with a promise from the artisan Mustapha that he wouldn't copy the lamp for general distribution in the souk—a practice that had burned Bill often—one of the more distinctive pieces of the "real" Rick's Café came into being.

In September, as soon as the house was mine, Bill made his first working visit to Casablanca. He wanted to get in the mood for the project and stay in one of the old hotels. He mentioned the Transatlantique and the Excelsior, built respectively in 1922 and 1920. After looking at both, I booked Bill into the Transatlantique, somewhat restored, but certainly not to its former glory. Renovation had stripped away much of its Art Nouveau decoration and furniture, but the rooms appeared comfortable and were reasonably well appointed. Little had changed at the Excelsior, on the other hand. It was like a time capsule, reflecting the better days it had seen. (I found out later Bill's insistence on these cheap hotels was to save me money.)

Waiting at the hotel for Bill to arrive wracked my nerves. We'd been talking a lot about the project, but this would be the first time that he, Hakim, and I would sit down to make key decisions. Slimane, Bill's draftsman, drove them from Marrakech, and when they arrived Bill was a nervous wreck from more than three hours on the road in horrible traffic.

We both needed a drink, so we repaired to the hotel bar. Bill tried for a Jack Daniel's but settled for Scotch and I had a gin and tonic. Decorated with colorful *zellige* tile, the room had a service bar of dark wood with copper trim on one side of the room and a baby grand piano on another. We sipped our drinks and talked of the work ahead. I showed Bill photos of the house, interior and exterior, but they only gave him a superficial feel for the space.

Once we had relaxed a bit more, we went on to one of my favorite restaurants, a French bistro called La Bavaroise, located behind the Marché Central. Hakim Benjelloun joined us. We had a laugh-filled dinner, lubricated with several bottles of wine that encouraged Bill's hilarious observations and stories of previous visits to Casablanca. We mutually agreed to start our work session the next day on the late side . . . noon.

Bill in the old kitchen of the house on his first visit, September 2002.

Before I left my apartment to pick Bill up the next day, he called me, frantic.

"Kathy, can you call the restaurant? I must have left my cigarette holder there. I have another at home, but Paul Getty sends them from London. He's not well—I can't bother him to send me a few more."

If Bill was worrying about finding his cigarette holder, he might not be able to concentrate on the house. I called the restaurant, spoke with the *maître d'hôtel*, who remembered where we were sitting. He didn't find anything. No one sat at the table after we left, and no one had turned anything in. Still, I stopped at the restaurant on the way to Bill's hotel, looked myself, and verified that his cigarette holder wasn't there.

At the Transatlantique, Bill was grouchy. He had numerous complaints: the sheets were starched and uncomfortable; he'd been unable to get ice delivered to his room at midnight; and they hadn't wanted to serve him breakfast at 10:30 a.m., although they finally relented. His mood changed in an instant as soon as he entered the house. Bill wasn't easily impressed, but the space awed him with its grand-size rooms and the galleries around the balustrades. He was particularly taken with the cupola and what he could do with the natural lighting. He criticized nothing, seeing only possibilities.

We sat down on plastic chairs at a wobbly Formica table left by the Ghattas family and discussed the entrance. Bill, Hakim, and I were all thinking along the lines of "palace formula" restaurants in the Marrakech Medina, particularly Dar Yacout, which, after all, Bill had designed. A meandering drive through narrow streets, dodging pedestrians, motor scooters, and donkey carts, culminates at a seeming dead end where djellaba-clad greeters holding lanterns guide guests to a modest door. When the door opens, a sumptuous space right out of *The Arabian Nights* appears: pools, palms, fireplaces, dramatic lighting, Gnaoua musicians, and waiters serving heaping platters of Moroccan food.

We worked on the initial assumption of using the impasse, the short back alley that leads from the Medina to the house. Parking was close, and the walk would be brief, nothing like the scary ride to Dar Yacout. But that decision made it hard to direct the flow of the space inside the restaurant. Stuck at this new impasse, we broke for lunch to clear our heads—off to the Taverne du Dauphin on the edge of the Medina.

Hakim and I drank water while Bill opted for beer as we crowded into the popular seafood restaurant presided over by Jean-Claude, the third generation of the French founders. Even though it was 2:00 p.m., the room clamored with the voices of other late diners, clanking plates and silverware. Bill kept complaining about the noise and commenting about what our restaurant's acoustics should be like. Then he ordered another beer and raved about his swordfish, lamenting the lack of fresh seafood in Marrakech. After coffee, we got back to work at the house.

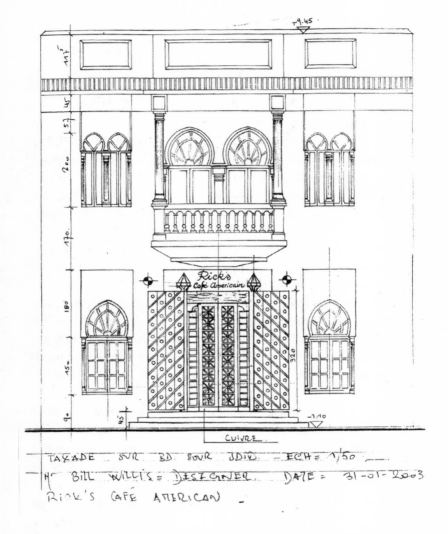

Bill's lovely rendering of the front facade captured the classic look of the film. Rendering by Bill Willis for The Usual Suspects

"I don't know what I was thinking about this morning," Bill said as soon as we sat down. "It's obvious. We have to put the entrance on the street side. Then we can recreate the same sort of doors and entrance you see in the film. I must have been stuck in Marrakech this morning, but the lunch was just the jolt of reality I needed to focus on Casablanca."

With that, everything fell into place. It was easy to imagine the entry, then the courtyard with tables, the bar and the kitchen behind, leaving the impasse door as the service and delivery entrance. Slimane took numerous photos for reference, but Bill had a way of absorbing a space and later added design touches to small nooks and crannies that I didn't think he'd even noticed. More than once his recall left me speechless.

The next day I met Bill at the Transatlantique to settle the bill, thank him, and set up our next meeting in Marrakech.

"It's been a great visit, my dear. I confess I am so eager to start designing the restaurant. Oh, by the way, I found my cigarette holder. It was in my suitcase. When I came back from dinner the first night I must have leaned over to get something out of my bag and it slipped out of my pocket."

Bill's second visit to the site, in February 2003—before construction had even started—didn't go as well. Indeed, that meeting with the architect and the subcontractors portended things to come. Bill had created striking designs using the finest materials. As I carefully noted the details he had specified, blank, unconcerned faces stared back. Even Hakim, the architect, wasn't taking it seriously.

With Bill churning out spectacular drawings at a furious pace from his studio in Marrakech, and Hakim spending more and more of his time there with other projects, I steeled myself for what lay ahead. It wouldn't be easy to keep this group of what I termed "miscasts" mobilized to follow their contracts. I had to be on site to follow the action . . . or lack of it.

Trouble hit when talk turned to lighting and I described the table lamps that Bill had conceived, the sconces and lanterns we were having made, and the antique floor lamps and lanterns I'd been finding in the souks of Casablanca and Marrakech. The technical consultant heaved out an electrical supply catalog with cheap rudimentary sconces and hanging light fixtures. I sharply told him to put his catalog away. At the end of the meeting, I realized that I had been the only person taking notes, but it was vital that Bill's ideas come to life. I must admit, I felt a little like Ilsa supporting Victor Laszlo!

In addition to the grand front entrance, Bill designed a central stairway, five fireplaces, new window treatments, wood paneling and floors in a private dining room, an intricate black-and-white marble courtyard, a skylight over the cupola, a fabulous bar with glamorous gold-sculpted palm pillars dividing mirrored shelves that display the bottles—and forty-two brass lamps with beaded shades.

Rick's Café was Bill Willis's last project. He died on January 8, 2009. Former ambassador Frederick Vreeland was in Casablanca and came by that evening to console me. We sat at the center table in the courtyard drinking Jack Daniel's and exchanging stories about Bill. Ambassador Vreeland, who lives in Rome and Marrakech, recalled Gore Vidal commenting that Bill was the most expensive designer in the world after hiring Bill to do some work on his villa in Ravello. I knew Bill had reduced his fee for me, and I finally understood the magnitude of that generosity.

Our contract was one piece of paper in his handwriting that I still keep in a Japanese chest next to my corner at the bar. On top of the chest sits the amazing brass lamp that looks part Moroccan, part Chinese, with a brass base covered by painted enamel and a brass dome shade inlaid with colored glass. It was delivered to me anonymously several months after Bill's death.

FIVE

Vultures

When the sale went through in September 2002, we rushed to complete engineering studies, architectural drawings, and all the bureaucratic paper-shuffling needed to apply for the building permit. Driss's secretaries helped with appointments, advice, and encouragement. They welcomed me to stop by for coffee or just a rest—and I frequently took them up on it.

Their office lay at the end of a hallway across the open gallery from the wali's corner office, the first point of contact for those seeking an audience. Fatima and Leila went about their business while I sat on a vacant chair making calls on my cell phone. Invariably one of them looked my way and asked, "Coffee?"

I nodded and prepared for a very . . . innovative service.

A smiling figure soon appeared on the balcony that surrounded the exterior of the Wilaya. Fatima or Leila opened the window and took the tray with the cup of steaming coffee. They devised this alternative after the aide found it more than difficult to navigate through the sea of people crowding the hallway leading to their office door.

Driss would often have a free minute in the late afternoon when he was doing busywork. He usually sat at a conference table, signing stacks of passports and other documents, muttering that he really did have better things to do with his time.

Why did he have to sign each passport personally? Through how many other hands had those documents passed before they reached his desk? As they say in Morocco, *le système, ça marche.* The system works.

Well . . . maybe. Even someone like Driss, who wanted to change *le système,* had to go along with it.

Another frequent phrase that I heard too often was: *C'est le Maroc. Il faut adapter.* This is Morocco. You have to adapt. But the worst possible mistake would be for me to adapt. If I adapted every time a curveball flew my way, I'd still be sitting in a dilapidated mansion, cooking over a Bunsen burner.

Morocco's public administration takes after the French system. Papers, usually accompanied by the commensurate bribes, work their way through numerous offices and levels of bureaucrats. More than once Captain Renault's line from the film about being a poor and corrupt government official ran through my head. France, I'm told, has made some improvements in automation and efficiency, if not transparency, but here the system remains unchanged and often causes unreasonable delays or demands.

The most tedious procedure is something called *légalisation* which translates to notarization in English, but in the hands of the Moroccan bureaucracy it has become a true art form. The communes and various administrative offices have a Legalization Depot or Annex where you must take signed documents for authentication as official. These offices overflow with lines having no apparent order—except for those who have slipped money between their sheets of paper to hasten service.

But there were exceptions as I discovered when my friend and house godfather, Mahir Tammam, introduced me to Ahmed Fachtal at the Commune Sidi Belyout. Mahir led me up a wide, winding staircase to the second floor where crowds of people were standing behind barricades outside a string of offices. (The barricades improved upon the usual Moroccan method of crowd control, which is none.)

He tapped on a door and entered, motioning me to wait. A minute later he ushered me in and presented Mr. Fachtal, the chief of the

Legalization Office. Quickly donning his sport coat, Fachtal shook my hand with a welcoming smile, immediately putting me at ease. Friendly and sincere, he asked for my I.D. card, some coins for the official stamps, and the document that I needed legalized. He gave everything to an assistant who left the room to hand-carry the paperwork through the system.

While we waited, Mr. Fachtal continued to listen attentively as I described my project, while signing paper after paper after paper. His aides scurried in and out of his office, delivering stacks of documents and retrieving others. The whole scene had a Charlie Chaplin or Mel Brooks quality to it.

Finally an assistant brought my legalized document back along with a register book for me to sign. As I was leaving, Mr. Fachtal made it clear that he had given explicit instructions that in the future I was to be ushered directly to his office for any and every notarization. His reward?

"One day I want to sit at a table close to the piano with a glass of wine," he said. That I could do.

The engineering studies required for the building permit unearthed more than the basic structure of the old house. First, because the house lay near the port, we had to check the foundation. (Aicha Ghattas insisted that the waters used to come up to the Medina walls, so it was probably a good idea. Besides, we were considering digging a basement, so we had to know what awaited.)

This same process in Prague often uncovered archaeological treasures, so it intrigued me to see what the dig would turn up. A young workman carefully dug three holes three feet deep. Good news: the house was built on rock.

Not so good news: his excavation uncovered human bones.

For a moment it looked like we couldn't continue, as sometimes happens in other countries when bones or artifacts come to light. But we reported the find to the caid, who acknowledged that this strip close to the sea had once been a cemetery. So we delivered our bones in black plastic bags to his office for proper reburial elsewhere. To this day, the palms don't thrive in that space, but the head of the company who carried out the survey work comes often and always sits in that corner.

Another surprise came up during the initial study. When the professional measurements of the site were completed, we had 16 square feet *more* than the title recorded. It turned out that the title didn't include our back stairs. The property next door, Le Cheval Blanc, had been a bordello, so, armed with blueprints of both sites, I met with the director of the Land Registry. As we compared drawings, I suddenly realized that our back stairs slipped into a slot behind the old bordello entry. Records showed that the Cheval Blanc owner had purchased a small piece of land from the public domain for an entry door but the corresponding space behind that was never purchased from our side, even though the stairs were built on it. Some sort of "negotiation" at the time must have left no documentation. Fine for a bordello, but not for a restaurant. Time to go to the office of Public Property for resolution.

Not one of Casablanca's Art Deco treasures, the building was cold, both in terms of design and comfort level. Since the temperature rests at a moderate level year-round, there was no central heating, like a lot of public buildings in Morocco. But it retained the cold during fall and winter, and it wasn't unusual to see men working at their desks in heavy overcoats. In fact, they milled around a lot and avoided sitting, I think, to keep their hands in their pockets.

Unsmilingly the division chief of the Public Property office motioned me to take a seat, though he himself never sat down throughout our entire conversation. He paced back and forth, wearing his heavy duffle coat and a deadpan expression that reminded me more of Buster Keaton than a midlevel bureaucrat. As he paced, he lamented the seriousness of the problem, as if it were somehow my fault. After he'd exhausted himself and the subject, he informed me that he and his technical assistant would come by the construction site the following morning at 8:30 a.m.

Early the next morning, I phoned my regular taxi driver, Mr. Mourabit, affectionately nicknamed Mr. Bojangles because of a vague resemblance to Sammy Davis Jr. Mr. Mourabit was no entertainer, but he sure could tap dance his way out of trouble. He'd been my personal driver from my first days at the Consulate. (Salah drove me only during the week and only on Consulate business.) Mourabit drove a private taxi, a white, old-model Mercedes.* Our trips while I was still at the Consulate were fairly simple and routine, but since I had begun creating Rick's we took six, seven, eight trips a day within the city, to the suburbs, from meeting to meeting, supplier to supplier. The constant traffic and awful parking problems resulted in much wear and tear on Mr. Mourabit and his Mercedes. If he hadn't been so busy with me, he could have made the same amount of money on three or four round trips to the airport—a lot easier.

Moroccans are gracious and accommodating, but they find it hard to say no. It's much easier to ignore the difficulty or just disappear. That's exactly what Mr. Mourabit did: He disappeared. Even though I knew about this national character quirk, I wasn't prepared to be stood up on the morning of such an important meeting. He didn't answer his phone despite repeated calls.

---

* In Morocco, *petits taxis* are licensed within towns and color-coded; Casablanca's petits taxis are red. *Grands taxis* travel fixed routes between cities. Private taxis have no restrictions.

A red petit taxi brought me to the site just minutes before the division chief and his assistant arrived. They walked around, compared the two blueprints, confirmed helpfully that we had a problem—but had no idea how to resolve it. The division chief continued to glare at me as though I had plotted deviously to ensure that our back stairs ended up inside the neighboring building sixty years ago. The solution was obvious to me. My suggestion to appeal to the wali met with sighs of relief. The wali immediately wrote a letter granting us permission to use the (formerly) public domain space with a requirement to pay a nominal quarterly rent. Once the first quarter was paid, we never received another notice.

Just as my meeting with the division chief ended, Mr. Mourabit called to apologize. He'd been at the airport when I phoned and "didn't hear the ring."

"I'm a bit tied up right now, Mme. Kriger," he said, "but I'm sending another driver to pick you up and take you back to your apartment." Taxi drivers have their own network that rivals the coterie of businessmen surrounding city officials; they do favors for each other, expecting to call in those favors at a later date.

The relief taxi arrived, took me home, and promised to return at 2:00 p.m. to take me on my afternoon errands. At 2:00 p.m., no taxi driver. When I telephoned to check on his whereabouts, the substitute driver told me that Mr. Mourabit himself was on the way. With Mr. Mourabit nowhere in sight after a reasonable amount of time, I hailed another red cab. Mourabit called later to reassure me that he had been just at the nearby intersection and noticed that I'd found a red taxi. I interpreted this as a sure sign that it was I who was driving him—crazy—and took the hint. I phoned Aicha, a woman who had driven me once, who was quite agreeable to assuming the role of chauffeuse.

Neither of us knew what lay in store.

⌐

The months leading up to construction certainly weren't dull. A Usual Suspect friend from Prague came for a visit. After a few days in the Marrakech sun, we went back up to Casablanca. He loved the site and the plans for Rick's.

"You're sitting on a gold mine," he said.

He wasn't so positive about me, however.

"Have you thought about what sort of image you want to project, running Rick's?" he said on the way to the airport as he was leaving.

"What do you mean?"

"Let me put it this way: Would you rather appear to be a femme fatale or a mama-san?"

"Well, neither . . . but certainly not a mama-san."

"Then you're going to need to lose a stone."

But fourteen pounds were only the tip of the iceberg. I immediately started walking a mile in the morning, tried a laser treatment, and went on the Atkins diet. Between that and the stress of creating Rick's, the pounds flew off.

As I began shaping up, I was anxious for the gin joint to start shaping up, too. We just needed the building permit to get going. Rachid El Andaloussi and Mahir Tammam submitted our application in early December and then shepherded the file through the various city agencies. We received our permit at the end of that same month—exceptionally fast, I was told.

What an amazing year it had been. To celebrate, I threw together a New Year's Eve party in the empty house. It was a little rough, with furniture rented from an antiques dealer friend, some of my lamp purchases, and a boom box playing Glenn Miller and Cole Porter—but

Rick's Champagne Cocktail

Preparation time: 1 minute
Serves 2

In the hundreds of times that I watched *Casablanca*, I often came up short on menu and cocktail ideas—with the exception of the champagne cocktail. I love the proportions of the old champagne coupes and created our version of the classic cocktail to fill them.

2 raspberries

4 dashes Angostura bitters

6 ounces Veuve Clicquot champagne

2 splashes cognac

Place one raspberry each in the center of two chilled champagne coupes and sprinkle with the bitters. Add the champagne, and top with a splash of cognac.

the ambience of Rick's was there. Tears welled up in Yasmina's eyes as she and her husband climbed the back stairs to the grand salon. Nancy Reynolds, a Usual Suspect visiting from Santa Fe, contributed the champagne. I fixed tamale pie, and Yasmina and Ali brought a yule log from Lenôtre.

As we celebrated the arrival of 2003, I never imagined that it would be more than a year before Rick's opened.

Before a single wall came down, we carried out "negotiations" between the architect and the subcontractors. Hakim asked for bids on ten specific areas. The bids were "evaluated," and I "selected" the firms—but really Hakim orchestrated the whole process and received commissions from most of the "winners." In addition to his fee, which was twice Bill's.

Construction began in earnest on March 3, 2003. For the first four months, the site was a maze of wood planks, metal scaffolding, cement, and a lot of noise. The whole cupola came apart for repairs, and the contractors had to break out the small basement for bathrooms with jackhammers. From below ground, you could look up to the sky, three stories above. Working alongside the construction crew were the contractors for electricity, plumbing, and heating/cooling.

Visiting the construction site was exhilarating. Progress, even though slow, was coming along, and here at least I came face to face with problems that I could tackle in the same way—totally different

The early construction site was a web of supports and planks with blowtorches blasting away at the basement level.

from working with banks and capital risk firms where I never knew who lay behind a problem. I not only kept track of contractors, sub-contractors, and all eighty-two workers on site, but I doggedly drove them to follow Bill Willis's evocative designs. It was irritating to have to keep always one step ahead of each attempt to cut corners, but an Arab proverb goes, "The barber learns to shave on the orphan's face," and I didn't want them to take me for an orphan. Those who tried invariably discovered that it didn't pay to cross me.

Fueled by mistrust and never knowing what some of the contractors would try to slip by me, I rose every morning mentally armed for battle, following another Arab proverb: "Open your door to a good day and prepare yourself for a bad one." Some of the bad days happened because of my refusal to roll over and pay bribes to various officials. The pressure to do so became more intense after Driss Benhima was no longer the wali. Without my protector, I was fair game for bureaucratic vultures—like the two men from the commune who showed up one day shortly after construction began, unannounced and dressed casually, to do a "routine inspection" of the site. They asked to see the construction site record book, but for some reason it wasn't on the premises. Then they turned their attention to the working drawings taped to the wall.

"These plans aren't the same ones that were stamped with the building permit," one of them said, waving his hand at the drawings.

As soon as Hakim saw the direction of the conversation, he drew the commune bureaucrats out of my earshot. They exchanged words, threw arms across shoulders, patted backs, shook hands, and left, seemingly reassured.

Perplexed at this sudden intervention, I cornered Hakim.

"Well, there were some parts included in the building permit that we decided not to do, so the working drawings should be fine," he assured me. "We're not doing anything over and above what was approved, and we'd forgotten to do a *cahier du chantier*, but we'll get that done tomorrow."

His words would come back to haunt me.

⁓

Bill Willis had particular requirements for the floor tiles, the wood elements, and the fireplaces. His fireplace designs in particular were legendary. He introduced the application of tadelakt over the base and framed the soft polished surface with zellige or terra-cotta bricks. Starting with his work in Marrakech, fireplaces became his trademark—one that, alas, hustling entrepreneurs who followed the latest design trends quickly "adapted."

A traditional Moroccan decorative finish used for the walls of palaces, riads, and hammams, tadelakt is today a distinctive and popular wall treatment. Pure lime plaster from Marrakech is mixed with water and natural pigments. Applied to a wall, it is polished with a river stone, making the surface smooth and shiny. It was fascinating to watch the workmen stir up batches of it, first lining recesses in the ground with plastic bags, and creating the beautiful pistachio green for the private dining room, the robin's-egg blue for the Blue Room, and the champagne beige for the downstairs restrooms.

Bill and I were operating on the same wavelength while the architect and the subcontractors were on another. The architect showed up for our regular Thursday meetings, but he seemed to be spending the rest of the week in Marrakech, where he had other projects—no doubt more lucrative and conventional than mine. So I became the general contractor supervising everyone else, the *maîtrise d'ouvrage*. It wasn't easy.

The same conversation took place again and again.

"This is not what the plans call for," I told the contractors, rattling the drawings in their faces.

"We've never seen that," they responded automatically.

And actually they probably hadn't. The architect often "forgot" to forward Bill's updated designs to the men on site. My solution: Fax everything to the construction contractor, and get a confirmation report for every fax.

On one of his visits, Bill, aghast, spied an air-conditioning duct cutting diagonally across the ceiling in the large formal dining room upstairs. Rather than let it mar the room, he designed a decorative molding that rimmed the four sides of the ceiling. His answer didn't detract from, but rather accented, the heightened ceilings and allowed even heating and cooling temperatures.

This design formula was to be followed throughout the restaurant, but Abdullah, the A/C contractor, never followed instructions. Either he ran a duct in the wrong place or used shortcuts that ruined the aesthetic. The construction contractor once roughed him up when he routed a duct through the peak of an arch. Abdullah's mistakes added to the delays and haunted us even after opening: He had fed the bathroom exhaust vent directly into the air conditioning intake on the roof! Before we learned what had happened and fixed it, someone rushed out into the Medina one afternoon and dragged in an incense seller, dressed in a flowing djellaba, who wandered through the restaurant, swinging a smoking incense burner like a lost Catholic priest to waft away Abdullah's mistakes. I penalized him for his shoddy work, but Abdullah frequently showed up at the bar after we opened, already drunk and expecting to be paid.

When it came time to tackle the geometric design of the black-and-white marble courtyard, Bill's assistant, Slimane, showed the craftsmen how to lay the pieces starting from the center to ensure the design would extend evenly all the way to the exterior boundaries of the courtyard. Two weeks later, they finished. At our regular Thursday meeting, the architect, the contractors, and I were talking upstairs in the back when the head of the company who had contracted to do the tile work looked over the balustrade at the marble floor. The next thing we knew, screaming in French, he dragged off the foreman of the crew doing the work downstairs. We all looked over the balustrade and gasped. Ignoring Slimane's instruction, the workers had started at one edge and at the end found it uneven. On the opposite side, they'd cut the tile at odd angles to make it fit. They had to do the entire floor over again.

The marble floor wasn't the only "retake." After much discussion and pressure from the tile contractor and Hakim that we use factory-produced terracotta tile from Spain, Bill and I decided on handmade terra-cotta tiles for the other floors in the restaurant. Bill and Slimane knew the company in Marrakech making the tiles, and Slimane agreed to be on hand when the tiles were picked up. We soon discovered that

The graphic design of the black-and-white marble courtyard is one of Bill Willis's most stunning creations. Photo by Issam Chabâa

113

our contractor had subbed out the floors and walls to another company without going through the procedures and approvals required by our contract. That's why the tile work evolved into a series of finger-pointing arguments and shoddy attempts at cost-cutting.

When the first delivery of the tiles arrived from Marrakech, the illegal subcontractor had ignored instructions to fill the truck bed with hay to cushion the layers of tile, and they hadn't called Slimane to supervise. A truckload of clay powder, chips, and rubble arrived, sparking one of my frequent eruptions in French directed toward men who no doubt understood my tone if not my actual words. Their explanation: They didn't have enough money to buy hay, and a delayed start meant they were in too much of a rush to call Slimane to have him inspect the shipment. Yet another Moroccan proverb came to mind: "Where there is a will, there is a way. Where there is no will, there is an excuse."

When work finally began on the terra-cotta floors, much complaining ensued because the tiles, handmade, had to be treated with more care, especially when cut. Bill had an idea for a natural finish as well: a mixture of turpentine and linseed oil. The idea vexed the workers. The manufactured tiles already came with a finish: a gaudy high gloss totally unacceptable to Bill or me. We asked them to do a sample corner with the linseed-turpentine finish, and it was beautiful—so beautiful in fact that all the doubters resigned themselves to the handmade tile.

But it was one thing after another. Soon after, Hakim, the architect, called to say that the terra-cotta was posing yet another problem.

"I'm worried about chairs and tables on the uneven floor," he said. "Ask Bill if this has worked in other restaurants." Then he added, "I think you should still consider some alternate tiles from the supplier here in Casablanca."

Just in case, I looked at some other tile samples. Nothing compared to the tiles from Marrakech.

When I called Bill to ask, he told me that it was only the second time he'd used the tile in a project. "The first was in a house I just did in Tangier," he said.

Hakim didn't need to know—and I said to Bill, as Ilsa said to Rick, "Your secret is safe with me."

"Just continue with the terra-cotta," I told Hakim, still fuming over the subcontracting deception. "Bill will design tables with adjustable legs."

These mistakes and delays, of course, were preventing others from doing their work. Painters stood by with rollers at the ready . . . only to have to wait for the dust to settle from contractors laying the tile, weeks over deadline. The workers at the construction site were mainly Berbers who didn't speak English or French—although they understood my anger or frustration perfectly.

If someone did make headway, as if on a prearranged cue everyone left on vacation. As soon as the workers returned from their August holidays, we had to brace for Ramadan in November. Those who remained were fasting and left each day at 2:00 or 3:00 p.m. A two-day holiday for something like the Aid Al Kebir—the sheep feast 40 days after the end of Ramadan—became a full week for the Berber workers to go back to the *bled*.

The pressure to keep moving caused me to make one big mistake: the subcontractor for the woodwork. Bill had redesigned a beautiful front entry door and vestibule, reshaped windows and frames, designed wood panels between open arches, and in the VIP room had done an oak floor with inlays and paneling halfway up the walls. On top of that was metalwork, including two skylights.

When Hakim found a supplier who presented a bid that he said I'd have to approve, I was worried. He'd had enough confidence in the others not to ask my opinion. I inspected the company's atelier in the Bourgogne section of Casablanca, and the work they were doing looked fine enough (not that it had anything to do with what Bill had designed). In parting, the owner proudly gave me a carved wood box he'd made himself. As I muttered my thanks, a knot formed in my stomach. The box was ugly and badly made, the carving rough and the pattern basic. I should have taken it as a sign and found someone else.

Later I met a woodworker with a beautiful atelier in the Ancienne Medina. The space had belonged to his grandfather, the same artisan who did all the original woodwork when the house was built in 1930. I didn't have to think twice about giving him a side contract to build the bar. I couldn't bear putting Rick's bar in the hands of the "butcher" from Bourgogne.

Morning raindrops through the first skylight foreshadowed the results of a "water test" that allowed me to turn the job over to another contractor.

The "butcher," Abdesalam, was also doing the metalwork on site. We had specified black aluminum for the skylight, a very precise geometric piece covering the cupola, and a smaller version of the same design over the central stairs. He used silver aluminum that had to be painted. But the color was the least of our problems. We suspected the

116

skylights weren't watertight, and on the day of the test, we had a sneak preview. It had rained earlier in the morning, and raindrops had flecked the courtyard floor. When we dragged the hose up to the roof to test the skylight for water resistance, water of course poured through.

Abdesalam shrugged off my fury, but his work was unacceptable, so legally I didn't have to pay him. I did have to find another metal contractor at the last minute, though, with no room for negotiating his fee. I was also penalizing delays with not-insignificant fines thanks to clauses in the seventy-five-page contracts. The laggards erupted in outrage. Clearly this was never done. But then most developers in Morocco didn't have the same level of personal financial commitment and concern that I did.

With a million shifting details to consider, one innocent question usually led to another task.

"How are we going to know how many tables and chairs we'll need?" I asked Bill one day.

"Oh that should be easy. Just rent some square, rectangular, and round tables and fold up chairs from a caterer. You can put them in various settings and use that as a measure of what the space allows."

Brilliant—of course.

The system, which I suspect Bill had never used, worked.

There were some bright spots in the chaos.

Assigned to the worksite as the representative of the construction contractor, Houssein coordinated the subcontracted workers and directed traffic between the ten different lots of work on the site. He slept on site for the last eight months—most of the time on a dirt floor—and only rarely took time off to visit his family, in a Berber village two hours outside Marrakech. Toward the end, when he asked if I'd be interested in hiring him as my maintenance chief, I jumped at the chance. He'd always been the go-to guy at the construction site, so I knew I could rely on him, in casting terms, as my best boy. He knew the place so well that you could say that he knew where the bones were buried—literally in our case.

Meanwhile, tempers continued to flare, especially when it came to the five fireplaces that Bill had designed. I had already compiled Bill's plans for the fireplaces, numbered them, and had them witnessed and distributed. And yet *somehow* they were misplaced, lost, or not delivered, so the construction contractor took it upon himself to form them in concrete using one mold. They had to redo all but one of them.

They had almost finished with the first marble fireplace when Slimane noticed that a top ornament of a column was missing. The subcontractor denied that there was an ornament in the plans, getting so agitated that he almost hit Slimane. Houssein brought the plans, giving his boss from the construction company a wary glance as he handed them to me. The ornament was clearly there. You could have cut the silence with a knife.

When it was all over, I knew more than I ever wanted about fireplaces, subcontractor contracts, terra-cotta tile, air-conditioning vents, and a certain woodworker with an atelier in Bourgogne.

"Kathy, this has been a real important project for us," said the Frenchman in charge of construction just before Rick's opened, "but I must say, you are extremely difficult."

I took it as a compliment. "Pierre, if you had said I was a pleasure to work with, I would have been disappointed."

SIX

Raising the Bar

Normally, in order to get an alcohol license, someone opening a restaurant or bar had to get the venue to a point where it was ready to open. Only then could the application go before the Authorization Commission and the project undergo inspection by city and police officials, who hemmed and hawed over details that . . . weren't quite right.

They would tsk-tsk over a neon sign with the words "Restaurant—Bar," commenting that really the word "Bar" should be smaller. The applicant would point out that nothing in the regulations stipulated this ratio, and, in the "negotiation," money changed hands before approval was granted.

Driss Benhima, when still the wali, had a new approach designed to give developers confidence in choosing to invest in Casablanca—and I was a test case. My application was submitted in January 2003 to the new Regional Investment Center, which acted as my go-between with the Authorization Commission. Driss called me in March, just three weeks after construction began, with the good news that the Commission members from the Wilaya, Police, Tourism Ministry, and Investment Center had met that morning and approved my application.

"Come with five photos, your I.D. card, and 250 dirhams [$25]," he said. "You can pick up the papers in an office on the ground floor of the Wilaya."

For all the time that I had spent and was spending there, the Wilaya, a beautiful Neo-Mauresque structure built by the French

119

in the 1920s, was like a second home. A lush courtyard in celadon-green tile with palm trees and fountains leads to two grand staircases, each boasting a dramatic painting by Jacques Majorelle. Zellige tile of varying colors and designs decorates the upstairs halls and corridors and gracious galleries overlooking the central courtyard. This second floor was my usual destination, so the contrast with the ground-floor office, where the alcohol permits were administered, surprised me. It was dark and musty, and the people working there had little experience with foreigners other than the French—and certainly not with a woman getting an alcohol license.

When I spoke in my American-accented French, the man at the front desk nervously responded: "*Je ne parle pas l'Anglais.*" I don't speak English.

While my heart wanted to scream, "*JE SUIS EN TRAIN DE PARLER EN FRANÇAIS!*" instead I took a deep breath, smiled, and spoke slowly: "*Je suis en train de parler en français. Excusez-moi pour mon mauvais accent.*" I am speaking in French. Pardon my bad accent.

That seemed to calm him, and we completed the simple and straightforward process. He took my photos, gave me a receipt for the 250 dirhams, and said I could come back in an hour or the next morning. Driss had warned me to act fast, so I said I'd return in an hour.

Upstairs, Fatima and Leila offered me a celebratory cup of coffee. Driss popped his head in, and, as soon as he heard that I'd submitted everything and was just waiting to pick it up, he called one of the uniformed couriers standing by in the hall and barked out some instructions. Ten minutes later the license was mine.

Some weeks later, a messenger arrived at the construction site with a notice to appear at the Police Commissariat at 10:00 a.m. the next day for an appointment with the chief of the Alcohol Enforcement Brigade. My face must have registered fear or apprehension because the messenger said, "Don't worry. They just want to have some information on your project."

Even more puzzling. Hadn't they received copies of all the materials I'd submitted in my application? Floor plans, financial information, marketing plans . . . everything was there.

It took a while find the office and some minutes before a passerby muttered "*toujours en panne*" (always broken) at the elevator bank and guided me to the stairs. Once in the office, the chief of the Brigade asked me to describe the restaurant. A discourse on my grand vision wasn't what he wanted. He searched his desk, found a blank piece of paper, and pushed it toward me.

"Can you draw me a plan?"

I asked him if he hadn't seen the plans in the license application. His blank look told me that perhaps the deliberation over my license had taken place at a higher level. I began to feel nervous. He told me to give them a rough idea of the floor plans, the number of square meters, and the location of the bar.

Then we talked about timing. I told him that construction had started recently and we figured that it would be seven months at least before the work was done. (Oh if only.)

When I asked questions about late closing hours and how they enforced the Ramadan and holiday alcohol bans, he was reassuring. "You're not going to be open soon. We have plenty of time to talk. Why don't you give us a call one or two months before you plan to open, and we'll talk about all our procedures then."

I should have known better.

⌒

Innocently confident after the nice reception at the Police Commissariat, I set about finding our Sacha, the bartender in the movie. A friend teaching in a hotel and tourism school in Rabat suggested Darryn, an itinerant Australian living in London who had spent the winter in Timbuktu. He'd put out the word that he was interested in tending bar in Morocco, so our mutual friend introduced us by e-mail.

I didn't want to hire him sight unseen, though, so, when I found out he was managing a workingman's bar in East London, I asked my English lawyer friends Robert and George, more Usual Suspects, to visit the bar and interview him.

"If he can manage that bar, he shouldn't have any trouble managing your bar in Casablanca," Robert said.

I offered Darryn the job but told him that he had to wait until a month before we opened. It was looking like December, but it could be later, I said, emphatic that he shouldn't make travel plans until I gave him the green light. Imagine my surprise, then, when he showed up at the end of September and wondered why I wasn't overjoyed to see him. I found out later that, although he had managed the London bar at one time, "it hadn't worked out." He'd talked the owners into letting him come back and pose as manager for a night to pass the interview with Robert and George.

So there was the answer: He came because he was unemployed. It's cheaper to be unemployed in Casablanca than in London, and the "letter of transit" for his sojourn in the UK was about to expire.

Of average height and build but a little paunchy, Darryn was glib, charming, and very social—but he drank heavily and was given to exaggeration, easily distracted, and totally incorrigible. He ensconced himself at the youth hostel in the Ancienne Medina, about ten minutes' walk from Rick's. His first "job" as he saw it was to introduce himself at all the bars in town, meeting people and dragging all sorts of locals and tourists to the construction site to see "his" bar.

A very agitated Houssein called me from the construction site one day. "Madame, you've got to do something about Monsieur Darryn. He just brought some people by the site, and you know they're pouring the concrete for the front steps, and there's a wood plank over them that's not very stable. One of the ladies almost fell into the concrete mold, but I caught her arm just in time. Monsieur Darryn told me I should put in a better support on the wood plank."

It was just the excuse I needed to tell Darryn that he couldn't bring people inside the site. He could show them the outside, but he couldn't come in without me. Which of course didn't stop him from parading people by, saying, "There it is, my bar," and waving to all the workers.

Ramadan, which fell in November that year, threw him for a real loop. While restaurant-bars that catered to the local business community, foreign residents, and tourists might close for a week or two, few closed for the whole month. But bars that, by their sparse furnishings, limited selection or lack of music, food, or other distractions, drew exclusively a Moroccan clientele, similar to Darryn's workingman's bar in East London—with a big emphasis on "man" since women customers were rare—closed for the entire month because alcohol was their only product.

Without the bars that comprised his stomping ground—the ones providing cheap beer and a minimum of ambience—Darryn was in bad shape. So he took to dropping by my apartment. He was staying now at a cheap hotel in the same neighborhood near the Marché Central, having been kicked out of the youth hostel because he continually failed to meet the 11:00 p.m. curfew. Nor could he comprehend the total ban on alcohol for Muslims that went along with the sunrise-to-sunset fasting during Ramadan.

"The Moroccans take this month very seriously maybe because, during the other eleven months of the year, there is more tolerance of drinking," I explained.

He frowned. "Well, we don't have to follow this at the bar do we?"

The comment scared me. "Darryn, you have to understand something very important. The alcohol license is in my name personally, and I am responsible for enforcing the regulations. We will be told when to stop serving Muslims and when we can begin serving them again. We can serve non-Muslims, and there is nothing that prevents Moroccan clients from eating together with a group of foreigners who might be drinking wine with dinner or drinking fruit juice or soda at the bar. But I suspect we won't have many Moroccan customers during Ramadan."

It was too heavy for him, and he quickly changed the subject back to his work in London. During these flights of nostalgia, I peppered him with questions, trying to see if he had any potential.

"Tell me about the place," I said. "What did people do in the bar?"

"What do you mean, 'What did they do?' They drank."

"Was there food?"

"Customers ordered ready-made sandwiches that we'd heat up in the microwave. Sometimes there was soup or stew. People really didn't care what or if they ate. Most had their dinner at home and dropped in at the bar later. There were sausages and pickles and spicy, salty snacks to make people thirsty."

"There may be people who want to hang out at the bar all night, and we have to feed them—but not sausages and pickles," I said.

Darryn's face registered a knowing look of "experience."

"Well, you're also going to have bottle specials, aren't you? We used to make a brilliant return on whiskey by the bottle, along with whatever mixer they wanted, ice, and peanuts. Those guys always sent me drinks, and there was many a night where we all staggered out after closing together. We have to save some tables for the drinkers. That's where the money is, and these people, believe me, don't care about food."

I sighed. "Rick's bar will be sophisticated and reflect the mood of the film. We'll have cocktails and create a house drink plus all the cocktails you need to learn. It's not going to be like East London. We will not tolerate letting customers buy you drinks."

He looked crestfallen, and yet a glimmer of confidence crossed his face, revealing a certainty that eventually he could navigate around my rules. "Well, you're the boss, of course, but we'll just have to wait and see what our customers want."

Our customers? He was going to need a lot of training.

He wasn't a bartender by profession—having been a lower level bureaucrat in the Australian tax department—and bar service to him involved plunking down a bottle, a glass, and a carafe of water on the bar or table and joining the patron. Still, I waited until my son Kyle came for a visit in December to have Darryn audition officially. We enlisted the help of another friend and Usual Suspect, Delphine Park, and her boyfriend, Marc O'Rourke. At my request, they brought the *Four Seasons Cocktail Recipe Book* from New York for Darryn to use as a textbook.

Even though he exasperated me, I still felt a bit protective of Darryn, so I asked him to do a dry run on the Sunday night before his official audition. Kyle served as his second. There was a lot of laughing and joking in the kitchen as I steeled myself for the first drink. It was a Manhattan. Darryn had bragged that he knew that a Manhattan was the same as a martini only with red vermouth. So I was stunned when the Manhattan—made with my favorite Jameson Irish whiskey but otherwise conforming to the Four Seasons rye-based recipe—came out perfectly. Then he made a mojito, cosmopolitan, piña colada, and martini.

The results impressed me. Despite my sense that he'd been doing a good bit of tasting during the process, he seemed adept at following the recipes. After Darryn staggered out the door, Kyle confessed that Darryn had begged him to make the Manhattan. Though he tried making the other drinks himself, Darryn left it to Kyle to measure, mix, and prepare the cocktails for presentation.

The next evening, Delphine, Marc, Kyle, and I assembled at the scheduled time, 8:00 p.m.—but Darryn was late. He was also still hungover, casually explaining that he had been so relieved he'd done well the night before that he hit the local bars to celebrate. Kyle had strict instructions to let Darryn make the drinks this time.

The night before, the mojito had been by favorite. This time, the sprig of mint was the size of a branch. It tasted like drinking a garden. Each drink was a disappointment, and they came quickly. We had no sooner taken a sip, raised our eyebrows, and rolled our eyes than another cocktail appeared.

He rushed through the repertoire as fast as he could. Apparently he was still so hungover from the night before that he wanted to get out of my apartment before he got sick!

"Kathy, you have to get rid of him," Delphine said bluntly after he left.

She was right.

A solution to my dilemma conveniently presented itself in the form of Morocco's visa regulations. Darryn's ninety-day tourist stay was about to expire, so he wanted to go to Algeciras, Spain, to re-enter Morocco with another ninety-day permit. He needed $100 for transportation and promised to return in early January. I sent him on his way with a warning to think long and hard whether he was up to

Gin Joint Martini

Preparation time: 3 minutes
Serves 2

Darryn claimed that it was his idea to add rosemary leaves to the shaker. I suspect, however, that he got this inspiration from the Four Seasons cocktail book. Either way, the earthy hint of rosemary marries well with the sharp juniper of the gin.

ice

2–3 rosemary leaves

4 ounces Tanqueray gin

$\frac{1}{4}$–$\frac{1}{2}$ oz dry vermouth

2 pitted green olives

Chill two stemmed martini glasses. Fill shaker with ice, add rosemary leaves and gin. Shake well. Divide the vermouth between the two glasses, and swirl. Shake the gin again and strain into the two glasses. Garnish with olives.

my expectations before coming back, taking a gamble that I was giving him money for his exit papers. Sure enough, he took the money and ran—along with the Four Seasons cocktail book.

The Darryn debacle forced me to consider what I really wanted. Having a foreign bartender now seemed like a bad idea. He had taught me a valuable lesson, and it was money well spent. So the search continued, this time for a Moroccan bartender.

January presented a light at the end of the tunnel: Beautiful spaces unfolded all around me, and, while I might not have a bartender, the bar itself was emerging from the chaos in the careful hands of

Not minding the hard seat—barstool modeled after those in El Morocco in New York City—I stake claim to my future favorite spot at the end of the bar. The beautifully sculpted bar, along with the piano, would grab the attention of guests as they entered the downstairs courtyard.

the original woodworker's grandson. Thanks to Bill's creativity, it was going to be even more luxurious than the one in the film.

Quite by chance, just as work was starting on the bar, Ira and Nita Caplan, Usual Suspects from my Tokyo days, sent me a furniture catalog that included a line called the Bogart Collection. With Bill's approval, we created bar stools styled like those in New York's old El Morocco. The bar in the film has mirrored shelves with wood columns separating the sections, but Bill designed lovely carved-wood palms for columns. Finding the right wood to make them was looking like an extraordinarily long and expensive process, so we considered making the palms of plaster. Our plasterer made a small model and mounted it on the concrete wall for Bill to approve on one of his visits.

"I just can't see plaster holding up with the bartender constantly bumping into it as he works," Bill said.

He; his assistant, Slimane; and I were standing looking at the sample when a mischievous smile came over Bill's face.

"Hand me that piece of wood on the floor, Slimane," he said, and we both knew what was going to happen. Bill casually tossed the wood at the palm, and of course the frond chipped off. Back to the drawing board.

Slimane contacted an artisan friend in Casablanca for help. Ingeniously, the artisan made the palms of polyurethane—which we didn't tell Bill until they were done—and painted them with a special gold paint. They still look incredible.

Mine actually hadn't been the first Rick's in town. Another American had created a Rick's Café in the 1950s. From 1952 until about 1955, James Alexander (Jimmy) Smith owned and operated the Original Rick's, a private club that therefore operated under the radar and offered not only alcohol but also gambling. In fact, said Jimmy, the legal status of private clubs represented a gray area. They operated under what they called rules of tolerance, that is: "We'll tolerate you . . . for a fee."

In 1955, Jimmy decided to get a full license and in the process changed the name to Basin Street. He had more luck with his foreign bartender, Jerry Mandilow. Both men provided fodder for great stories, and their characters took on mythic proportions as the anecdotes unfolded through the years. Jerry had an extensive collection of jazz records that people still talk about. He was like a brother, Jimmy said, and the employees at Basin Street were like a family. When the waiter left, the dishwasher had done enough apprentice work to master the job, so he became the new waiter. There was no artificial hierarchy. Jimmy recalled the musicians that circulated through Casablanca. Once, he brought the renowned Memphis Slim from Paris. Slim lasted two nights, got a big head, and went on to one of the expensive cabarets.

The Basin Street Bar became a famous Casablanca watering hole, helped in part because of an American air base in the city, which meant the American military, diplomatic, and private sector population were much larger then. It was a less troubling time to be sure—at least in this part of the world.

After Jerry died and Jimmy left Morocco, the subsequent owners became locked in a bitter battle among themselves and local authorities over unpaid taxes. The building sits frozen in time on the Boulevard de Paris, its Art Deco grillwork covering windows that never open. But Moroccans who went to Basin Street still recall the friendships they established with the American owners and customers. Rollicking times with friends over drinks and music, jokes and burgers gave these young Moroccans a chance to know Americans, helping them to understand today that policies don't define America, people do. Perhaps my Rick's could do the same.

—

After Darryn left, I started meeting with prospective liquor distributors, my first appointment with the commercial director of the group that distributed, among many brands, Veuve Clicquot champagne, Hennessey cognac, Johnnie Walker whisky, and Budweiser beer— the "basics." He remembered me from the Consulate and organized a meeting in their office with all the brand representatives. I brought my alcohol license with me just in case they asked to see it. They didn't, but later they admitted surprise that I had received it before everything was "set up."

Before the group meeting, though, the commercial director took me to meet the director general. This American woman who was finally opening up a Rick's Café in Casablanca intrigued his boss. We reminisced about my days in Tokyo, where the company for which I

Elaborate front doors encourage the visitor to leave Casablanca and walk into *Casablanca*. Photo by Issam Chabâa

Table 1, just inside the front door, provides intimacy and a luxurious ambience with the marble and zellige fireplace, decorative lamps, and dramatic lighting. Photo by Issam Chabâa

At my corner post at the bar. Memorabilia in the background includes the original lamp that Bill Willis used as a model for the beaded table lamps.
Photo by Aziz Maradji for The Usual Suspects

The bar, with its golden palms, beaded lighting, green marble top, and leather trim.
Photo by Issam Chabâa

Music lovers adore these tables close to the piano, where they often strike up conversations with Issam. Photo by Issam Chabâa

A Syrian wood screen, just like one in the film, gives way to the grand
central stairway designed by Bill Willis. Photo by Issam Chabâa

A roulette table with the chips placed on Number 22 dominates the upstairs lounge with its little bar. Framed posters of *Casablanca* make this a favorite spot for movie buffs. Photo by Issam Chabâa

This tadelakt and zellige fireplace dominates the Salon Bleu, a formal dining room with Syrian wood screens and beaded brass lamps. Photo by Issam Chabâa

This lantern overlooking Table 6 was created in Marrakech to resemble one in the film. With five similar lanterns encircling the courtyard and a large one at its center, they cast dramatic shadows on the white pillars surrounding the balustrade. Photo by Issam Chabâa

Mustapha's vegetable stand is command central for Rick's Café and a reliable provider of everything from bok choy to quince.

Zohra is our source for fresh oysters and crab no matter what month of the year.

Khouiled, our trusty porter, has been plying his trade at the Marché Central since the 1940s.

worked also had a Wines and Spirits Division that handled the same brands. There was a special spot in my heart for the champagnes.

"Do you know that Veuve Clicquot is the only brand mentioned in the film?" I asked.

He didn't know Captain Renault's line about the 1926 vintage. I told him I couldn't wait to promote their champagnes at Rick's.

The meeting went well, and it felt good finally to be talking about supplying the bar rather than building it. As I was leaving, the commercial director was waiting with a gift from the director general. A box in orange and black could mean only one thing—a bottle of Veuve. His note said: "To another inspiring woman entrepreneur."

Another?

Inside wasn't just a bottle of champagne—but a bottle of Grand Dame, the top-of-the-line champagne of the house that honored its founder, the Widow Clicquot.

It was also up to me to find vendors for the cash register and bar control systems, telephones, sound system, and security. As usual, I ran into some bizarre people and lots of problems. Mr. Mernissi, supplier of the cash register and bar doser, turned out to be a hapless wheeler-dealer.

We discussed having one register behind the bar and another on the second floor. The two systems would be networked together, and I added a management/inventory software package that would run on our computer at the front desk. I gave him an advance of around $4,000. When the engineers were ready to install the cables, Mr. Mernissi was unreachable . . . and I wasn't the only one looking for him.

I left a long, detailed letter with the kitchen supplier who had recommended him. (Apparently he'd passed them a bad check, and they were expecting to see him.) No answer. Online, I found the head offices of the suppliers of the cash register and bar doser systems, one in France and one in Germany. Same answer from both: They were looking for him, too. I asked a restaurant friend who supplied their cash register system, got the contacts, and paid them a visit. Turned out my deadbeat supplier used to work for the company, and they were well versed in his "history." They offered me an alternative cash register and software system, a bit more expensive, but the bar doser would be the same. They could not, however, help me locate Mr. Mernissi.

I was not going to kiss $4,000 goodbye.

Somehow, as I was making the rounds of suppliers and talking to the director of Lavazza coffee, Mr. Mernissi came up. The director knew him and offered to find him.

He called me a day later with an address. "He's operating a snack shop called Fast Snack," he said.

In front of the snack shop—which I visited during lunchtime to be sure to catch him—I recognized his car with its "For Sale" sign in the window and a new mobile number that I jotted down. Mr. Mernissi was none too happy to see me, undoubtedly amazed at my audacity. He whisked me upstairs and unloaded the usual sob story. Did I want to buy his computers? Did I want to buy his car?

No, I wanted my $4,000 back, or he could give me the merchandise that I had ordered. We compromised. He gave me the one bar doser he had. It was still a difference of $500, but better than the alternative. The new company agreed to do the installation along with their cash register and software system.

No sooner had that crisis passed than the telephone rang.

"This is the police division of alcohol enforcement. Come in tomorrow morning at ten a.m."

SEVEN

Opening Night

During the making of *Casablanca*, no one knew until the final day of filming whether Rick would leave with Ilsa or give the second letter of transit to Victor Laszlo. The movie's cliffhanger reflected not just the director's indecision but also the writers' struggles with an ending that would have the most dramatic impact.

Nor was it by any means a foregone conclusion that we would open on our final target date. Our uncertainty came thanks to workers with no particular sense of urgency and the local authorities' indecision in supporting my project.

Patience was in short supply when, in an effort to add some pressure to the pot, I ordered 5,000 postcards saying "Opening March 1, 2004, after 60 years of renovation" with a photo of me dressed in a white tuxedo standing in front of the doors. I showed the cards to the workers, who seemed content to

Reopening 1 March 2004 ... after 60 years of renovation !

RICK'S CAFÉ
CASABLANCA

Réouverture le 1ᵉʳ Mars 2004 ... après 60 ans de travaux !

I showed workers this postcard announcing our opening day in hopes of pressuring them to finish by the deadline. It had limited effect. Courtesy of The Usual Suspects

make Rick's their life's work, and told them, "Unlike you, if I put something in writing, I mean it."

But pushing the workers to finish was a cakewalk compared to protecting my alcohol license. The police had rubber-stamped the initial approval back when Driss was in charge and then called me six weeks later to establish our file—the complete opposite of how the process should have happened. At that point, Driss had only been gone from the Wilaya for a month, and these bureaucrats didn't know how the system would work under the new leadership. Would Driss's reforms remain in place? Clearly the answer was no.

In early January, the Police Commissariat, which controls the alcohol licenses, telephoned and asked me to come in the next morning. They had been so friendly months before, so I greeted them warmly and showed them the latest newspaper and magazine articles about the impending opening of Rick's Café.

"That's all fine," the brigade chief said, "but we have bad news. Your license has been canceled."

"On what grounds?"

He pulled a worn, folded photocopied paper from his back pocket and handed it to me. The paper cited a law stipulating that a developer must open the business within three months of receiving the alcohol license. Nowhere on my license did it say anything like this. I quickly returned it to my tote bag. There was no way I was going to let them get their hands on it.

"The license makes no mention of this law," I said, my throat tightening. "I warned you in April that construction would take at least seven months. You told me then to come back a month or two before opening and you would answer any questions."

"Our job is not to interpret the law but to enforce it," the brigade chief said self-righteously. Instantly flashing to mind came the scene in the movie where, as Captain Renault closes Rick's down because he is shocked to find gambling, the croupier hand-delivers his winnings for the night.

Screaming in French, I started crying hysterically. I couldn't help it. My sudden dramatics caused the room to tense, and the men, all in parkas or duffle coats, began pacing the floor—except one. My teary eyes met some sympathy as I looked at the officer typing, on a manual typewriter, what I presumed to be a transcript of the meeting.*

"Well maybe you could try to see the wali and ask for a temporary license while you reapply for a new license," the brigade chief offered none too earnestly.

"*Oh no!*" I screamed. "I will *not* do that! I don't know the wali, and I don't expect he'd want to help me."

In front of the typist, I called Mahir at the Wilaya. "What can I do? They want to cancel my license, and I know it's a trick!"

"Keep up the crying, and call Driss Benhima."

"But he can't help," I said, still blubbering.

"He'll be able to tell you what to do," Mahir explained.

I dialed Driss's cell, but there was no answer, so I clumsily thumbed a text message: HLP AM AT POLIC. THEY CXLD MY ALC LICENSE

Translation: Help! I'm at the Police Commissariat, and they just canceled my alcohol license.

He called immediately.

"Leave the Commissariat, call your lawyer, then write a memo to the Regional Investment Center," he said. "They're the ones who shepherded your application. Make them do their jobs."

---

* These transcripts, called *procès-verbals,* dominate all legal and corporate proceedings.

By this time, the officers, quite subdued, suggested that maybe their superior could intervene. We went into his office, my face streaked with tears and completely distraught. He seemed quite inured to hysterics of this sort. No doubt he would have been reasonable only if I'd pulled out wads of dirhams and flashed them before his eyes. Useless.

Back in the first office, I gathered the magazines and newspaper clippings that I'd so proudly shown earlier. The brigade chief meekly asked me to read the *procès-verbal* and sign it. It stated, among other affronts, that I acknowledged having broken the law by not opening my restaurant the previous June.

I refused.

They asked me to turn over my license.

"No," I said as I walked out the door, still crying. "As far as I'm concerned my license has not been canceled."

I walked fast, not looking back, went down the stairs, and got nervous only when I had to stop at the reception desk to retrieve my I.D. card. Fortunately I wasn't detained.

Outside, I called the lawyer assisting me with the capital risk contracts.

"I was just going to call and invite you to lunch with another associate in the firm," he said. "I'll do some internal consultation, and we'll have a game plan hatched by the time we meet."

Over crab salad at Taverne du Dauphin, my lawyer told me that a senior member of the firm would write a letter to "someone" in Rabat. My job was to give them that afternoon a recap of the process from when I'd received my license, through my first meeting with the police, and to the meeting I'd just had.

In the memo written quickly after lunch, I thought it would bolster my case if I mentioned the National Tourism Convention coming up in Casablanca. Wouldn't it be embarrassing if I held a press conference during the event to reveal the traps that authorities set for investors? I hand-delivered copies of the memo to the law firm and to the Regional Investment Center.

A few weeks later, at the beginning of February, a staff member from the Police Commissariat came to the site with a written summons to appear the next morning. He laughed when I said that it must be good news.

"When you do good things, you notify people in writing," I said, "and, when you're trying to do bad things, you use the telephone."

The next morning, the brigade chief was all smiles. "Good news. Your license is not canceled on instructions of the big boss in Rabat!"

He was doing the bidding of the man who controlled his professional destiny, and I was happy that this charade had ended. The same sympathetic man was typing up the transcript of this meeting, and after the others left the room I asked him what had caused the attempt to cancel my license. "You were all so nice to me before. Has your section turned on me?"

"No, that's not it at all," he said. "We do like your project and understand that the previous wali was trying to change things. But after he left, the guys were more comfortable going back to the old system."

More comfortable because more lucrative, I thought.

"There was a restaurant also late in opening, and, when they were called in to cancel their license, they complained that we hadn't done anything to that American lady with her restaurant in the Ancienne Medina."

"I guess all my good publicity finally started to work against me," I said, relieved and happy to sign the transcript.

Then I asked a few questions of how things used to work under the old system. He understood correctly that I was wondering if I'd have to tip the local police.

"Everyone in this building knows your story," he said. "You are golden. No one is going to touch you. Don't even open those doors a tiny bit."

＝＝

Months earlier, a similar farce had also drawn me in, also thanks to forces beyond my control. The same inspectors from the commune had visited the construction site again, this time well after Driss's departure. The wood contractor was delivering cheap, manufactured bands of inlaid flooring rather than the artisanal design that Bill had specified, and I forgot to ask later what they had wanted.

The answer came soon enough when Hakim's office delivered several documents for my signature, one an attestation that I was who I said I was! The form had to be notarized at the Consulate. Another attested to a salary that I wasn't receiving.

I called Hakim. "Why all these documents?"

"Oh, didn't you know? The commune is making us resubmit our application for the building permit. You're the *maîtrise d'ouvrage,* so you have to sign all these papers. Don't worry"—famous last words—"the construction can continue. This is just paperwork to put everything in order."

Not so. All the agencies urged to give quick, positive approval of my project back in December 2002—when Driss Benhima was the wali and Rachid El Andaloussi and Mahir Tammam had made our case before all the various committees—wanted to see what they could squeeze from me now that I didn't have the wali's protection. First the

Fire Department called, then the "Aesthetic Committee." To each, I forwarded the documents required.

One afternoon Hakim hung up the phone laughing. "You're not going to believe this, but the project is now being held up by the Ministry of Tourism. You'll have to go speak to them."

The phrase "*incroyable mais vrai*"—unbelievable but true—often comes up when recounting my story in French. If any one event of the entire process suited that phrase, it was surely that the Ministry of Tourism was trying to block my project. Shouldn't we have been discussing how to make Rick's a destination point for visitors to Casablanca?

I'd been to the office of the Casablanca representative of the Ministry in a small, nondescript building on one of the backstreets once before during the application process for the alcohol license, and the man with whom I'd met had been very nice. What was the problem now?

The resident architects who had filed the complaint—two women, relatively young, dressed in business attire—should have been enthusiastic about Rick's Café. Their demeanor was anything but, however, and they radiated jealousy. One stood with arms folded, looking stern, while the other handed me a creased, worn, photocopied regulation establishing the prescribed size of a kitchen in order to serve X number of customers. According to their antiquated rules, our kitchen was too small to serve 135 people.

I asked why this was the first time I'd seen this formula, when earlier they had given their approval to our building permit. They hedged and denied ever seeing plans. They were trying to steamroll me—and, once again, I wasn't going to let them.

"I delivered plans to your office," I said, trying to keep my anger under wraps.

They finally found the plans but still refused to withdraw their complaint.

A call to the secretary general of the Ministry of Tourism in Rabat got me a meeting with a Mr. Fatihi, the chief of the Ministry's Casablanca Annex. Just talking with him on the phone revealed that he was afraid of the two architects, but he set up a site visit for the three of them the next afternoon.

Mr. Fatihi—slight, pale, dressed in a rumpled suit, tie slightly askew—stood meekly beside his colleagues. With Hakim and the various contractors, we started in the kitchen. Again the folded paper with the old-fashioned formula for number of seats versus size of kitchen went around. In all my dealings with unsympathetic bureaucrats, I never once saw a clean, clear official version of whatever rule or regulation they were throwing at me.

Hakim hadn't seen this regulation either and reiterated that the plans had included a narrative that mentioned the seating capacity. I emphasized our different approach, that we weren't thinking of serving hundreds of orders of couscous, roasting lamb shoulders, vats of *harira* soup or pigeon *pastilla* for the masses. We had a different menu, more international, with dishes prepared to order. The two ladies didn't want to hear any of it.

Moving into the courtyard, I led them to the space in front of the bar, forcing them to look at the restaurant. Impressed, Mr. Fatihi gazed at the skylight, gracious arches, and rich decor. He searched the faces of his colleagues for a common, appreciative reaction, but, finding their looks grim and dismissive, he quickly resumed a deadpan expression. Hakim made the case for the quality of the restoration and the architectural details. I emphasized what an important tourism project Rick's Café was for Casablanca, and wasn't boosting tourism their main objective? Unmoved, the two women held firmly to the raggedy piece of paper with the formula, while looking at me with nothing but contempt and running roughshod over their boss.

Finally, as we were standing at the bar, which had been formed *in concrete*, Mr. Fatihi, his knees shaking, said, "Couldn't the wall behind the bar be moved a few centimeters forward to make more space in the kitchen?"

"Not if we want to have a bartender behind the bar," I sniped.

We had come to an impasse, but by now I'd become adept at improvisation when my back was to the wall. In this case it literally was.

"All right," I said. "We'll comply with your formula. I think, if we just serve drinks downstairs and the food upstairs, there won't be any problem with your ratio."

M. Fatihi looked relieved; the two architects scowled, still determined to find another way to stop the project. Of course I had no intention of honoring the compromise, but finally I understood how to play the game to my advantage.

⌇

In between all these bureaucratic obstacle courses, I was having difficulties casting the role of chef. In *Casablanca*, the only food we see being consumed is caviar, so here the film was of no help at all. Around the time I found Darryn, the barman who didn't get the part of Sacha, I met a Moroccan chef who'd returned after ten years in San Francisco. Finally tired of the delays, he went back to the US in January. My friend Omar sent a brilliant chef from Marrakech who came complete with a barman. The chef said he'd give a month's notice and be ready to start on or just after opening day. I was keen to hire them both.

Two days later, Omar called with bad news. "He was too embarrassed to call you himself. He didn't think his boss would be so upset,

141

but it seems that he signed a contract, and they're not going to let him out of it. Kathy, it's time to think of hiring a caterer for your opening and take your time finding the right chef."

"I think you may be right. The food is important, but no one will be coming here for the food at the beginning," I admitted without any enthusiasm.

We interviewed a caterer who worked out some simple plates with me. I feared being drawn into the kitchen myself, and so at least this arrangement would keep me in the front of the house.

Not everything was finished by any means, but at least downstairs was ready: The piano was in place, and I had two barstools, twelve tables, and thirty-six chairs. I threw a preopening party to thank those who helped—investors, bankers, lawyers, contractors, and friends. It wasn't all fun, however. It was during this event that all the paperwork for transforming our corporate structure to permit the participation by the capital risk firm was finally completed, so several of us were closeted upstairs in the VIP room initialing and signing document after document.

One investor over-imbibed and crashed on the one banquette we had for display in an empty dining room off the VIP space. The plumbing/heating contractor merged with one of the barstools, determined to take the remainder of his fee in beer. It was a stressful evening, to be sure, but one additional emergency gave me the chance to use a classic line.

Just as all the papers were being signed in the VIP room, the electricity went out. There had been a surge somewhere. Houssein restored the lights, and I went to the balustrade, replaying the scene in the film where, after the Peter Lorre character is arrested, Rick apologizes for the disruption and tells his clients to go back to having a good time.

It was one thing to have a small private party in the restaurant, but I couldn't open for business officially without a building permit . . . and time was running out. On February 22 the *New York Times* travel section had run an article, "A Casablanca Landmark Is Ready for Its Debut," complete with the picture of me in front of our doors dressed in white dinner jacket, tuxedo pants, and heels. We had to open on March 1, one way or another.

A final hurdle in the permit process came with a visit from the Aesthetic Committee. Everything was fine as we walked through the restaurant—until we reached the terrace. The head of the committee asked about the second terrace, a small space over my apartment, where we had installed the air-conditioning units, the kitchen extraction vents, and the satellite dish.

"*Aha!* Just as I suspected," the head of the committee said as we reached the stairs. "You have stairs to this terrace."

"What do you mean?" I said. "Of course we have stairs."

"But the plans submitted for the building permit don't have stairs. We discussed this with your architect over a year ago, when we were concerned you would use this upper terrace for the restaurant, and he assured us then that the second terrace would be accessed by a ladder only when necessary."

The committee clearly could see the space was full of equipment, making any commercial use impossible, so they made a note that the architect would remove the stairs but gave no date or indication of enforcement. I wanted to point out the dangerous and clearly unauthorized "additions" tacked atop the building next door: rooms constructed out of rough cement, plastic sheeting, and rusty metal. But I had to bite my tongue. There was no denying that we had misled the authorities. They left, but they weren't happy about what they had seen.

Furious, I gave Hakim an earful for putting me in this position by not giving me all the information at the beginning.

"Well, you had both sets of plans," he shrugged. "You should have noticed."

That retort merited only a disdainful glance with no time to waste on more substantial recriminations as the permit needed sorting out. We scheduled a final meeting in which all the various agencies would convene at the Agence Urbaine (Planning Office) for the approval. After all the running back and forth, my determination had finally impressed someone there. Mr. Haji liked my spirit and was enjoying the way I got recalcitrant bureaucrats—even in his section—to do their jobs.

I arrived at the appointed time for the final meeting, but of course no one else did. This isn't surprising in Morocco. Punctuality doesn't have much importance in daily life. Mr. Haji arrived, and soon the representatives of the Aesthetic Committee showed up, then some others wandered in. The Fire Department and the Ministry of Tourism didn't send anyone. Mr. Haji called the Fire Department first, and they said they had a conflict. Haji's side of the conversation went something like this:

"If you have a conflict, you send someone else. . . . I don't care if everyone is busy. If you can't send someone, give your approval over the phone. . . . Oh, you don't want to do that? I'll pass the phone to Mme. Kriger."

Heavily dramatizing the situation, I finally got an OK from the weary official, then passed the phone back to Mr. Haji to note the man's name and title. It was a good warm-up for the Ministry of Tourism. Again, Mr. Haji's side of the call:

"Mr. Fatihi, are you sending a representative to the meeting at the Agence Urbaine for Rick's Café? . . . Yes, right now. We're all here. . . . Oh, you don't know if you'll be voting to approve the project? Why?

I thought the situation was resolved. . . . Mme. Kriger is going to be very upset. . . . Yes, she's right here. Would you like to speak to her? . . . All right, but call me back in *five* minutes."

Using what little time we had to maximum advantage, I phoned the secretary general of the Ministry in Rabat, threatening a press conference that would call into question the Ministry's support for tourism in Casablanca. He sighed, tired of me—and I didn't blame him; I was getting tired of myself! He said he'd make a call.

Within two minutes, Mr. Haji's phone rang, and Mr. Fatihi took the responsibility for giving the Ministry's approval. We finally had our building permit, just *days* before opening.

March 1 arrived. The article in the *New York Times*—complete with picture, phone and fax numbers, and our website address—was driving reservations our way. But the delay in granting the building permit had held up our operating permit. Mahir at the Wilaya had helped me with the wording and had his secretary type it. Usually approved permits go to the architect's office, so I was after Hakim Benjelloun all morning. Naturally he had no information, so I went directly to the director of planning for the commune. He said the permit had been approved and sent along to the vice mayor for his signature. When nothing came through by lunchtime, I called again and was told to go to the vice mayor's office at 3:00 p.m.

The vice mayor had a unique management style for Morocco. He didn't make appointments; he'd see anyone who showed up in his office. So I arrived and introduced myself to his chief of staff—the gatekeeper. "In four hours, I'm opening my restaurant, but we have no operating permit. I expect the mayor of Casablanca to attend. It will be very embarrassing."

That got me right in. The vice mayor, anxious to help, explained that he didn't have the file. He sensed my urgency and grabbed the phone. His telephone manner was just as direct as his management style. I sat there while he screamed at people in Arabic. Finally he slammed the phone down, rolled his eyes, and said, "Your papers have been 'found.' They are still at the commune, in the planning office. I'll send someone for them immediately." He paused. "Better yet, you go pick them up and bring them back here."

For the next few hours, I felt like Victor Laszlo chasing the elusive letters of transit. I raced to the commune and picked up the documents from the hapless paper pushers without a word but with my best withering look. If this was a last ditch attempt to extort money from me, it didn't work. Papers in hand, I rushed back to the vice mayor's office, ushered into his office past benches filled with waiting petitioners.

The vice mayor signed the papers with a flourish. "You're in business!"

Once again saved from the brink of disaster, I was as grateful to him as the Bulgarian girl was to Rick after he allowed her husband to win at roulette.

It was 6:00 p.m. when I delivered signed copies to the commune and the police and rushed back to my apartment to shower and change into my black tuxedo pants and white dinner jacket. I told Aicha to floor it, and we gleefully sped to the restaurant.

I dashed up the steps, through the beautiful wood doors, and into the role of Madame Rick. I turned on the sign, and with very little fanfare Rick's Café assumed its role as a backdrop for the daily dramas of Casablanca.

At last, after sixty-two years, an iconic Hollywood fantasy had become reality.

ACT II

The Legend Continues

EIGHT
A New Director

In the early days, Issam and I eased into an evening routine. After his last set we sat down to eat and talk about the funny or infuriating events of the night's service. Then, the house lights down and the soundtrack still playing, we dragged two chairs from behind the piano to face the courtyard. I sipped a glass of Jameson's, Issam a gin and tonic while he smoked his Marlboros. We laughed over the latest pratfall of the hapless *maître d'hôtel*, Abdallah Ghattas, or lamented Chef Abdou's most recent power play. Eventually we always came around to sharing our life's stories.

As we exchanged family backgrounds, struggles, hopes, frustrations, and goals during those early evenings, we had no idea what might lie ahead, but those moments alone in the dimly lit restaurant created a bond between us. Early on, I fantasized over a romantic relationship, and he let me pretend, just as Rick says in the final scene of the film. Over the years, however, we've found a way to mesh our disparate personalities into our own beautiful friendship and effective partnership. In our movie, I may take the role of executive producer, but Issam is the brilliant director.

The one and only chess game we played eight years ago defines our relationship to this day. One lazy summer Sunday, I decided to burnish my Madame Rick persona by learning to play, and Issam agreed to teach me. First we set the scene by moving the antique table with an inlaid chess board from my apartment to a space behind the piano. We added the two old Spanish embossed leather armchairs that reminded me so much of Bill Willis's Marrakech sitting room. Finally we trekked to the souvenir shops on Rue Félix Houphouët-Boigny, just outside the Medina, and bought a wooden chess set.

Back at Rick's, Issam arranged the board and explained the hierarchy of the pieces and how each could move. Hmmmm, this wasn't checkers. Each move caused me pain. It seemed impossible to think that far ahead, and I couldn't fathom a strategy. Used to following my impulses, I grew anxious about taking so much time to think about how to move.

"But Issam, how do I win?" I finally blurted out, frustrated.

He sat back in his chair, probably not surprised by the remark. By then, he had no doubt about my personality. He knew I was impetuous, used to making decisions based on emotion, inclination, or a zest for adventure. He'd also heard enough of my stories to know of my determination, persistence, and occasional brazenness when going after a goal. The consummate cautious strategist, he, on the other hand, looks at all angles, studying the ramifications. He won of course, and I never asked to play again.

One of Morocco's foremost modern artists, Issam's father, Mohammed Chabâa, belonged to a group of avant-garde cultural figures in the 1970s who presented their thoughts in a literary digest called *Souffles*. World tensions in the late '60s and '70s from Vietnam to Palestine, plus the socialist alignment in Algeria, led King Hassan II to quash anything that looked like political dissent.

When Issam was seven, his protected life with parents and baby sister, Nadia, suddenly ended when his father came under suspicion because of certain friendships and was taken to prison. Issam's mother put her fear and worry aside to care for her children, but the pain of that year had an indelible effect on Issam. After Mohammed was declared not guilty and released, the family, which eventually included his brother, Tarik, and another sister, Qods, grew especially close.

Now retired from the faculty of the École des Beaux Arts in Rabat, Mohammed Chabâa still paints, and he has not lost his old revolutionary zeal. His son, on the other hand, is pragmatic and middle-of-the road, which sometimes leaves Mohammed shaking his head.

Issam's parents believed in the importance of intellectual freedom and encouraged curiosity and self-expression. In 1978, the Chabâa family moved to Tangier, and at sixteen Issam taught himself the guitar. After the guitar, he learned to play the piano, again without formal instruction.

Two painful and frustrating years at the Faculté des Lettres in Rabat with its confusing maze of satellite buildings spread around town, disengaged professors, and students marking time left Issam feeling as if trapped in a Kafka story. He finally escaped, returned to Tangier, and with his friends Farid and Nabil started a band. Nabil eventually moved to Geneva, and in 1992 Issam and Farid regrouped in Rabat with the Souissi brothers—Hamza, Ali, and Hassan. At the end of 2003, after that group broke up, Issam did production work and picked up musical gigs here and there, but he had come to a personal crossroads, wondering what to do next.

As we approached our opening, I had to find a pianist even if I didn't yet have a chef. After all, no one remembers what people were eating in the movie, but can you imagine Rick's Café without Sam?

I'd always planned on bringing Lennie Bluett, a well-known figure in the world of piano bars, from Los Angeles to play at the opening and for the first month. Lennie's mother, Mae, was Humphrey

Bogart's cook, and Bogey insisted that the then-twenty-one-year-old have a chance to audition for the part of Sam. Even powder in his hair didn't help; Lennie was too young. Now, some sixty years later, he had his chance to play the role.

But Lennie could only be temporary. I had to find Sam.

I put out feelers, and two weeks before opening Karim Benkirane, an amateur jazz guitarist friend, called. "I've finally got the phone number of the pianist I told you about. Here's his number. His name is Issam."

"Uh, repeat that name," I said.

"Issam" (pronounced EYE-sam).

"I may have to hire him whether or not he can play the piano," I said, marveling at his name.

Most Moroccans hadn't seen the film, so Karim may not have understood, but Issam was familiar with the movie and had heard of the pianist.

"You've already got a good chance at this job because of your name," I joked, "but I do hope you can play the piano, especially the songs of the forties."

"Yes," he said simply. "I can play."

That turned out to be a major understatement.

Issam came in a few days later for an audition. He looked just like a classical musician with his round, open face and neat moustache and goatee. Quiet and formal, his English perfect, he marveled respectfully at the Pleyel piano, commenting that it was the best brand of the '40s. Then he sat down—back straight, hands poised—and played songs from the era of the film.

Ilsa Lund never quite says, "Play it again, Sam" in the movie, though, recognizing him from happier days in Paris, she does ask him several times to play "As Time Goes By." Of course I asked Issam to play the song at his audition, and he did—so well that it could have come from the soundtrack.

"Did you know the song before I called, or did you rush out to learn it?" I asked.

"I played it in Tangier at the birthday party of Malcolm Forbes," he said.

Well, I certainly hadn't expected that!

Nor had I articulated what exactly I wanted in a pianist, but once I met Issam and heard him play I knew he was perfect. Once more, destiny had taken a hand to make Rick's Café more than a dream, another case of life imitating art.

Issam was living in Rabat at the time and needed to move to Casablanca. In the meantime, we limped along with *Ella Fitzgerald Sings Cole Porter*, a two-CD set I'd been listening to every night for nearly two years. When Issam arrived for his first night, I apologized that we didn't have a proper piano bench for him. He had to use one of the dining chairs.

"The seat doesn't matter, but could I have a lamp?" he asked.

"Well, you came to the right place," I said. He had no idea yet that buying lamps was my specialty—and drove my bankers crazy. "What sort of lamp do you want?"

"Something small that I can put right above the keyboard."

I showed him my stash, and he selected a small brass lamp with an antique parchment-fringed shade that still sits on the piano today and gives off a warm light. I thought he wanted to be able to see the music, but he was self-taught, so he never used sheet music. He understood intuitively the importance of ambience.

Lennie Bluett arrived in time to play for St. Patrick's Day, and he and Issam played back-to-back sets. From having no piano player, suddenly I had two with such a contrast in styles. I wasn't at all sure how it would work out, but clients loved both pianists, and the two men did become friends, sharing jokes and stories of the music business. Lennie, with his showman's patter and repartee, introduced himself—"Hi, I'm Lennie Bluett from Hollywood, and I'm sharing the stage with Issam from Rabat!"—and slid into one of his signature numbers, such as the familiar Sinatra ballad with a change of lyrics. "Strangers in my tights . . ." he bellowed into the microphone, and the crowd broke up. One evening, before singing "La Vie en Rose," he told the audience, "If you can't understand my French, you can throw beer at the piano!"

Issam, poised, serious, and smooth, tailored his repertoire to the audience. On Bill Willis's only visit to Rick's, six months after we opened, he and I sat upstairs looking down on the courtyard. All of a sudden I was petrified. What if he didn't like the palms? What would he say about the lamp purchases and the lampshades I'd commissioned in Casablanca? And the food?

But he loved everything. Except one little detail. He chided me for wearing a blouse under my tuxedo jacket. "You should try for Marlene Dietrich, not Humphrey Bogart."

"You know, my dear," he said as we dined, "I've never had children, but I've come to think of each of my projects as a child. I'm sometimes so disappointed when my work is bastardized by the client either to save money or to assert their bad taste. I can sense this is a child that's going to turn out just fine."

As Issam started his set, I continued to prattle, but—

"Be quiet, my dear," Bill said. "We're listening to a piano concert."

When Issam started, he faced the room, but that arrangement distanced him from our guests. He waited until New Year's Eve 2006 to turn the piano around so that people could see his hands on the

Issam shared the stage during our opening month with Hollywood's Lennie Bluett, the son of Humphrey Bogart's cook—who, at twenty-one, auditioned unsuccessfully for the role of Sam in the movie.

keys. I took it as a sign that he was feeling more comfortable, but looking back it was probably dawning on him that I had no inclination of ever letting him go——no matter how difficult business became.

Issam later revealed that, when he first started, he could see how much we were struggling with the banks, personnel, and the somewhat fickle tastes of early clients. He knew that restaurants hired pianists to open the place and usually kept them for the first couple of months. Then, when the money became tight, the pianist was first to go. As he saw us go through all sorts of financial problems, he kept waiting to be fired, amazed that *not* having a pianist was inconceivable to me.

I never tire of seeing looks on faces when Issam takes his seat and begins to play. There's not a client who doesn't stop talking, eating, or drinking to look up as he begins his first set. His ability to play music according to the mood or nationality of the clients still makes me marvel. He carefully reads the audience and always determines the tone and repertoire by the feeling in the room. A set may begin with the upbeat "Lady Is a Tramp," move into jazz with "A-Train," go back in time with Dietrich's "Lili Marlene," or Piaf's "Hymne à l'Amour." If he hears Spanish, "Aquellos Ojos Verdes;" to an American crowd, "New York, New York;" and for certain regulars, "La Vie en Rose." He knows what music will work here and what won't. But no matter the mix of clients, most want to hear the inevitable "As Time Goes By," which he plays, beautifully, again and again.

Invariably clients compliment the music and wonder at the coincidence of his name. He smiles good-naturedly when someone approaches him with what he or she thinks a novel command, "Play it again, Sam, or whatever your name is." In fact, he's so gracious that he's been known to apologize for the disappointment that he causes by not being black!

But Issam is an artist in his own right, not an impersonator, so he's not building a reputation as the real Sam playing at the real Rick's. Just as our Rick's Café has developed its unique identity and image, so has Issam.

He chose Monday as his day off, and at first I had difficulty adjusting. He compiled a soundtrack that served as fine filler between sets, but listening to it all night long was boring. So I improvised. One night, I put on opera music, trying to suggest that Issam's place was being taken by Maria Callas. Stupid idea.

A more depressing solution was a trio of Spanish guitarists wearing gaucho outfits and trying to model themselves after the Gypsy

Kings. After their first—and last—performance, they became known to the house as the "gypsy fakers."

One Tuesday afternoon I said to Issam, "It's so painful when you have a night off. I'm worried that clients will be angry that you're not here, and we have to have some music. I don't know what to do."

Issam was practical, as usual. "It's better just to run the soundtrack. It still gives the right mood, and most people who come on Mondays are relieved we're at least open." And he was right about that. At first we closed on Mondays but gave up that idea after three weeks. Not just for financial reasons either, as I received a few e-mails from people who'd been in Casablanca only one night and were disappointed to find us closed.

Still I framed a picture of him that said in French: "No piano tonight. Day off for the pianist."

Issam never liked the photo—out of modesty, I thought. Only years later when we finally retired the photo did he give the real reason. "It's never a good marketing idea to tell people what they're missing."

Practical and premeditating, Issam is also extremely diplomatic when clients request a song he doesn't like, try to foist sheet music on him, or insist on singing along. A man once asked him to play "Chattanooga Choo-Choo," and Issam said he'd never heard of it. Later in the evening, after the man had left, Issam ended another number with a riff on the song—and a devilish little smile.

A friend bringing an important group to Morocco really put his tact to the test when she asked if one of the group, world famous in another discipline, could make her singing debut at Rick's. I agreed enthusiastically, thinking we'd scored a coup. What a mistake.

When the woman started warbling, my friend, whose face had shown such anticipation, suddenly registered shock. "Can you tell her not to hold the microphone so close to her mouth?" she asked through clenched teeth.

The rest of their group, sitting at tables facing the singer, stared stoically ahead, not daring to exchange glances with neighboring tables. Their champagne consumption increased notably during the four-song set—which ended, of course, in a rendition of "As Time Goes By" that included some, how shall we say, previously undiscovered lyrics. Issam, ever the showman, played beautifully and did everything he could, short of singing himself, to minimize the damage.

⌇

Because Casablanca is more of a business center than a tourist city, restaurants tend to close on Sunday rather than Monday, but at first we had no business on Sunday despite being one of the few places open.

One evening, the late Dr. Abderrahim Harouchi, civic leader and a former minister of health, reminisced about a group of friends who gathered informally at a different club or restaurant on Sunday night to enjoy the last hours of the weekend fighting off what they called *le syndrome du lundi* (a case of the Mondays). They liked to listen to live music, so they always were searching for the right combination of music, food, and ambience. Hearing this, Issam tried an idea he'd been considering—motivated by more than nostalgia.

"We have to do something to get word-of-mouth going," he said. "Let's introduce our own Sunday jam session."

It was a genius idea. Some of our first and most avid clients were owners or chefs of local restaurants on their one day off. Over the years, the Jam Session has evolved a bit. From the beginning, Issam engaged his old bandmate Hamza Souissi and Xavier Sarazin to accompany him on bass guitar and drums. More recently, saxophone player Gilbert Dall'Anese has joined the group, and Issam's friend Najib replaced Xavier on the drums. Rick's has become the place to come in Casablanca for jazz, and professionals have started to drop by when in town, attracted both to the mystique of the film as well as the positive vibes from great jazz improvisations. Sunday at Rick's literally jumps until the wee hours.

One evening I ventured out to the opening of a friend's new jazz spot in downtown Casablanca, which led to an unforgettable night. I wasn't really checking out the competition since there can really be only one Rick's Café, but I was curious to see their jazz setup and look at the menu. Dr. Harouchi was there, the same friend whose memories of Sunday nights in decades past encouraged our Sunday Jam Sessions, as were other familiar faces. I didn't stay long, soon returning to my corner seat at the bar in Rick's when the reception desk called to say that Dr. Harouchi and his wife were coming from the club opening with a group of friends. The ten of them were all prominent members of Casablanca society, a number of our regular clients among the group. Issam started playing the French classics: "La Vie en Rose," "Non, Je Ne Regrette Rien," and "Hymne à l'Amour." Soon the group gathered around the piano and sang along as they raised their glasses. I toasted them myself, again feeling as if living my own version of *Casablanca*.

Despite his diplomatic, gentle nature, Issam doesn't let his colleagues manipulate him. He's no pushover. An expatriate French saxophone player once showed up expecting to play but found himself instead just sitting at his table, listening to Gilbert's masterful artistry for set after set. When one itinerant musician offered that he would be happy to grace Rick's with his presence, Issam calmly replied, "We'll get in touch with you if we need you." The musician walked out in a huff.

British trumpet player Guy Barker further validated Issam's musical stature in Casablanca when he selected Rick's as a jam site for part of a series for BBC Radio that ran in July 2005. Guy's travels with his trumpet had taken him to Jamaica, Cuba, and South Africa. He had musician contacts everywhere but Casablanca. He found us through our website.

Issam coordinated a local brass band, costumed in blue robes, normally hired for weddings and special events, to play with Guy. He found some young musicians experimenting with traditional Moroccan music and jazz fusion. He also contacted an eighty-year-old Gnaoua master in the Ancienne Medina.* One afternoon, Issam led Guy through the narrow alleys to the master's apartment and an intimate jam session. In Guy's words

the visit to the master and that area by the mosque really gave me a lump in my throat. . . . I felt like I was in another world. And playing with him, it was like nothing else. A musician gets accustomed to playing certain scales, and you can usually sense the flow, but as we were playing together I hit one note and thought—that's not right—and he looked at me, smiled, and we went on. For me that was the most formidable moment . . . the master and his wonderful attitude and presence. I asked him about two well-known Gnaoua musicians. His response was so right. He said, "These people are younger than me, so therefore I cannot credit them. I can only credit those who have passed before me and passed along their knowledge."

---

* Gnaoua, the most traditional of all Moroccan music styles, originated in West Africa and is played with castanets, drums, and a three-stringed lute.

In the radio coverage and an accompanying article in the *Guardian*, Guy's praise of Casablanca's music scene was effusive, and he rated Casablanca the surprise hit of the four-country tour. "Without Rick's Café this would never have happened," he said.

Issam's skill and experience also impressed Harry Connick Jr. He and his entourage came for a private jam session for a documentary being filmed in Morocco, with Gilbert, our sax player, joining Harry's bassist and drummer. Harry was most interested in talking with Issam and Gilbert about the music scene in Casablanca and Morocco.

"I've always been interested in doing jazz fusion with Moroccan music," Harry said.

"I've done it," Issam replied. Blown away, Harry asked Issam lots of questions.

Toward the end of the conversation, Harry mentioned how impressed he was with Gilbert's playing. "I hear Gilbert play, and I realize I still have a lot to learn. That's the great thing about jazz."

Issam agreed. What he liked about jazz was that it kept a musician innovating and always looking for ways to improvise.

Before Harry left Rick's, he gave a very credible rendition of "As Time Goes By," even though he had never sung it before.

Issam with Harry Connick Jr. after an impromptu jam session.

Issam's contributions don't end at the piano, though. Bit by bit he's put his mark on Rick's, pursuing something I might mention but more often taking the initiative in anticipating something I might like. He's never wrong.

In the early days he showed up impromptu in the afternoons, helping out because, as he said, "There's so much to do." I knew that. He was right. I was drowning in details and didn't have anyone on whom I could count.

One day I was in the car with Aicha, our driver, and we saw Issam walking by a travel agency near the Royal Mansour Hotel.

I called him on his mobile. "Were you coming from the travel agency?"

I was afraid he was leaving town.

"No, I have a room in the Hotel du Centre, around the corner."

He had moved from Rabat, but he was still living in a hotel, which made me worry that he wasn't planning to stay with us for long. He said later that he came to Rick's so early so the hotel staff could make up his room. I didn't care why he came early; I was just so grateful that he did.

On our second anniversary, Issam conceived a superb gift, a small book with a narrative and wonderful photos. Especially memorable, it came at a time of intense financial pressure when Issam and I were attempting to work out the best way to mesh our different talents.

He had the total vision for the book, took the photos, and did the layout. Even though I wrote the chapter headings and most of the narrative, I respected his editorial control and followed his suggestions. Sometimes I believe he knows how I think and want to express myself better than I do. Issam delicately and warily points out to me those times when I've been too hasty, and I've so much respect for his judgment that I take his words to heart. Under his influence, I may have become better at thinking just a little bit before opening my mouth and saying something I may regret later. For those who know me—especially men—this is probably shocking.

For the first couple of years, I had the edginess of a veteran fresh from combat, struggling to adjust to normal society. The demanding confrontational attitude that had served me so well during construction obviously wasn't appropriate for the restaurant's working environment. But I had developed a tough shell. I was so determined not to show weakness or rely on anyone but myself that I absorbed this persona as I faced all new problems that came to Rick's. I was hard on everyone then but hardest on Issam, the one person trying to help me the most. In August 2006, he e-mailed that he needed a break and that I shouldn't contact him. It was the wake-up call I needed.

Afraid he wouldn't come back, I was relieved when he did. The week he'd been gone had been truly sobering. We had a series of long, frank conversations that usually left me in tears. Still, I knew it was as hard for him to confront me as it was for me to process what he was saying. The years of combat had passed. The people around me were on my side. My automatic defensiveness had to go; I had to adapt. I promised to change, heeding the Arab proverb always to "Follow the advice of the one who makes you cry, never the one who makes you laugh."

So Issam and I started over, step by step. It's not often in life that you get the chance to replay a scene, but that's what happened. I concentrated on keeping my mouth shut, and Issam adapted to and guided me through my impulsive schemes and ideas.

He completely redesigned the terrace in time for the 2007 summer season. A beautiful wood pergola dominates it now along with a brick planter full of geraniums and terra-cotta pots holding palm and olive trees. Rattan tables and chairs fill the space along with a bar and all the necessary refrigeration and cooking equipment. Issam mixed a soundtrack of old Cuban and fado music. After I'd taken to reading and having lunch at the terrace bar, Issam came by from time to time, and we talked over coffee. It reminded me of the early days, when Issam would just appear "because there was so much to do."

There still was.

One day Issam came to me and said that he'd reached a point where he was ready to make a bigger commitment to Rick's. He had some ideas and some plans that we could discuss, but he wanted me to agree that once we started, "there was no turning back." Issam was sounding a lot like me. It had taken huge efforts on both our parts to rebuild our relationship, but we'd reached a new level of understanding.

From that summer day on the terrace back in 2007, there has been no turning back: Issam redesigned the small kitchen to improve efficiency; hired a mature, disciplined manager with no cooking experience to be our chef; designed software allowing our menu to change and be printed daily; not to mention designing furniture to enhance the decor, an oyster bar, a marble-topped buffet table, a full bar for the lounge and—best of all—a roulette table.

Issam took a bare film set and used it to express his myriad talents: music performance and compilation, graphic and product design, merchandising, marketing and branding, architecture and furniture design, software and website development, personnel management, carpentry, and managing a freewheeling American entrepreneur. Just as I did, Issam has found himself at Rick's.

He and I sat down recently after my son, Kyle, and his wife, Sarah, had visited. Amazed at the changes, they clearly recognized that Issam

House Cocktail Sour Jdid

Preparation time: 5 minutes
Serves 4

"Whatever you do with drinks, you have to serve a *sour jdid,*" said a friend looking at the restaurant's address. *Sour jdid* means "new walls" in Arabic, and he was right: We needed a tart cocktail to amuse and bemuse our clients.

Just a few weeks after we opened, inspiration struck and I created this refreshing cocktail. Issam designed a poster for it, and we sell House Cocktail Sour Jdid old-fashioned glasses in our Rick's Gear souvenir corner.

8 or 12 lemon slices

ice

6 ounces Johnnie Walker Red Label scotch

1 ounce red vermouth

1 ounce lemon juice

sparkling water

Divide lemon slices and mash them in four old-fashioned glasses. Add ice. To each glass add 1½ ounces scotch, ¼ ounce vermouth, and ¼ ounce lemon juice. Top with sparkling water and stir.

Note: It's impossible to drink just one!

is as much a part of Rick's as I am and that we are both committed to making the legend continue. I told Issam that I wanted to formalize his position and make him a *directeur*—the French spelling, but it works in English, too. He calls the shots, so he should be recognized for it. He's the Michael Curtiz to my Hal Wallis. Since then there's

Issam at the Pleyel, in one of his many roles as general manager. Photo by Aziz Maradji for The Usual Suspects

been a subtle change. He exhibits a pride of ownership, a more easy familiarity with clients, and even more focused attention on our staff and strategies for the future.

Today, Issam always seems to be three steps ahead of me in making sensitive decisions, and he's always right there with a teaching moment when I need a little technical adjustment. Recently he kept me from publicly chastising a waiter for what I perceived to be insubordination.

"Think about the young staff, people who are just starting out and haven't worked with you and don't know you yet," he said. "You don't want to have them feeling on edge because they see how quickly you react to something that seems to them a minor gaffe."

"You're right," I said. "I hadn't thought of it that way. I'll take him aside and clear the air. Thank you, Issam, for helping me to see this from another side."

He smiled. "It's my job."

By now he has become used to what I euphemistically call the "dance," which he more practically calls the "negotiation," involved in getting me to come around. All I need to say is "I've finally decided that you were right," and he flashes a knowing smile. Handling areas that I can't, familiar both with my way of thinking and Moroccan attitudes, he has brought balance to the restaurant and given me a sense of calm, the trust that comes from working with the same shared purpose.

And there's still nobody in the world who can play "As Time Goes By" like Issam.

NINE
Do or Die

Within days of opening, former American ambassador to Morocco Frederick Vreeland stopped at Rick's en route to his home in Marrakech. One of the Usual Suspects, he scampered up the front steps and stood in the central courtyard, his eyes wide, taking it all in.

"Kathy, you were born to do this," he said.

That's exactly how I felt. All of my previous life experiences had prepared me to play Madame Rick, and I loved the role—even though it didn't exactly start out according to the script.

Fans of the film will recall the heartbreaking scene in Paris when Rick reluctantly boards the train to Marseille alone after receiving Ilsa's farewell letter in the rain. We next see him eighteen months later in Casablanca. Dressed in a white dinner jacket, he has a commanding presence in his classy, sophisticated, and from all appearances financially thriving gin joint. I'd already spent two and a half years bringing my dream to fruition, and it was going to take yet more time for my Rick's to be running as smoothly.

But for the first few weeks, I allowed myself to celebrate. The doors were open, the final tranche of money from the capital risk firm had arrived, and we were busy. Tourists holding the *New York Times* article came. Groups of Casablanca's fickle movers and shakers, who made the rounds of new restaurants, came, but so did the *Casablancaise* who loved the city and wanted it to regain its cosmopolitan image, tarnished by the attacks of May 16, 2003. One night a woman grabbed my hands and said, "Oh, thank you, thank you for giving Casablanca people a reason to go out at night again."

Rick had a policy of not drinking with his customers, but I didn't follow his lead in those heady, early days. Usually found in the middle of a group gathered at the downstairs bar with a glass of house wine, Ksar Bahia, in my hand, sometimes smoking a mini-Cohiba, I finally relaxed and let down my guard, reveling in the praise for creating both Rick's Café and a new me: thin with short curly hair. The new me got a lot of attention, including a proposition to become someone's mistress and lots of leering looks from amateur lotharios.

The new chef, Abdou, encouraged my relaxed mood . . . for a while at least. He came for an interview two days after we opened with quite a buildup: He had been the executive chef at a major hotel in Agadir for more than a decade. He wasn't a roly-poly, jovial, dough-boy kind of chef, but a tall, lanky, darkly handsome man with a distinctive mole on one cheek and a square face. At first his piercing eyes were intimidating, but as soon as we engaged in conversation I had an entirely different impression. He charmed me in his perfect English, making jokes about the restaurant business. When he called a waiter over in the middle of relating a story and ordered a vodka, it seemed entirely natural. He offered to take over all the responsibilities in the kitchen, including hiring cooks and assistants.

"Once I am in charge, madame, you will never have to step foot in the kitchen again." My guard may have been down, but it wasn't gone. I mentally filed that comment away.

I asked when he could begin. We needed him sooner rather than later because we had a group of forty-five from the Chicago-Casablanca Sister City organization coming for a cocktail-dinner in four days.

"Sunday's my day off," he said. "I can do the dinner if you can do the marketing from a list I'll give you right now."

I was sold. That Sunday I brought my own pots and pans, he pulled in some colleagues, and we organized a memorable party.

Once he started, Abdou equipped the kitchen, hired cooks, and made decisions about the menu. For a long time his histrionic personality completely mesmerized me. He dominated any space he occupied—which was increasingly the dining room. He loved mingling with customers, but his humor could be biting, especially when it came to the waitstaff. Asked once if he'd seen the *maître d'hôtel*, Abdou said, "Oh yeah, I just saw him out in the courtyard faking—oh I mean *taking* orders."

But I couldn't fake our financial situation, which was getting pretty grim. We owed the bank, suppliers, various contractors—many of whom I had no intention of paying—to say nothing of operating expenses and salaries. Bouchra, our lucky catch of a financial assistant, had previously worked for the group that owned my favorite Casablanca restaurant, La Bavaroise. She'd just returned from a year in Italy and promised to get our financial reporting system up and running. She may have brought a bit of the Italian temperament back with her from Europe; she was often at odds with some of the staff. She and my driver, Aicha—now functioning also as my secretary—had become bitter enemies. If Bouchra gave her checks to deposit at the banks, Aicha found some way to lose the deposit slip.

Aicha was also getting on my nerves. It all came to a head one morning as she, Abdou, and I were returning to Rick's from the Marché Central. As we turned onto a main street, she nicked the handlebars of a bicyclist and made an angry gesture indicating that the cyclist was at fault. As she sped away, I exploded, telling her that she had to be careful, that she was driving a car representing Rick's Café, not a taxi.

That did it.

She unleashed a stream of insults and railed against my complaints about her fast and aggressive driving while speeding to the restaurant, ignoring everybody else on the road. If we made it back to the restaurant alive, I vowed to fire her on the spot—and I did.

Meanwhile, we had a restaurant to run. One day a self-assured young man wearing an Indiana Jones fedora, white shirt, and chinos walked in, took a table, and sent a waiter to me with his card and a message that he wanted to talk. Intrigued, I greeted him with my own card.

"How did you get the name Maximillion?" I asked.

"Eccentric parents."

Maximillion Cooper runs Gumball 3000, an international company based in London that, among other pursuits, organizes car rallies. The latest was coming up in May and was going to pass through Casablanca.

"I'd assumed there was a Rick's Café in Casablanca, and it was already put into the program as the checkpoint," he said. "But I was amazed when I checked into my hotel last night to find out you'd just opened."

Cooper said that we'd have to feed lunch to, and handle parking for, about 350 people in 160 cars in a four-hour span. Abdou came out from the kitchen and created a basic menu on the spot: tuna salad, sautéed chicken breasts, Rick's Cheesecake, lots of fresh orange juice and sodas—but no alcohol, per Max's instructions. Everyone set to work planning for the event, which was six weeks off.

We didn't have nearly as much notice for a dinner in honor of Monika Henreid, daughter of Paul Henreid, who played Victor Laszlo in the film. A call came on a Monday in mid-April from my friend Said Mouhid, the director of the Regional Tourism Council asking if we would comp a dinner for forty-five people that Wednesday night. A distributor would donate the beverages and champagne; we had only to provide the venue and food. The occasion was Monika Henreid's birthday, and in addition to the wali a royal counsellor would attend along with other public officials and figures from the Moroccan film industry.

How could we say no?

"Welcome, Monika," I said at the door. "I'm Madame Rick."

"And I'm Victor's daughter," she replied.

The dinner, held upstairs in the Blue Room and patio, was a great success. At the end of the evening, after birthday cake and champagne, when she hugged me goodbye, Monika said, "Never in my wildest dreams—and I do have wild dreams—could I ever imagine celebrating my birthday in Casablanca, let alone at Rick's Café."

We'd no sooner recovered from her visit when a call came from Al Goodman, the CNN bureau chief in Madrid.

"I'm coming to Morocco to do some pieces on the first anniversary of the May 16 attacks and wanted to have something uplifting and positive," he said. "I tucked the *New York Times* article in my Morocco file, and I'd like to do an interview with you at Rick's."

Al and his cameraman, Scotty, arrived at the end of April. During the interview, which was great fun, Issam played "As Time Goes By." Al asked me where I'd put Rick if he ever walked into the gin joint.

"I'd probably put him over there in the corner of the bar," I said. "That's where I like to sit so I can keep an eye on things."

A perfect vignette, the CNN piece aired worldwide on Headline News all day on May 6. I couldn't have wished for better PR. CNN posted an article on their website, and the demand on our site was so great that our domain host in Rabat crashed. There was no time to sit around congratulating ourselves, however. The next day was the Gumball rally.

The cars were crossing from Spain to Tangier and scheduled to arrive at Rick's around noon. Moroccan police were providing escort, but with 160 cars the police couldn't do much else than just keep the drivers on the right course. We applied to the wali for a special parking permit to use all the space around the neighboring Jardin Zerktouni plus the street in front of our restaurant.

Abdou prepped the tuna salad in giant washtubs where it was kept, shaded, under awnings set up in the dead-end alley that used to be the main entrance to the house and now was the service entrance. The cheesecakes alone took up all our available refrigerator space. The kitchen had prepared the chicken breasts for cooking, and the accompanying pasta was coordinated to accompany the chicken, again kept in plastic washtubs. We crossed our fingers that the cars wouldn't all arrive at once.

They didn't.

At noon, when regular customers started arriving for lunch, there was still no sign of the Gumballers. The advance team relayed that there'd been a delay in the ferry crossing. Perhaps transporting 160 cars had something to do with it!

"Don't expect the first car until around 2," we were told.

Around 2:30 p.m., the squeal of rubber and motorcycle sirens heralded the first car, a yellow Lamborghini. Over the next four hours came a parade of Ferraris, Humvees, and even a New York City police car. Maximillion drove a classic restored Morgan. Some drivers got lost and had to hire taxis to lead them in; others had parts problems that required hasty calls to Europe. The funky Garage Neptune next door offered a natural spot for photo ops, putting a smile on the eccentric owner's face that lasted a full week.

Abdou and his sous chef, Hicham, were smiling, too, and spent most of the day outside. I trusted that someone was back in the kitchen getting lunches served—but I was cautioned to stay outside. Toward the end of the afternoon, I finally took a look inside the restaurant and saw what you might expect when 350 people had been served a three-course lunch over four hours in a space that accommodated 135.

The last of the Gumball drivers left at 6:30 p.m. just as we were welcoming the first of our evening customers. The staff was totally exhausted, but there was no time to rest. I ran upstairs for a quick shower and wardrobe change only to find Rick's packed to the gills when I came back down. Crowds of people had seen the CNN piece, among them the AP correspondent, who had come from Rabat after receiving an urgent call from his bureau chief in the US to do an inter-view. His photographer had been at Rick's during the afternoon and taken photos then. When the article hit the wire that weekend, papers all over the world ran their article on Rick's with a photo of Chef Abdou and his sous chef, Hicham, in front of a cluster of exotic cars.

The Gumball 3000 rally represented the pinnacle of Abdou's ten-ure and our relations with Khalid, proprietor of the Garage Neptune. It went downhill after that. Khalid had been very "helpful" parking cars in the evening, not shy about asking for tips. I soon put a stop to that. With no car-parking duties, he turned his attention to dissuading our clients from parking in front of the garage at night . . . when the garage was closed.

But he was happy to advertise his expertise as a mechanic. One day at lunch, some diners mentioned that they had had some car trouble and had asked the "garagiste" to work on their car while they were at Rick's. I said that I had never seen any car work take place there, and the client quickly rushed next door to discover that Khalid had removed some parts, checked them, and put them back—sort of. There were some odd pieces left. The car ran, however, so the client put the extra pieces in the trunk and took the vehicle to another garage.

Vol au Vent de Poulet (Chicken Pot Pie)

Preparation time: 30 minutes
Cooking time: 20–25 minutes
Serves 4

A comfort-food favorite in any language is a popular choice for those at the end of a long tour or weary of tagines. High quality ready-made puff pastry simplifies the preparation, and the abundance of fresh vegetables elevates this dish to center stage.

prepared puff pastry

3 tablespoons butter

1–1¼ pounds boneless chicken breasts, cut into bite-sized pieces

2 medium white onions, chopped fine

1 clove garlic, crushed

¼ cup chopped parsley

½ sweet red pepper, chopped

3–4 white mushrooms, chopped

1 tablespoon white wine

1 cup cream

salt and pepper

pinch nutmeg

¾ cup shelled peas, blanched

2 carrots, chopped and blanched

PUFF PASTRY SHELLS

Prepare four flat rounds of puff pastry each about 4 inches in diameter; these are the bottoms of the pastry shells. On top of each, to build the sides, place 3 rings $1/2$ to $3/4$ inches wide. Bake the shells according to the package directions along with four slightly smaller flat rounds of puff pastry, which will top the shells.

FILLING

In a deep frying pan, melt the butter. Add chicken and cook on medium until it turns white. Add garlic, parsley, pepper, and mushrooms and cook 2-3 more minutes. Deglaze with white wine, then add cream, seasonings, peas, and carrots. Lower the heat and reduce for 3-5 minutes. If it appears too dry, add more cream. Season to taste.

To serve, place a pastry shell on a dinner plate, fill with chicken and vegetable mixture—it's fine if it overflows—and crown with the smaller pastry round.

Note: The puff pastry shells can be prepared in advance and reheated in the oven just before composing.

Then Khalid decided to mount a protest of sorts. First came the baby chicks. As they grew and grew accustomed to their habitat, they were released from their cage to parade back and forth on the sidewalk between the garage and the restaurant. Not a good advertisement for our poulet au curry, vol au vent de poulet, or salade de poulet tropicale. Then came the "garden"—potted plants, the chicks well on their way to being chickens still parading, and laundry hanging out to dry from time to time. He crossed the line when he cemented in a planter on the sidewalk where our property ends, put up a wire grill, planted some green stuff, and placed in the middle of it a brightly colored pot containing bright fake flowers.

When I asked what could possess him to do something like this, Houssein, our maintenance manager, said, "He's doing it to get your attention."

Every day I was learning something new.

The CNN and AP stories brought more interviews with American and foreign press, lots of curiosity seekers, and a generous gesture from a man who wanted to add to the decor. The assistant of Aziz Dadas, governor of a district in Casablanca, called to invite me to meet the governor in his office. My phone French was still a bit rusty, but apparently he wanted to present me with photos. The appointment was set of course for the morning that I fired Aicha, so I had to hail a red petit taxi. Before we could leave, though, Houssein had to explain to the driver, Youssef, exactly where I was going and to wait for me and bring me back to the restaurant.

Governor Dadas's office clearly wasn't used to having guests arrive in petit taxis, but they politely accommodated and directed Youssef to a shady area to wait. The governor I recognized from a recent visit to Rick's. He told me how impressed he'd been with the decoration and architecture. Then he confessed to having embarked on a special project, inviting me into his conference room to have a look. Spread out, one by one, around the long, oval table were 21 framed posters of the film *Casablanca,* some in foreign languages. The posters had been reproduced from the Internet in letter size and nicely framed.

I thanked Governor Dadas for his gracious gesture, and he offered his chauffeur to drive me back to the restaurant with the posters. I explained that the petit taxi driver was waiting, and I was uncomfortable letting him go, so we loaded the pictures into the governor's Mercedes, and his chauffeur followed us back to Rick's. Houssein paid Youssef and, seizing the moment, arranged for him to report the next morning to help bring back the order from the Marché Central.

Issam and I were both . . . "overwhelmed" . . . by the governor's gesture, but we had no idea where the posters would go best—somewhere unobtrusive. We chose nine of them to hang on the walls of the upstairs dining room, where the film plays on a loop. That dining room has since become our lounge with its own bar and the roulette table. The posters give just enough flavor of the film for those still looking for Humphrey Bogart and Ingrid Bergman.

Youssef, in his own way, also fit in—as our driver. I soon learned to avoid being in the van we bought when he drove it during Ramadan, when cigarettes were banned until sundown. His impatience showed as soon as we hit the road. His driving was erratic at best, swerving past cars, careening around corners, and screeching to a halt just in time at red lights.

One morning, several weeks after Ramadan, we set out early for Casa Milano to buy Parmesan cheese, and he took off in the opposite direction. I asked him where we were going, and he quickly cut in front of oncoming traffic to pick up a street that took us through the center of town, trying to convince me it was a shortcut. My nails dug into my palms as we threaded our way through tight traffic and honking horns. Parmesan in hand, I got back in the car and noticed a distinct smell of hashish. Youssef seemed calmer and more in control. The trip back to Rick's was direct and uneventful.

I cornered Houssein as soon as I got back, though, and confided my suspicion that Youssef had smoked hashish while waiting for me. Houssein exchanged a knowing look with Adil, our stock controller, and they both chuckled. "Oh no, madame, you have it wrong. Youssef can't function if he doesn't have his hashish in the morning before he starts work. Unfortunately you needed him a bit too early this morning, and, well, you see what happened."

Somehow these things always seemed to be my fault—but I couldn't help but laugh.

Smoking hash daily, however, hardly suited Youssef for long-term employment. We denied his requests for salary increases, and at the end of one month I heard him yelling at Houssein, the sound of keys being thrown, and Youssef was off in a cloud of . . . smoke.

Other Casablanca characters made a lasting impression on Rick's as well. Serge, a former party promoter—with "happenings" featuring horseback riders and belly dancers—now owned the Atlantic Beach, a relaxed beachside restaurant thirty-five minutes south of Casablanca. He came in late one night with a large group. They all seemed drunk, except for Martine, the manager of the restaurant. With her short cropped hair, she reminded me of Claudette Colbert; managing Atlantic Beach for Serge was probably a never-ending madcap comedy. She spoke English and explained they'd just come from the restaurant and wanted to have a late dinner if we didn't mind. Well, of course I didn't mind and welcomed them.

In Serge's limited English, on the other hand, he kept coming up to me during the evening, his face a little too close, saying, "You are lovely."

At the end of the night, Martine approached the cashier alone and picked up the tab for everyone. She said they'd be back next Friday . . . with friends.

And they were.

Arriving again at 10:30 p.m., they had dinner and then ordered champagne. Bottle after bottle of champagne. I was enjoying their patronage but watching the clock at the same time. Closing time, 1:00 a.m., came and went. Still more champagne. Finally, at 4:30 a.m., I announced that we only had one bottle left, apologizing that it must be a sign that the evening had to come to an end. They happily took their leave at 5:30 a.m. by way of the service door at the impasse to avoid drawing attention to violating our closing time.

When I awoke later that morning, Ilsa's line after Risk kisses her, questioning if her emotions are triggered by cannon fire or her beating heart, came to mind, but in my case it was my head that was pounding. I made a mental note never to do that again.

Serge and Martine, with an entourage of friends and grifters, became regulars for quite some time, adapting in their fashion to Rick's rules—until the night Serge brought his long-lost friend Bob, an American saloon singer who'd been performing in Paris for twenty years. They strutted in together, weathered and dissipated versions of Jean-Paul Belmondo and Johnny Hallyday. Without asking Issam, Serge gestured for Bob to take the microphone, and Bob sang the rest of the number the group was playing. After this unexpected treat— applause limited to Serge's table—Issam ended the set, and the musicians took their break.

The evening tumbled into a tailspin as Serge, not to be deterred, encouraged Bob to get his guitar from the car. Their whole table joined him in—of all things—"Old MacDonald Had a Farm"! Well, at that point, they had gone too far.

Before I could throw them out, Issam thought fast. He brought the musicians back to play Brubeck's "Take Five," drowning out "an oink oink here, and an oink oink there." The audience gave a loud hand to the jazz combo, leaving Serge and company grousing in their corner, looking quite like Major Strasser and his men after Laszlo's "La Marseillaise" had drowned out their "Die Wacht am Rhein."

Rick's was really on a roll, and I mistakenly assumed it would continue—but in June we noticed fewer clients. There was always an explanation:

"People are on vacation up north, where they have apartments on the Mediterranean."

"They've all gone to the Sacred Music Festival in Fes."

"They're at the Gnaoua Festival in Essaouira."

"It's raining; people don't like to go out in the rain."

"There's no rain; the people don't want to go out, in solidarity with the poor farmers whose crops don't have water."

As I was fretting about the numbers, we started to get some complaints about the food. Some of the comments we took with a grain of salt, considering the sources, but others seemed sincere. They did have one positive effect: Chef Abdou no longer spent so much time in the dining room schmoozing with the clients. I kept a closer eye on him, more careful about inspecting dishes that came out of the kitchen.

In those early days, we ambitiously introduced weekend brunch, featuring eggs Benedict among other specialties. After one Saturday service, I went into the kitchen between shifts to get something from a refrigerator and spied a dinner plate piled high with pre-poached eggs! I asked Abdou why we would poach eggs in advance, for one, and why on earth we would keep them after the service was over.

"Oh, I was trying to economize and thought we could use them tomorrow," he said. He probably thought I'd believe his feeble attempt to cover up his lack of oversight and swallow the egg story as a logical way to save on expenses.*

Abdou was right about one thing, though: I was having to analyze costs. The reserves from the capital risk firm were dwindling as business slacked off. I drew a salary only for the first two months, and began to resent the high salary I'd agreed to pay the chef. We called in some of the original staff and asked them to take cuts. I knew I had been overpaying them when they readily agreed. Abdou, though, was making more than the rest of the cooks in the kitchen combined, but, too afraid of the scene it would cause, I couldn't ask him to take a cut. Clearly I'd put all my eggs in one basket when I hired him, but finding them stacked on a plate in the refrigerator was the last straw. I started looking for opportunities that might encourage his exit.

Abdou forced the situation himself by lying about a ten-day sick leave—which he actually spent at the annual music festival in Essaouira—then trying to finagle another couple of days off to care for his hospitalized son, or so he said. When I refused, knowing full well that he probably just wanted more time off, he made good on an earlier threat to take his knives and leave.

That left his sous chef, Hicham, in charge. He was stocky and had a cherubic round face, though not the personality that might have gone with it. He didn't feel it was necessary, for example, to keep his uniform clean or shave regularly. The days of the chef interacting with the clients were over, and I told him to stay in the kitchen.

---

* Another eight years passed before we gathered the courage to reintroduce a Sunday brunch with eggs Benedict. Now, however, it's a sumptuous buffet in the Blue Room upstairs—and the eggs Benedict are cooked to order.

Still, he found ways to annoy me. When he brought me the market list at night, he was supposed to walk behind the bar not in front of it. He'd "forget," and I cringed watching him walk toward me, a sauce-stained towel tucked into the belt around his rumpled uniform. The first time this happened, I hissed at him to approach from behind the bar. He shrugged, said, "Ok, madame," and handed me the list. As he walked off, he scratched his rear end. Maybe it was his way of scratching his head. *Oh*, I thought, *this can't last long*, and I got out the short leash.

On top of finance worries, kooky cooks, and slow business, the capital risk firm insisted that we have a board meeting. I was chairman, and the directors were Driss Benhima, who acted through a power of attorney for his son Taibi; Rachid El Andaloussi; Pamela Loring, a Consulate officer Usual Suspect; and two directors of the capital risk firm. We met in the courtyard of Rick's between lunch and dinner service. The director general of the capital risk firm immediately took over. He complained that business was slow and tried to propose ideas for promoting the restaurant. He didn't want to hear about Issam's work on the website and how successful it was. He also paid short shrift to the media coverage we'd achieved through CNN and AP. My friend Mr. Bakkali, the capital risk deputy director, looked embarrassed and said nothing.

Then, toward the end of the meeting, came another shock. Under the agenda heading of "new business," the director general wanted us to fire our accountant and take on one his firm was recommending along with a list of tasks for their proposed accountant.

"This doesn't look like he's working for us," I immediately objected. "I see very little day-to-day accounting here, but quite a lot of reporting to you. He seems like a spy."

Driss supported me, but it was hopeless. I drew up an additional list of responsibilities, and the accountant's confirmation was subject to my approval. But there was no way I could jettison him; the risk firm had too much control.

⌒

Abdou had promised that I would never have to set foot in the kitchen, but now with Hicham I had to provide more oversight, steering him away from mediocre plates of paella or fried calamari, his standbys from Atlantic Beach, where he'd previously cooked. Meanwhile, I was also juggling finances, chasing accounts receivable, and delaying payment to our suppliers whenever possible. The Marché Central remained the lone exception; we paid them daily.

The many different taxes we had to pay also surprised me. It seemed as if there were no incentives for small business owners. All of which required me to deal with inefficient and nontransparent agencies such as the CNSS, the Moroccan equivalent of Social Security. The accountant foisted on me by the capital risk firm knew less than I did about the system.

Into this chaotic scene, Kyle and his fiancée, Sarah, arrived at the end of August with their two cats and all their worldly possessions in tow. They had both just graduated from the University of Chicago, and Kyle suggested that they come to Casablanca and spend a year helping me with the restaurant. It was a generous, loving offer, and I couldn't wait to see them.

When the cat carrier tumbled out onto the baggage carousel with all the other luggage, Kyle and Sarah knew they were in for a wild ride. They spent their first few days doing a major overhaul of my old apartment near the Marché Central. On their first Friday in town, they came to Rick's for a couscous lunch. Visibly relieved that they had come to give me moral support, Issam had an instant, natural rapport with Kyle. Issam may have assumed that would be their main job and that their year in Casablanca would be a long vacation. It was anything but.

The Friday they came for the couscous lunch, Bouchra, our financial administrator, and Adil, our stock controller, had a disagreement over the meat invoice. Bouchra cascaded into a hysterical fit, crying and screaming in the front entrance in full view and earshot of all the staff. Adil just stood there, his head bowed. People came running from every direction and ogled the disturbance.

"I quit! I can't work with the people here!" she screamed in front of everyone. "That's it! I'm leaving!"

Bouchra had the last word in the argument, but she had made a bad move.

"All right," I said. "Just gather your personal belongings together, and we'll expect your official resignation."

But that wasn't the end of it. Instead, Bouchra went over to her desk, rifled through some papers, and resumed working at her computer.

"Bouchra, didn't you hear me? Pack up your things, and leave."

She started crying again, so I suggested we go up to the VIP room—in her case, Very Irritating Personnel—so we could talk in private. Upstairs, she apologized, said she had overreacted, and wanted to stay.

"Bouchra, you were the one who said you were resigning," I said. "I can't let you stay. Other staff will think I'm a pushover."

We talked in circles for an hour until she finally understood that I wasn't going to change my mind.

Kyle and Sarah were waiting downstairs, wondering what on earth was going on.

"I'll tell you the gory details over couscous," I said.

As I recounted the story, describing Bouchra's job and some of the difficulties in recording and tracking bills for deliveries, Kyle suddenly said, "I think we can help with this. I can do an Excel spreadsheet, and Sarah and I can split the tasks. We can also take over the shopping at the Marché Central since we're living in your old apartment nearby on Mohammed V."

By the time we finished the last grains of couscous, Kyle and Sarah each had rough job descriptions.

Life outside the restaurant, where everybody loved them, wasn't easy. Because Sarah is young and pretty, she constantly had to fend off unappreciated advances. Kyle felt as if he stood out as a foreigner. In fact, he said, leaving the apartment every day took an effort of will and emotional preparation. They almost never went out separately. I could sympathize. Even though Kyle and I lived eight years in Tokyo and three years in Prague, we always had a social network in which we fit, whether the expatriates in Tokyo or the Embassy community in Prague. I'd felt the loneliness myself when I was "addressee unknown" after leaving the Consulate.

Kyle also felt responsible because it had been difficult for Sarah's family to let her come. There was a family story about Morocco—told, retold, and no doubt embellished throughout Sarah's childhood—that lurked in the background as their plans progressed. During World War II, Sarah's grandfather had spent some time in Casablanca as a Navy pilot based on an aircraft carrier. The sailors were warned that only designated parts of town were open to them, and certain areas were to be avoided at all costs. Most important, any contact with Moroccan women was strictly forbidden.

As Sarah's grandfather recounted, one sailor broke all the rules, jumped ship, and disappeared into the town. The next morning his

Kyle and Sarah enjoying an evening at Rick's. They provided much needed moral support for me, and their smiling faces show the fun of it all despite problems and irritations.
Photo by Issam Chabâa

body was dropped dockside, his mouth stuffed with severed appendages. Her grandfather had observed firsthand, like Major Strasser in the movie, that human life can be cheap in Casablanca. He was enough of a realist to assume things had changed, but he still wasn't in favor of her coming. And here she was, working in the Ancienne Medina across the street from the Port.

Having Kyle and Sarah around was good for me, though. We had lunch together, and sometimes Issam joined us. They provided a source of positive reinforcement and helpfully acted as intermediaries between me and the staff. There was a good crowd when they arrived on a busy night in September and joined me in my corner at the bar for one of the Sunday night Jam Sessions. They were enjoying the music and having a great time—until Serge and his entourage arrived, drunk, loud, and moving into our corner as if they owned the place. Serge gave Sarah an appraising look, sidled over, and said, "You are lovely." I could brush off Serge's routine, but Sarah had no reason to tolerate him, so we hurried off to a table for dinner. Kyle and Sarah avoided Jam Sessions after that.

No sooner had business finally started to pick up when Ramadan began in mid-October. Nothing passes the lips of devout Muslims from sunrise to sunset. But not only could we not afford to close, I didn't want to. Having no place to go out to eat during Ramadan had been frustrating during my days at the Consulate, and I imagined we'd get good business from the foreigners in town even if we were open only in the evening. Following the advice of other restaurateurs about our alcohol service during the holy month, we removed all the bottles from the mirrored shelves behind the bar, keeping them out of sight.

To emphasize the point, we put up a sign that read, "We do not serve alcohol to Muslims." I was still paranoid that eyes were watching us, some people trying to trap us, so that first year we were all overly conscientious. The waiters were instructed to ask for passports and verification of religion if they weren't sure. With Moroccans, the waiters could tell from a passport if the name was Muslim or Jewish, but with other Arab nationalities, such as Lebanese or Egyptians where there were Christians, it was more difficult. Many times during the month I had to intercede, either arguing with clients or apologizing for not being able to serve them.

So for once the daytime was more enjoyable than the evening. Taking advantage of having a full kitchen to ourselves Kyle, Sarah, and I fasted in our own fashion, with a morning breakfast at a normal breakfast hour, and spent the day preparing ftour, the traditional meal served at the breaking of the fast. In Paula Wolfert's cookbook *Couscous and Other Good Food from Morocco,* we found a delicious recipe for harira, a hearty soup made with beef, tomatoes, onions, fresh cilantro, parsley, chickpeas, and thin vermicelli. Harira is the main dish of the ftour, which also includes chebakia, a honey dipped pastry; m'semen, square flat pancakes somewhat like Indian naan; and little

Berber crepes. Other elements of the ftour might include dates, a hard-boiled egg, and cumin and lemon wedges to spice up the harira.

Often Issam and our maintenance manager Houssein came by, and we all gathered upstairs at the balcony window watching the minaret of the Mosque Hassan II to see when it would come alight, signaling sundown. Then we ran downstairs to the set table and—*bon appétit!* We had mint tea, but Houssein and Issam usually started their meal with espresso, missing their coffee even more than the food. One day, Issam told us just to make the soup and surprised us by bringing the crepes and chebakia along with some traditional Moroccan pastries.

In November, when we had an election-night party that didn't turn out the way I, half of America, and most of the world had hoped, Kyle and Sarah met a group of Americans teaching at the Casablanca American School and started to widen their social circle. Kyle soon was attending poker parties, and they were invited to excursions and outings with their new friends. They were settling in.

        ⌇

Hicham managed to squeak through Thanksgiving with a stuffed, rolled turkey breast recipe that I'd found on the Internet and New Year's Eve with foie gras and one of my baked salmon recipes . . . along with plenty of champagne. But he took constant monitoring.

On one occasion I heard shouting in the kitchen and raced back from my corner at the bar. Rachid, our calm and professional barman, was screaming at Hicham, and Hicham was screaming back.

"What's the problem?" I asked.

Rachid, still furious, blurted out the explanation. "Madame, I asked Hicham for some celery to garnish a Bloody Mary, and he ignored me. I kept asking, and finally he just threw it at me and said, 'Next time, address me as chef.'"

I left them to sort it out and managed to keep from laughing until safely back at the bar. But Hicham's delusions of grandeur were wearing thin, especially since they usually corresponded to a demand for a raise. Issam's intuition that Hicham would quit if we held our ground against a raise proved correct—just before our first anniversary.

We hardly had a strong bench, but El Baz, the pastry cook who'd moved into the sous-chef position with Hicham's promotion, seemed the only possibility to step into the head cook position. At least he looked like a chef: graying hair, moustache, clean whites. He could also speak French and read recipes. He would be temporary, but we could only deal with one challenge at a time. The money problems weren't getting any better, and the capital risk firm was breathing down our necks. Not that Mr. Belkabir, the new accountant who had made his first appearance back in September, was providing any useful advice or guidance.

Mr. Belkabir had bags under his eyes, glasses, was slightly balding—a Homer Simpson resemblance, but not at all funny. Even with my unfamiliarity with the intricacies of Moroccan accounting, I could tell he wasn't looking for ways to save us money. He never answered any of my questions about invoices or taxes or Social Security. When I said his response was unacceptable, he said, "Très bien," to which I screamed back, "Ce n'est pas très bien!" It's not very good! It was his way of shrugging off responsibility, similar to the phrase that acted as the motto of public and private sector functionaries, "Ce n'est pas grave." It's not really serious.

He operated solely by mobile phone and shoe leather, always dropping by unannounced to pick up and deposit documents because his "fax wasn't currently working." As preparations for our first year's balance sheet were under way, I finally found out why.

In the months we'd been working with him, several people had delivered documents to his office, but I'd never set foot in it. One afternoon I brought down some additional invoices that he'd forgotten to include in our accounts. The office building was nice enough from the outside, across the street from the Sheraton, but apparently the elevators sometimes didn't work or, worse, stopped in mid-ascent. The concierge directed me to the one working elevator.

Safely off the elevator, I rang the bell of the firm on Belkabir's card and was buzzed in to reception. The receptionist gave a blank look and asked me to repeat the name of the accountant I was there to see. She shook her head and asked me to wait. Soon she reappeared with a man who asked me the name again and then said, "He doesn't work at this firm."

Confused, I went back out to the elevators. At the end of another corridor lay an office with a light on, and there he was, Mr. "Très Bien" himself, sitting at an empty desk, no telephone line and consequently no fax machine. There was no desk for the secretary that he'd clearly never had, but he wasn't alone. A man was working on what looked like a portable computer and printer arrangement in a cabinet on rollers—probably a "have computer, will tabulate" part-timer that Belkabir had hired to input the figures for the year-end formal balance. Belkabir possibly had worked at the accounting firm once, but he no longer had any association with them.

That was it.

I called Mr. Bakkali at the capital risk firm.

"Your boss unloaded a fake accountant on us. You're trying to put us out of business."

"I'm going to give you some instructions," Bakkali said calmly. "First, the director general is leaving in a few months, and they have already identified his replacement. He'll be someone you can work with. My advice to you is write a letter immediately to the director general, while he's still here, and lay out all your complaints about

Belkabir. Put everything in writing, and notify the firm that if there is no improvement you will fire him. Get a receipt of reception for the letter. No doubt you won't hear from the director general before he leaves, and I know there will be no changes in Belkabir's performance. You will have the comfort knowing that letter is in your file. Once the new director general is on board, do whatever you want."

Mr. Bakkali's advice was a relief. Even though we were in bad shape financially, I was regaining some control over our situation. When the time came, I took great pleasure in telling Mr. Belkabir that his number was up.

Our next accountant wasn't much better, though. A sax player at the Sunday night Jam Session, Jamal talked a good game, but I should have been more observant of his style. A big lug, he reminded me of a little boy who never cleans his room. I was constantly tripping over the open sax case that he left on the floor next to my seat at the corner of the bar. His jam session persona foreshadowed his accounting style: sloppy, disorganized, rote, and anything but creative.

His firm, CompteCo, rescued us from Belkabir's incompetence and made things right. At least they had an office and staff, and for a while there was an assistant, Said, who stayed on top of things, coming into our office and going through our invoices. But whenever I had to meet with Jamal, he was invariably in his corner office, talking on the phone, his feet on his desk. As unfamiliar as I was with Arab ways, even I knew that showing the soles of your feet to a visitor is highly insulting. Still, we had a "honeymoon" period of about a year and a half before our marriage hit the rocks. Did competent accountants even exist in Morocco?

As often happens in our story, Issam came to the rescue. He created a customized data center that revolutionized our internal financial information, giving me instant access to all our accounts at once.

So, as I tearfully said goodbye to Kyle and Sarah, there was a program in place putting sales and expenses, payables and receivables at my fingertips. Kyle and Sarah were proud of what they'd done to help me, and I knew they were anxious to get back to their future in America, but I will be forever grateful for their help when I needed it most.

After they left, we took another step in the right direction, this time with the kitchen. Issam knew I liked El Baz, and he worried how I'd react when he said one day, "I think we need to look for a real chef."

"Was it the birthday cake that did it?" I joked.

We had surprised Issam on his birthday, and El Baz had demonstrated his flair for kitsch with a cake boasting a carved chocolate grand piano on top. But I agreed. We had to put someone in charge of the kitchen again, and Issam said he'd talk to some people.

Just before Ramadan, at the end of September 2005, Issam said a former chef from one of Casablanca's seafood restaurants was available. He met with Chef Houcine twice before he finally asked me to meet him. Probably forty and very well groomed, Houcine always wore white and didn't drink or smoke. He had a nice easygoing manner, and from his résumé we knew he could cook. He started during Ramadan so he could get to know the staff and spot problem areas during a quiet period. He proved very effective in the post-Ramadan high season and took charge of New Year's Eve planning.

Again, he was just what we needed at the time. Both Issam and I knew he wasn't going to be our chef forever—we had aims that went beyond the standard fare—but he seemed capable of sorting out the staff in the kitchen, which had gone largely unsupervised with Hicham and reached a nadir of laissez faire under El Baz.

Now that operations were starting to stabilize, my attention turned to an employee who came with the house, so to speak.

TEN

Central Casting

Today a well-rehearsed cast with defined roles, the staff at Rick's didn't start out that way. In some ways, the years since we opened in 2004 have been a long-running reality show, with more than one employee voted off the island for reasons that range from the ridiculous to the absurd. One of the original members of the ensemble was Abdallah Ghattas, the son of the woman who owned the house. He was our first maître d'—and I couldn't imagine a more fitting relationship—but in the end he didn't fit in at all.

Skinny, with light hair, and glasses, Abdallah looked like Don Knotts as Barney Fife, but he moved like Chevy Chase channeling Gerald Ford. Whether tripping on a carpet or falling down stairs, he had a flair for a dramatic entrance.

Granted: I had gutted the house, but the architectural details and the overall structure remained the same and should have been familiar to him. He'd lived there in the early 1960s. Still, he kept bumping into pillars and banging his head on arches as if surprised they were in the way. I worried that he might be suffering from the horrifying experience of being in the lobby of the Hotel Farah on May 16, 2003, when one of the bombs detonated at the entrance. Unfortunately I learned pretty quickly after Rick's opened that Abdallah's pratfalls were not the result of post-traumatic stress disorder.

He was a drinker and none too subtle about it.

During one memorable open bar function on the second floor, Abdallah passed the bars and tasted drinks . . . repeatedly. When the event ended, he spied an unopened bottle of gin that he decided to sneak away. He slipped going down the back stairs, ending up with cuts and bruises, but he managed to keep the bottle intact—only to be greeted by the head barman, arms folded, at the foot of the stairs.

Abdallah handed him the bottle.

"I just didn't want this to fall into the wrong hands," he said.

Mmmm hmmm.

Even when sober, he had a natural talent for slapstick comedy, except we weren't trying to reproduce the Marx Brothers' movie *A Night in Casablanca*. At our first New Year's Eve celebration, we served a flambéed strawberry shortcake. Abdallah was in charge of the presentation, and we practiced delicately pouring the brandy into a spoon, lighting it with a match and sprinkling it over the dessert.

Faced with so many tables, so many desserts, and the hands of the clock moving toward midnight, Abdallah decided to cut a few corners. Gone was the grace of the presentation, replaced by a hurried glug of Napoleon into a spoon, the click of his BIC lighter, a quick *voilà*, and on to the next table. The pours were less and less measured, and I coined the phrase "flaming liberally" to sum up Abdallah's performance that night, although he fortunately did not set anything on fire.

As *maître d'hôtel* he recruited, trained, scheduled, and supervised staff. He was also the floor manager, responsible for reservations and overall service. In keeping with the film, we asked him to wear a tux. But clothes really don't make the man, and it became evident that Abdallah wasn't up to the task. The waiters and helpers he hired were real losers: young boys who never seemed to close their mouths; a waiter who purported to speak Spanish who couldn't even speak French; an extra hired for a party promoting a new perfume, caught more than once trying to steal samples.

We moved Abdallah to the reception desk, continuing to call and pay him as *maître d'hôtel*, but the real job went to someone else. In Morocco, it's impossible to reduce someone's salary without their agreement even if they are demoted because of poor performance or disciplinary measures. Many companies keep people on six-month contracts and don't even think of staff retention. I was trying to be different, but *le système* certainly wasn't encouraging.

At the reception desk, Abdallah settled into his routine, which included keeping track of the time left before he could retire. He grew a moustache and looked quite proud when some innocent tourists said he looked like David Niven. His debonair presence didn't last for long, though. Soon after, he needed dental work and showed up for work with a mouth empty of teeth. Somehow he didn't think I'd notice him greeting people with his hand over his mouth, insisting it would only be two weeks before his teeth were ready. Instead I gritted *my* teeth and sent him home.

At home for two weeks, while he waxed his mustache, he must have been waxing nostalgic over his career and upcoming retirement. He came back armed with photo albums of his glory days when he worked at the Hyatt Regency. In some pictures he was wearing the tattered tuxedo that he still wore, claiming dubiously that our cleaners had caused the stains and tears. He'd worked at all the major spots in town, and Casablanca old timers all knew him by name. He appeared to know everyone, too, or at least I thought he did until one day I heard him taking a reservation on the phone:

"*Bonjour*, Rick's Café. . . . *Bonjour*, Mr. Bennis. How are you? . . . A reservation for lunch or dinner? . . . Fine, a reservation for dinner, Mr. Bennis, of course with pleasure . . . And the date? . . . For tonight, that's fine, Mr. Bennis, and at 8:30 p.m. . . . Do you have a seating preference? . . . A table downstairs, Mr. Bennis? Yes, it's available. And your phone number please? . . . All right, Mr. Bennis, that's noted. . . . Finally, the name please. . . . Hahahah, oh, of course, we'll see you tonight then, Mr. Bennis."

Despite these occasional lapses, I thought he couldn't get into much trouble at the reception desk, but Abdallah Ghattas could always surprise me. I should have realized that, while transferring him to reception might cut down on stolen wine bottles, it would also diminish his tips. One evening just before the Aid, when he must have needed a little extra cash, he followed one of our most loyal clients—also one of the best tippers—out to the car. The startled security guard at the front door watched him receive a large wad of cash from the client, most of which went right into Abdallah's pocket. When he went back inside, he gave the headwaiter 200 dirhams to divide between three servers. (Usually each person received 400 dirhams from this client.) That was the last straw, especially for the staff who were used to covering for him. Even though he protested his innocence and acted insulted to be accused of stealing, I demoted him to the security detail at the front door.

That's when Abdallah had a chance to display his hidden talent for navigating through the Kafkaesque legal system. He refused to accept the job of security, even though we were still obligated to pay his *maître d'hôtel* salary. We had two acrimonious sessions with the Inspection de Travail, the labor office, which unfortunately for him ended with the inspectors screaming at Abdallah to accept our settlement for dismissal or accept the position. He took us to court instead, and it took three separate appearances before the Tribunal for our case to be heard. With all the evidence against Abdallah, particularly the drinking stories, we weren't surprised when the lawyer called us a few weeks later to say we had won and only had to pay him a month's salary.

Our relief was premature, however. We soon learned that Abdallah was appealing. This time we lost for reasons that I will never understand, although I suspect Abdallah's personnel history had taught him how to use the system.

~

That was my first but by no means my last experience with labor laws in Morocco. It's not as easy to vote someone off the island here as it is on those reality shows. It requires meticulous record-keeping, filing official written warnings, and enduring constant "mediation" by the impossibly opaque Inspection de Travail.

It took several *years* to ditch an employee who held on to his job despite a checkered personnel history that included a jail term and a shotgun marriage. Allal managed to rise from the ashes of his own destruction time and time again. Originally hired as a security guard, then promoted to cashier, he wore a gold necklace and often hummed to himself. On Saturday nights, he usually wore white pants, a black shirt, and a tie, heading to the discos after we closed. Perhaps he thought himself a Moroccan John Travolta. He certainly had a knack for stayin' alive.

I noticed he was somewhat of a skirt chaser after he befriended an American intern with us for a few weeks, but we had no problems until a new receptionist came along. Sarah spoke fluent French, Spanish, and English, so we put her in charge of groups working with the travel agents. But my woman's intuition told me there was something going on between her and Allal. I asked them to keep their relationship outside the restaurant, but instead it has become part of Rick's Café lore and legend.

When Sarah became pregnant, she named Allal as the father. He denied paternity, refused to marry her, and was remanded to a jail in a rough part of town where some of Sarah's relatives lived. The relatives could provide the necessary "incentives" to the police to ensure Allal's rough treatment—rougher than the potential of being married to Sarah.

His role as human punching bag notwithstanding, Allal stayed in jail for weeks, stubbornly refusing to marry Sarah. We hired another cashier, and I wasn't too keen about Allal coming back, married or unmarried. After two months, Allal agreed to marry Sarah, which was a condition of his release from jail, so ironically, or perhaps fittingly, he wasn't able to participate in the happy event. In true Moroccan fashion, with a procedure in place for every bizarre circumstance, he issued power of attorney for a friend to represent him and sign all the papers.

While I was hoping to live happily ever after *without* Allal, our lawyer informed us that the scandal had nothing to do with his performance, and therefore wasn't grounds for dismissal. It looked like we'd have Allal around till death do us part. We put him back at his old security job (at his higher cashier's salary), but instead of being grateful he started a vendetta. He took unexcused absences and "sick" days with a doctor's excuse while blatantly informing others that he was visiting family in the countryside. He took his three-day paternity leave three months after the birth of his baby girl—alone. Still, we didn't have grounds to fire him. Somehow with this checkered personnel history he was elected staff representative. To fire one of them, you need the permission of the Inspection de Travail. After so many infractions landed him as night guard in the back alley from 2:00 to 7:00 a.m., Allal finally was set adrift permanently when he threatened the security chief and his family in front of witnesses.

Throughout my career, I'd developed a management style: Management by Walking Around. My ears are always open, picking up whispered conversations in Arabic that usually signal that an employee is trying to hide something. In those situations, I walk over and ask, "What's the problem?" More often than not, I don't get a straight answer the first or even the second time around.

It's been a particular challenge to deal with what seem to be national characteristics of stealing or lying (or at least not telling the whole truth). The Moroccans have a proverb: An honest answer is like a kiss on the lips, and I haven't been kissed too often over the years. In fact, I've learned to translate sentences like, "Oh madame, I just narrowly escaped a grave accident in the car," into the truth: I ran a stop sign and didn't see a car coming straight at me. I spun the wheel quickly enough so that only the left fender is wrecked rather than the whole car.

My antenna has frequently picked up financial shenanigans, too. Brahim, another of our cashiers, was very young in age and behavior. He probably worked out, and he definitely strutted around like he was something special. Long as he was on ego, he was just as short on intelligence. He started as an assistant waiter, one step up from busboy. He'd been drafted into the role when the cashier who'd been hired when Allal was behind bars—rather than the bar—was fired for stealing.

It didn't take Brahim too long to make his own attempt. One evening, after the restaurant had closed, I was in the office counting the cash as I always do before putting the money in the safe. But this time, the total didn't match the sum on the receipt ribbon, so I sent Rachid Merzoug, our chief of security, to investigate.

Brahim had the money bundled in a rubber band hidden under a menu, next to the cash register. When he realized he'd been caught

201

he tried to save the situation: "Oh, could you give this to Madame? It wasn't included in the cash I gave her earlier."

Obviously he was hoping I'd put the cash in the safe without counting, leaving him to make off with what he'd stashed away. He never seemed to realize that even if I wasn't there Big Brother was watching. A wide array of security cameras has provided incontrovertible proof of many a fiasco—and plenty of entertainment as well. A few weeks later we caught Brahim on candid camera.

After signing out at 1:00 a.m., he left with the last bar clients—presumably to a nightclub, the only places still open. At 4:35 a.m., Said, the night kitchen cleaner, heard a knock at the service door, which is locked. After exchanging words with whomever was knocking, Said got the key from the night watchman and unlocked the door. In walked Brahim, laughing, just like he was entering his own home. Hours later, one of the housekeepers opened the doors to the VIP room, only to find Brahim asleep in an armchair.

It wasn't his first VIP room episode, either. The Casablanca American School often holds meetings or sessions there. They pay 500 dirhams for the room, extra for drinks, and we provide 500 dirhams of hors d'oeuvres. Going over the receipts one night after one such event, I noticed the tape didn't match their invoice. There was the 500 dirham charge for food but no corresponding 500 dirhams for the room rental. "Rental/location" is programmed in French, so it should have showed up under "miscellaneous/divers," but it wasn't there. We finally found it under "*Rhum*," which is rum in French. With shades of Peter Sellers as Inspector Clouseau looking on, Brahim must have thought the word was *room!*

This little escapade cost Brahim a three-day *mise à pied,* literally "put on his feet," better translated "take a hike." He lost three days' pay and—here's where Madame Rick got her licks in—the fee for his "rental" of the VIP rhum, 500 dirhams, same as the school, was deducted from his salary.

His final act, as an assistant waiter upstairs, came to an abrupt end the night I received an e-mail from an unhappy guest. She had never before made a complaint at a restaurant and thought the food and service were great. However: "When I asked one of the waiters to bring me the dessert menu, he felt it was appropriate to tell me that, 'Instead of having dessert you should work out more because you're very pretty but fat.' I really didn't feel that it was necessary." She felt humiliated and should have spoken to management on the spot but wanted to leave quickly before she started crying.

It didn't take much sleuthing to track down the culprit. In this case, we had all the legal recourse we needed to fire him but settled for his legalized resignation instead. Brahim became the first of our misfits voted off the island with the help of a client. He washed ashore once with a pitiful message on our website: "Please my boss, give me my old job back." He even managed to get the e-mail address of the woman who made the complaint and sent her a sob story claiming that her e-mail had got him fired.

Rick Blaine didn't have problems hiring staff partly because Casablanca had become a way station to so many refugees. Carl, the headwaiter, is German; bartender Sacha is Russian; Emil, the croupier, is French; and Sam, like Rick, is of course American. Rick is also a man, a decided advantage in Morocco. One of my biggest challenges was trying to establish my authority, especially with the male staff.

Houssein, our maintenance manager, has given me ample opportunity. As the construction company's liaison to the site, he knew every nook and cranny of Rick's. In fact, as soon as the interior demolition was complete, he moved his mattress and duffle bag to the site and lived in several of those nooks and crannies.

He came to Casablanca to work in order to support his wife and children living in his native village, two hours outside Marrakech. He often talked about the village, that it was a beautiful place but very hard living. When he described walking to the well and carrying water, it became obvious that it was really his wife performing this task, not to mention taking care of their children, keeping up the house, and tending to Houssein's mother, who also lived with them.

At the beginning, he rarely visited his family and had to be pushed to take time off to see them. When my Mohammed V apartment was empty after Kyle and Sarah left Morocco, I encouraged Houssein to bring his wife and kids to stay for six weeks. I had a skewed notion that once the family saw Casablanca and were together with Houssein they might consider moving. But it wasn't exactly a case of "How ya gonna keep 'em down on the farm after they've seen Paree?"

He brought his mother with them ("I couldn't leave her by herself"), so at first there were six in the two-bedroom apartment. His mother left after two weeks because she couldn't stand the city noise. The kids ran a bit wild, but then they were used to a life outdoors with open spaces and familiar neighbors and no constraints like traffic. Houssein's wife was simple and plain, probably younger than she appeared. She spoke only Berber. It's hard to accept that in the twenty-first century, women are still such second-class citizens in much of the world and certainly in the Moroccan countryside.

The most unforgettable revelation came during a couscous lunch at the apartment toward the end of their stay. As we ate, Houssein and his wife sat side by side on a couch opposite me, and he made conversation.

"What do you think of my wife?" he asked, slapping her thigh. "She's not much to look at, but she's strong and a real hard worker."

If she hadn't been present, Houssein would have been combing couscous out of his hair for days. I couldn't stop myself from blurting out: "That's not the way to talk about your wife, Houssein, especially considering she's shouldering all the burden of raising your children."

But my words wouldn't have any effect. Taking his wife's many backbreaking roles so casually reflected Houssein's upbringing in the bled, where wives are chosen specifically for their ability to work hard in a rough environment. His naive, guileless talk reflected the wild innocence of the countryside, exacerbated by his solitary construction job that presented no opportunity for developing personal values or social skills.

But he did know how things worked at Rick's and made the transition to maintenance manager fairly seamlessly. For the first few weeks, he continued to sleep in the restaurant until I finally had to put my foot down when one morning I went behind the bar to get something and nearly put my foot down on him.

"I think it's time you found another place to live," I said. "We're not a *chantier* anymore."

His insecurities became evident now that he was no longer the day-to-day boss of the construction site, and, worse, I—a *woman*—was *his* boss. He was most comfortable with others from the bled, many of whom were illiterate, and who looked up to him because of his perceived high rank in the hierarchy. Houssein grabbed opportunities when he could, taking on the supervision of the security and housekeeping staff after we canceled our service contracts and hired our own people. Even though he seemed well-intentioned by jumping in to fill these voids, he was taking on more than he could handle while Issam and I were sorting out our working relationship. He even kept some control over our finances, overseeing the cashier's daily reconciliation and acting as go-between with CompteCo, the accounting firm, shuttling files and papers to and from their offices.

The day that Mr. Belkabir's past sins, compounded by CompteCo's incompetence, came home to roost initiated a series of events that told me that Houssein had to go back to maintenance. There had been some tax inquiries about skipped payments during the Belkabir epoch, and the accountants had left it to Houssein to take the papers to the tax office and meet with them to sort out what was and was not paid. He gave me reports that they were "making progress."

A fax came from our bank at 5:30 p.m. one afternoon saying that our account was frozen due to nonpayment of tax, making it clear that there had been a lapse somewhere. Houssein was on his way home for the Aid, but I called him and told him to come back immediately for a meeting with the tax authorities the next day at 10:00 a.m.

We owed something like $20,000, and Houssein had been promising that he was negotiating with the tax office to see if we could pay in installments once they'd determined how much we actually owed. It was a critical meeting, and it was important to be contrite and apologetic to let the tax authorities know that I understood how serious this was. I wanted them on our side in dealing with the tax issue as well as with the bank.

The next morning, I chose my clothes with care: a Moroccan-style brown knit pantsuit, respectful yet businesslike. When I came downstairs, Houssein, wearing his usual jeans and duffle coat, was waiting in the office with Hasnaa, our bookkeeper. He gave her a nudge.

Clearly unhappy, Hasnaa said, "They think you shouldn't attend the meeting."

"And who are *they*?" I asked, glaring at Houssein.

"*Avec tout mon respect, madame*," Houssein said, "I was talking to Jamal, the accountant, last night and he felt, and I agreed, that you would be too emotional and scream at the—"

That did it; I erupted.

"*Listen*, Houssein, the only person I intend to scream at is you, the last person to tell me what to do. How could you think I'd speak to the tax authorities the same way I spoke to the workers at the *chantier*? We're in this mess because we all let things slip through the cracks. I am the president of the company and the only person with the authority to meet with the people we need to see. This is *my* meeting. If there are technical questions, Hasnaa will answer them. You will sit with us, and, if it's necessary to thank the official with an 'envelope' because the Aid is approaching, I'll leave that for you to present after Hasnaa and I leave."

We drove to the tax office in simmering silence. Once seated with the director, I explained the problem and showed him the fax we had received from the bank. The official said the bank was out of line and called the branch, running into one of the contentious officers always making trouble. I had to call a director at headquarters on my cell and pass the phone to the tax director, giving Houssein a *and-you-didn't-want-me-in-this-meeting* cold stare. After sorting out the bank, the tax director called the other tax office across town and arranged for Hasnaa and me to see them in the afternoon. He assured me everything would work out. We exchanged pleasantries on the way out, and I wished him a Happy Aid. I left Houssein behind with the envelope, and we met up back at the car.

Back at the restaurant I sat at my corner seat having a cup of tea, trying to calm down when Houssein approached me.

"Yes?" I said.

"Madame, I didn't intend to make you upset," he said. "You're just like a mother to me."

I cut him off flat. "Listen, Houssein, *that* is the problem. I am *not* your mother. I am your *boss*, and I feel sorry for your mother."

Later, when Houssein had suffered a terrible accident that severed the tendons of his right wrist, I visited him in the hospital. When I saw him, curled in his bed with pain written all over his face, I burst into tears. At that moment, I felt like I was his mother.

Shortly after the tax incident my friend Saad Berrechid introduced me to Mehdi El Attar, a licensed accountant and also a qualified financial advisor and strategist. He spoke perfect English, clearly competent in a way that I didn't know existed in Casablanca's accounting world, and I immediately made plans to work with him. It was past time to kick the capital risk firm off the island.

Earlier, when Jamal from CompteCo, who had always said he'd help advise me with the capital risk firm's exit, made a comment along the lines of, "I have no idea how you're going to get that amount of money," his days were numbered. CompteCo soon joined other accounting castoffs. Houssein was probably the only one wistful about their departure.

When Mehdi arrived in December 2007, I had already signed an agreement to buy out the capital risk firm. The contract—which I'd signed under pressure—listed a variety of formulae for determining the value of their shares when the time came to end their participation, and the firm had the right to choose the one most advantageous to their side. I wanted the buyout to take place sooner rather than later since the formula they selected was 50 percent of the average of three years' gross receipts. It had to be the first three years, taking advantage of the first partial year, and the low receipts of the second and third years. After that, our business started to pick up, making a small profit. As it was, I was going to have to pay them almost twice what they had invested, about $400,000.

Mehdi and I met with the capital risk firm, going over the figures and making one last attempt to negotiate or arrange to pay in installments. The answer was a firm "No."

Out in the hall, Mehdi reassured me. "We'll find a way, Kathy. I don't think much of them, though. Maybe it's the barking dogs that make them so mean." It was Mehdi's first experience with the canine acoustics from the racing track across the street.

After months of meetings and negotiations with banks and government agencies over details of appraisals, loans, real estate liens, and buyouts, the day finally came. On April 6, 2009, Mehdi, our real estate lawyer, and I gathered with the director general and the investment manager in the large conference room with the windows facing the street and the dog track. The familiar yelping provided a soundtrack for the momentous occasion.

After glasses of mineral water in lieu of mint tea and some small talk, the papers were signed, the checks were turned over to the capital risk firm, and the deal was done. For six years, they had been an albatross around my neck. They were either demeaning my role in the project, criticizing my management style, subjecting us to a worthless accountant whose advice brought further financial problems, tying my hands by limiting financial decisions I could make without their permission, or interfering with personnel issues. Their presence had formed a black cloud over me, and any meeting scheduled with them made me a nervous wreck before, during, and after.

But today the sky was blue, and Mehdi and I lingered awhile on the sidewalk, laughing about how quiet it was inside their office, the only sounds coming from the dogs outside.

"No phones, no voices. I wonder if they just let everybody go," I mused.

"In any case, we don't have them to worry about anymore," Mehdi said. "Now we can concentrate on making Rick's even more profitable. You know there is an Arab proverb that says: 'The dogs may bark, but the caravan moves on.'"

We were definitely moving on.

After Mehdi came aboard, we started planning for the future instead of worrying about the past. During the summer of 2007, Issam and I had taken a look at restaurant operations, particularly the kitchen.

Chef Houcine wasn't creative, but he was stable, and he had his seafood specialties. We had tried to add some variety to the menu with international favorites like Japanese tempura, Hungarian goulash, and fish-and-chips, not to mention Rick's hamburger, chili con carne, and an American breakfast. The menu had fifty-two different dishes. We were spread too thin, but we couldn't expand either the kitchen or the staff.

For several months, Issam had talked about a daily menu that could be printed up and also serve as a souvenir. I was lukewarm to the idea; it was a waste of paper, and how would we reduce the number of dishes? So Issam and I began our usual negotiation-dance, back and forth, about the issue.

A trip to London in September 2007 and a dinner at the fabled River Café was a revelation. There on the table were menus of the day that you could take as a souvenir. I came back and showed Issam the menu.

"I'm totally convinced now, so let's do this."

Issam smiled and went to work.

We talked in general terms with Chef Houcine and the young, talented cooks he had working with him at the time about our plan to change the entire approach to our menu.

"We can't have fifty-two dishes that are literally all over the map," I said. "What we want to do is choose the best and most stable dishes for a fixed menu and then have specials that the chef will propose, and we'll print it out daily."

The young cooks seemed keen to try it, but Chef Houcine had his doubts.

"We need to have a stable menu," he said. "I don't think the Casablanca people will go for this."

"Don't worry, Houcine," I said. "We'll approach it gradually and won't launch the new concept until we're ready."

But Houcine dragged his feet. On January 1, we announced that we would launch the new menu in a week. Our chef faxed a ten-day medical excuse that afternoon and voted himself off the island by the end of the month. Another chef guided us through this menu revolution, someone who was the most *un*usual suspect.

ELEVEN
Revolution of the Menu

When Kyle and I visited Marrakech before my posting, we quickly tired of Moroccan food—or at least Moroccan food as offered in restaurants that served only a set menu of typical dishes designed for a tourist palate: little plates of salads, a tagine either of chicken with preserved lemons and olives or of lamb with caramelized prunes, vegetable cous- cous and a pastilla (like sheets of corn flakes) and almond cream des- sert. It was good the first time but lost its appeal very quickly. After a few days, Kyle never wanted to hear the word "tagine" again.

On our final night in Marrakech, I offered to treat our taxi driver, Aziz, to dinner if he could find a Moroccan restaurant where we could order a la carte. He'd been driving us to and from restaurants nightly after I'd made reservations through the hotel concierge. Aziz told me that if he had made our reservations he would have received a com- mission and a meal. Paying commissions to taxi drivers, I learned later, was common in tourist enclaves. So I was making it up to him, and on the way to the restaurant he happily told me he would be receiving a commission even on his dinner. We arrived at a beautifully decorated restaurant, sat on banquettes, and received full Moroccan menus. There was no a la carte. Apparently that was available only upstairs in their Italian restaurant.

Kyle was ready to mount the stairs, but for our last night in Marrakech we should have a Moroccan meal. Once again, we duti- fully plowed through Moroccan salads, chicken tagine, and finally the couscous course, which was exceptionally tasteless—even Aziz agreed—so we rushed through dessert and Moroccan pastries.

On the way back to the hotel, Aziz said he wanted to prepare a couscous lunch for us at his apartment the next day before driving us to Casablanca for the flight home.

"Oh you don't have to do that," I said, feeling Kyle's penetrating gaze bore into me.

But Aziz insisted, and the next day he gathered us up and drove to what I thought was his apartment. We entered a simple courtyard, climbed the stairs, and sat down in a small sitting room lined with upholstered banquettes. Soon others arrived, and we moved into a larger room, sitting around a table. We met Aziz's father, sisters, and finally his mother, a colorfully dressed Berber woman with dark eyes, a rosy complexion, and wide smile.

"So I take it this isn't your apartment, Aziz," I said.

"No, it's my parents' house," he replied. "When I asked my mother this morning to come over to my apartment to make couscous for you, she insisted on preparing the meal in her home."

So we were going to have more than couscous. What followed still stands out as the best Moroccan lunch I've ever had. Her salads were innovative and delicious—especially one of beets and potatoes. Kyle had seconds. The tagine came next, very special—at least to us—because it was made with beef and tomatoes. We all oohed and ahhed over the couscous, the grains deliciously filled with the steam of the broth. It was an utterly fantastic, surprising meal and our first introduction to gracious Moroccan hospitality.

Moroccan society offered a complete change from what I'd found in Tokyo and Prague. Japanese society was closed, based on group structure, with family allegiance coming first, then networks developing out of college, and finally company employment. Invitations to Japanese houses were rare for this reason, but also because most people lived at least an hour's commute from central Tokyo. My social

Moroccan Beet and Potato Salad

Preparation time: 15 minutes
Cooking time: 30 minutes
Serves 6

2-3 medium-size beets

8-10 small new potatoes

¼ red onion, finely chopped

1-2 green onions, chopped, including green ends

1 tablespoon parsley, chopped

1 tablespoon fresh lemon juice

3 tablespoons olive oil

salt

1 teaspoon cumin

1 teaspoon paprika

½ teaspoon turmeric

Remove the greens from the beets, but leave the skins on. Boil them for around 30 minutes or until fork tender. Boil potatoes separately for 20-30 minutes, until fork tender. Peel the potatoes and beets, cut into ½-inch cubes, and combine in a mixing bowl. Add onion, green onion, parsley, lemon juice, and olive oil, and toss. Add salt and spices. Season to taste.

life revolved around the foreign community. The Japanese called us *gaijin*, outsiders.

Prague was closed for other reasons. Socially reticent and protective, the Czechs of course endured decades of Soviet mind-control that led neighbor to report on neighbor. They were still carrying the cynicism, burdens, and scars of the Warsaw Pact, slowly getting their lives back together again, opening up as a society little by little.

In Morocco, on the other hand, it's normal to be invited to private homes for business dinners. Even the simplest house had a room furnished traditionally and lined with brocaded banquettes along the walls, used exclusively for entertaining.

When Driss Benhima hosted a dinner at his family's architecturally stunning villa in Rabat, we entered the most beautiful Moroccan room I'd ever seen. There was zellige tile work on the walls, carved plaster panels, and lacelike sculpted moldings with an ornate carved cedar ceiling. The late King Hassan II came for a visit when it was nearly finished. A Moroccan room wasn't planned for the project, but the king is said to have been instrumental in the decision to add it. Friends of the family have said the king actually helped Driss's father build it, but either way the artisans who worked on the Benhimas' Moroccan room came from the Mohammed V Mausoleum, a dramatically beautiful national monument being built at the same time.

But enjoyable as Moroccan entertaining was, it was difficult at first adjusting to how late everything started. In both Tokyo and Prague, dinner usually started at 7:00 p.m. Here in Casablanca you would be invited for 8:30 p.m., most guests wouldn't arrive until 9:00 p.m. or later, and dinner came later still.

I learned this the hard way. Soon after I arrived, I was invited to a 9:00 p.m. birthday dinner that a local businessman was giving for a former US ambassador. A friend from the Consulate drove me, and I was concerned that she came to pick me up at 9:30 p.m. She said not to worry. We arrived to find just a few people and had a glass of wine.

216

Over time more and more guests filled the house and garden. There weren't any hors d'oeuvres, so we thought dinner would start soon.

A DJ launched into a program of dance music, more wine and drinks were served, and finally a few canapés. At 11:30 we sent someone inside to try to sniff out dinner cooking in the kitchen. He came back shaking his head. Maybe the dinner was being catered. At 12:30 another reconnaissance returned the same results. We were going to Tangier in the morning, so we begged off at 1:00 a.m. As we pulled out of the driveway, two large catering trucks pulled up. Dinner wasn't served until 1:30 a.m.

While Rick got by with caviar and champagne through the black market services of Signor Ferrari, it was going to take more than that to draw local Moroccans from their homes. I wasn't going to compete with Moroccan home cooking (or in-home catering for that matter) nor try to imitate refined French cuisine.

There was only one type of food I wanted to serve at Rick's: simple, straightforward dishes made with the freshest, best-quality local ingredients. Growing up in Oregon, I learned to savor fresh salmon, oysters, and crab. I looked forward to family outings in summer and early fall to gather peaches, pears, tomatoes, and cucumbers that my mother canned and pickled, letting my sister and me help.

Eating out while traveling was inculcated in me at an early age when we took a family trip to San Francisco—I was around seven— and visited a recently married cousin. We started out with cocktails at the Top of the Mark, a famous cocktail lounge of the time at the top of the Mark Hopkins Hotel, where my sister and I had Shirley Temples. Then off to North Beach and dinner at a typical Italian place called the Gold Spike, which served simple Italian food, family-style,

Crab Louis Salad

Preparation time: 15 minutes
Serves 4

Crab Louis salad originated on the West Coast—most probably debuting in 1904 in San Francisco, but there's also a claim that it was first served in 1914 at the Davenport Hotel in Spokane, Washington. Fellow Oregonian James Beard spoke highly of a Crab Louis salad he enjoyed in 1917 at Portland's Bohemian restaurant. Wherever it first appeared, this vintage West Coast salad has become a favorite of our Casablanca regulars.

SAUCE

½ cup mayonnaise

2 tablespoons cream

2 tablespoons chili sauce

2 tablespoons sweet red pepper, chopped fine

2 tablespoons green onion, chopped fine

1 tablespoon lemon juice

½ teaspoon Worcestershire sauce

on red-and-white checked tablecloths. Chianti bottles with raffia casings hung from the walls, and cats walked in and out of the kitchen. A restaurant in Chinatown, Shanghai Low, served lunch to our family of four in a little room we had all to ourselves on the second floor, with open windows looking onto the scene on Grant Street below us. Their identification with the city, an authentic atmosphere, and, in the best cases, the owner's presence made these restaurants special.

16 leaves of lettuce, butter or red leaf variety

16 leaves of mixed lettuce, julienned

12–14 ounces fresh crabmeat

4 hard-boiled eggs, quartered

2 avocados, cut in strips lengthwise, then halved

24 black pitted olives

4–8 chopped scallions

Whisk all sauce ingredients together and set aside. Place four leaves of lettuce on each plate and then divide the julienne of lettuce equally atop the leaves. Put the crab in a rounded heap in the center. Dress crab with ¼ cup sauce. Surround with the pieces of egg and avocado and the olives, and top with scallions.

Note: You may want to serve additional sauce on the side.

The 5th and Yamhill Market in Portland introduced me to farmers' markets—the smiling vegetable dealer and the coffee shop that had the old-style hamburgers with soft buns that had a sheen of grease on top. The Pike Place Market in Seattle became a favorite in my teens. The fish and seafood came from Alaska, the Northwest coast, and the Columbia River. Local growers brought in produce like shallots, which weren't yet so common. In Honolulu, at the market near the port, the cafés opened early for a breakfast of fried eggs with spicy Portuguese linguiça sausage. At the Mercado in Puerto Vallarta, I bought tortillas, cheese, and roasted chicken. I wandered through Barcelona's Boqueria, the Rialto Market in Venice, and in Tokyo the sprawling Tsukiji Fish Market, where I witnessed many a tuna auction at 5:30 a.m. followed by breakfast of the freshest sushi. Travels in Asia took me through markets in Burma, where I looked at the food but bought silk; Bangkok's Chinese market; and Calcutta's fragrant spice market. In Prague, the little French shop received its deliveries every week, and then Casablanca with my wonderful Marché Central and Marché Jamia, the spice market.

Morocco's bounty—anchovies, argan, capers, condiments, fish and seafood, fresh fruit, herbs, meat and poultry, olives and olive oil, preserved lemons, dried figs and dates, saffron, spices, and vegetables—reflects the color, exuberance, refinement, sumptuousness, and variety of the country itself. During the Protectorate, the sunny climate and year-round growing season made Morocco the breadbasket of France, leaving an agricultural legacy still reflected at the Marché Central in downtown Casablanca.

The Marché is the foundation of Rick's cuisine, and it's the Casablanca landmark that I love the most. Situated on the Boulevard Mohammed V, the sprawling indoor-outdoor Arabesque Art Deco expanse with its wide gated entrances was built in 1917 during the French Protectorate. When you walk through the arched central gate, the color and scent of the flower vendors' birds of paradise, dahlias, gladioli, lilies, and roses envelop you on both sides. The stalls, with the merchants' names written in French and Arabic, teem with fruits and vegetables in myriad shades of red, yellow, and purple. Varieties of green and black olives glisten in ceramic containers dished out by Berber women wearing djellabas and headscarves. Observant Muslim men can wash their feet in a patterned tile fountain before saying prayers. Second- and third-generation stall owners do business from dawn until 2:00 p.m., operating hours that haven't changed in a century.

Mustapha Légumes, our command central, provides all our vegetables and herbs. It's also the dispatch center for our porter, Khouiled (pronounced "Willy"), who has been plying his trade at the Marché since the '40s. Opposite Mustapha Légumes lies Mustapha Fruits, which supplies fresh figs for the house favorite, Goat Cheese Salad with Fresh Figs, and the papaya and avocados of the Tropical Shrimp Salad. In the fish hall, Zohra provides our fresh oysters and crab.

Before we bought our van, we called in orders to the Marché Central first thing in the morning, and the vendors took crates of fruit, cartons of dry goods, and baskets of oysters to Mustapha Légumes to join their crates of vegetables. Khouiled loaded everything onto a creaky, wooden handcart that he pushed through the busy streets on the thirty-minute route to our service entrance. Paid, tipped, and fortified by a stiff cup of espresso, Khouiled headed back to "base." Only his smile was bigger than mine on the day the van arrived.

The Marché Jamia, near the New Medina, is an amazing spice market, with colorful, fragrant, lush spices spilling from burlap bags: anise, cardamom, mustard seed, and rose blossoms. *Ras-el-hanout*, literally "top of the shop," is a Moroccan staple. It's a mixture of the best spices that a spice merchant has to offer, and each shop has its own secret recipe. My spice guy does a basic ras-el-hanout with seventeen spices and a deluxe mix with close to forty ingredients that include rose petals, saffron, tree bark, twigs, and various seeds. He arranges everything beautifully on a tray, smiles for a photo, then puts it all through a grinder twice and into a plastic bag. When I asked once for curry powder, he thumbed through his recipe book to find "kari" and followed the same procedure, putting cardamom, coriander seeds, cumin seeds, ginger, turmeric, and some unrecognizable ingredients through the grinder. On the way back to the restaurant, the warm bags filled the car with the most luscious scent.

I was lucky at the beginning that I was already buying from Mustapha Légumes, Mustapha Fruits, and Zohra. They all took a special interest in supplying Rick's with the best they could find. Other suppliers we winnowed out by trial and error—with an emphasis on the error.

Abdou, the first chef, thought it best—meaning easier for him—to order cakes and bread fresh from a bakery every day. While that may have been reasonable for the bread, the expensive cakes had been shuffled around from service to service, making them unfit to serve after a day. Today, our bread comes from Paul's, a French wholesale franchise, that provides the individual little olive bread, poppy-seed, and whole-grain rolls, frozen and half-cooked. Our pastry chef's desserts run the gamut from traditional (apple tart with vanilla ice cream), through creative (grilled pineapple in coconut milk), to decadent (chocolate lava cake).

"Madame, there's someone here who has a farm where they produce goat cheese," the receptionist said one day shortly after we'd opened. "Do you want to see him?"

Of course I did! Kamal Daoudi made a convincing presentation with delicious samples, but what absolutely sealed the deal was a photo album with pictures of silken-haired goats and his well-tended farm, Clos de Babette, between Fes and the mountain town of Ifrane.

Before I left the Consulate I had heard a bizarre story about Mexican nuns in Casablanca who made tortillas and even tamales by special order. For lovers of Mexican food, this was a godsend, so I repeatedly asked the American who hosted an annual Cinco de Mayo party to give me their address or phone number. It was always "*mañana.*"

Kyle and Sarah sleuthed out directions from one of the teachers at the Casablanca American School, and we set out to locate the sisters. It was a two-step process: first to a neighborhood grocery store for verbal directions, then to the convent. In true speakeasy fashion, we rang the bell at an iron gate, and someone answered on the intercom.

"*Si?*" the voice said.

"*Tortillas, por favor,*" I replied, using all of my Spanish.

After a few seconds, we heard footsteps and were welcomed into the convent. We gave our order for three packages of thirty, sat and waited facing a crucifix, and pretty soon the sister came with our tortillas. Because of them, we have a special Cinco de Mayo plate every year.

Our fishmonger, Hassan El Ofir, has been delivering our fish daily for five years now, helpfully covering us during Ramadan or the Aid Al Kabir, when the fishermen take their breaks. He selects the best John Dory, monkfish, sea bass, sea bream, sole, swordfish, and turbot with the occasional lobster making a live appearance. Our butcher, Boucherie Ilfoulki, provides filet mignon and Omaha-grade T-bones along with every cut of lamb—chops, racks, shanks, and shoulders.

Thanks to the quality and variety of the fish, meat, produce, and other specialties available, the kitchen has a real head start—but it's up to the cooks to follow the script.

Early on, I dredged out my old cooking class recipes and scoured my cookbooks for simple delicious recipes that I was used to making, my taste tests the only way to ensure quality and consistency. Appearing either on our regular menu or frequently as suggestions are: monkfish Asian-style; tropical chicken salad; and a shrimp, papaya, and avocado salad dressed with an argan oil, lemon juice, and honey vinaigrette.

Even though I suggested menu items, I decided early on not to interfere with the staff's execution. Sometimes I've had to intervene with a cook who's not ready for prime time and attempts to ad-lib. Of those rare occasions that drew me back into the kitchen, the most memorable was the night on which osso buco appeared on the menu for the first time.

Earlier in the day, I translated a very simple yet delicious recipe into French, went over it with Chef Houcine, who, unbeknownst to me, was taking the evening off. Which meant the osso buco fell into the hands of the sous chef and the meat/sauce chef, both of whom spoke little or no French. Because of my American accent, native English speakers seem to understand my spoken French best. But the recipe was written down, it was easy, and I was hoping for the best.

I went to taste the seasoning early in the evening. The shanks were swimming in liquid. I tasted the sauce—salty with an . . . inexplicable taste. Not good. We went over the recipe.

Had they dusted the shanks in flour and browned them in olive oil?

"Oui."

Had they added a cup of white wine and evaporated it off after 15 minutes?

"Oui . . . plus ou moins." More or less.

Then added the two cans of tomatoes?

"Oui."

OK, so far, so good—except that still didn't explain the liquid.

I referred to the part of the recipe which said, "If necessary to add more liquid during cooking, add bouillon or water."

Had they added bouillon?

"Oui!"

"Why?" I asked since it didn't seem to have needed it.

Because the recipe called for it.

"No, it didn't, only if the tomato liquid had evaporated."

So what did they add? A bit of water and *three* cubes of bouillon!
Well, no wonder.

We tried to rescue the sauce by spooning off the salty, bouillon
water (unfortunately rubber bulb basters aren't sold in Morocco),
adding juice from the canned tomatoes, redoing the spices, and
returning the meat to the pot to finish cooking. With a silent prayer, I
said I'd be back later to check the progress.

So at 8:30 p.m. there I was in my evening attire in the midst of a
small kitchen already in full service trying to salvage the osso buco.
The chefs had taken the meat out of the pan again. I told them to put
it back in to finish and to add some of the sauce. With my evening
bag over my arm, I mixed the *gremolata* myself. After adding it to the
sauce, I tasted it. It seemed pretty good—although by what compari-
son I wasn't sure.

A stickler to the end, I instructed the sous chef to find the marrow that had slipped out during the cooking and put it back into the
hollows of the bones. But I made the mistake of using the English
word "marrow" instead of the French word *moelle*. A panicked summons a few minutes later came from the sous chef who couldn't find
marrons, chestnuts, anywhere in the kitchen. It certainly would have
been a new turn on an old dish if we had had them!

Later that night, when we received our first order of osso buco,
the waiter said he thought the client was Italian. Oh no. I prayed he
wasn't. Turns out he was Venezuelan—and loved the dish.

Communication is obviously a two-way street, and I have learned
to clarify my instructions carefully, or, to be really efficient, I ask

Issam to review my translations with the kitchen staff. He can tell better than I can if a nodding head means comprehension or dizziness.

~~~~

Over the years we've had more than one strange personality in the kitchen. The so-called three musketeers—young, hot-shot cooks Youssef, Jamal, and Imad—could create blockbuster menus and deliver the goods.

But after learning that Jamal was taking over as *saucier*, Ghazouli, an older, illiterate cook, put a black magic hex of coded symbols printed on paper between some recipe notes, making the kitchen staff extremely nervous. A vestige of old tribal practices, black magic can wreak havoc in groups of believers, and we didn't want it to escalate. We sent Ghazouli on his twenty-one-day vacation and fired him when he came back. But that wasn't the end of it. Like Abdallah Ghattas, this unassuming character knew his way around the Tribunal as well, apparently from prior experience. He took us to court, and after four years of continuous delays and appeals we had to pay him about $7,500.

We do special menus for the holidays—New Year's, Valentine's Day, etc.—and occasionally we're approached to create a dish for a private occasion. I had to read this e-mail several times to make sure it was for real, but there it was: "I am the Pastry Chef and Personal Chef to Hugh M. Hefner at the Playboy Mansion in Beverly Hills, CA. Every year around Mr. Hefner's birthday, he has a 'Casablanca' night. This year I would like to serve desserts reminiscent of the movie. Do you have any ideas for me?"

As a matter of fact, we did. Our pastry chef at the time, Abdesalam, along with Youssef, came up with some innovative desserts with a Moroccan taste and feel: pastry with pistachio-almond paste, dates, and cinnamon cream topped by a banana wafer; and a fresh orange salad with cinnamon-almond cream. These two desserts still rotate through our daily menu.

The high points are great fun of course, but running a restaurant kitchen involves more than creating imaginative menus. It involves managing staff and training them in discipline, hygiene, punctuality, and stock control. Neither Youssef nor his predecessor, Houcine, was really up to the task.

Between piano sets, Issam took up a usual post at the end of the bar by the door of the kitchen. He monitored the comings and goings from there and kept an eye on the bar. He was planning the kitchen remodelling and building two cold rooms but didn't see Youssef trying to retrain the cooks with bad habits to have more respect for the space in which they were working. As Issam was mulling over these plans, he watched Rachid, head barman, performing his job impeccably.

Rachid had come to us through the national employment service. I'd approached them before we opened, looking for waiters and bar staff. They sent about thirty résumés, but only Rachid's impressed me. When I interviewed him, I knew he'd be a good addition to the wait-staff. Shortly after we hired him as a waiter, our barman at the time added an extra bottle to Atlantic Beach Serge's champagne bill, so we fired him on the spot.

The next day Rachid offered to try his hand at the bar. Whether monitoring Abdallah Ghattas's attempts to pilfer bottles or developing a loyal following of regular clients, Rachid was every bit the consummate professional. Always neat and well dressed, he came to work on time, had his station set up well *before* opening, and kept firm control of his stock. It had been Rachid who, when asking for a stalk of celery, stubbornly refused to address Hicham as chef.

Issam was watching Rachid performing his job night after night at a level he knew Youssef could never manage. "I wish you were the chef instead of the barman," he said to Rachid one night. As soon as Issam had said this, he started thinking, *Why couldn't Rachid be a kitchen manager and not necessarily a cooking chef?* The "chefs" we knew were creatures of their own bad habits: demanding commissions from suppliers, stealing merchandise, flouting hot tempers and big egos.

In September, I went to Paris, and Issam asked me to bring back some books from the Librarie Gourmand: *Technologie de Restaurant* and *La Cuisine Professionelle*. He gave Rachid the books to study over the month of October and told him to think hard about whether he wanted to take on what was going to be a momentous challenge. We were thrilled (relieved) when he finally said yes.

Rachid's recipe for running his kitchen was like making a soup. Start with old stock and add some young sprouts, discarding what might overpower the dish. Add green beans and a few crazy tomatoes to smooth out the taste. Mix well. Let it come to a boil, then simmer. Correct for seasoning and skim off anything that resists mixing in. Remove from the heat, and let cool. Strict and inflexible from the beginning, his approach for the undisciplined crew became somewhat like military boot camp.

November brought more than the good news of Rachid's new position in the kitchen: America had a new president-elect. My little world and the big world changed for the better at the same time, and we celebrated with an inauguration party at the restaurant. After the excitement was over, we needed to brainstorm ways to revolutionize the kitchen's approach to cooking, to move away from the traditional French approach and look at the California cuisine model of using fresh ingredients and simple presentations. We needed someone to give Rachid and his staff some new ideas.

Like a bolt of lightning, the ideal person came to mind. Leah Caplan, the daughter of Ira and Nita Caplan, dear friends from Tokyo days and among the first Usual Suspects, fit perfectly. A graduate of the Culinary Institute of America, she had recently left her position as chef-proprietor at the Washington Hotel, Restaurant, and Culinary School on a small island in Lake Michigan. She was finishing up some consulting work, but luckily for us her first three weeks of March were open. She agreed to create the menu for our Fifth Anniversary dinner and work with Rachid and his kitchen crew on a two-week training program.

Chef Leah Caplan (left) and her eager pupil, Rachid (right), who began as a kitchen manager and very quickly became our chef. Photo by Issam Chabâa

Her visit precipitated a cultural revolution. It was amazing to see the positive effect on our kitchen staff, who willingly worked extra shifts just to learn more. They responded so openly to Leah—even if it meant throwing plating symmetry to the winds. The code word in the kitchen became *sauvage*, wild, but thankfully only as far as presentation. Under her influence, they paid more attention to uniforms, kept stations cleaner, respected equipment more, and showed increased self-discipline.

We always celebrate St. Patrick's Day at Rick's, but it rarely goes beyond Irish coffees. Leah offered to prepare corned beef, bringing the preserving ingredients with her. Finding a brisket was an adventure.

Armed with a diagram of beef cuts from *The Joy of Cooking*, we went to the kosher market and talked to the butcher.

"This won't be like going into Zabar's," I warned Leah. "They may sell matzo meal, but you won't see bagels, and they won't know what corned beef is."

I was right, but the butcher was keen to find the cut of beef. He took us to his back room, where we compared anatomical diagrams, American versus French, finding the particular cut we needed in a hybrid of two French cuts. (You learn something new every day!) He gave us one end part and said to come back the next day for the full

---

Chef Leah's Casa-Mopolitan Cocktail

Preparation time: 5 minutes
Serves 2

Leah Caplan took a real shine to harissa, Moroccan chili paste, and introduced its spicy touch to meat loaf, oyster stew, and our hamburger sauce. In no time, she added it to a bottle of vodka, providing the base for this delicious, pungent cocktail.

ice

3 ounces vodka

3–6 ounces fresh-squeezed clementine juice

1/4 teaspoon harissa

2 pickled red peppers for garnish

Combine ice, vodka, juice, and harissa into a shaker, and shake vigorously. Strain into two large, chilled martini glasses, and garnish with pickled pepper.

Note: If you can't find clementines, substitute tangerines.

---

brisket. It took several days to cure—another fascinating project for the kitchen.

It was sad to say goodbye to Leah, but she left a lasting legacy at Rick's Café. Issam and I worried at first about how our little experiment would work out, the chemistry between the credentialed female American chef and the Moroccan ex-barman turned kitchen manager. The formula succeeded far beyond our expectations.

Rachid became a true chef during Leah's training sessions, and their daily one-on-one conversations. He never had had formal chef training, so, completely open, he wanted to absorb everything. She had become his mentor, and to this day he quotes Chef Leah, chapter and verse. With the confidence to start cooking himself, he took to the stove like a natural. The ultimate compliment came when Leah took me aside just before she left.

"If I were opening a restaurant in Casablanca," she said, "I'd steal Rachid away from you in a minute."

Leah had helped found the chapter of the Slow Food movement in Madison, Wisconsin, and it turned out there was a meeting in Rabat while she was in Morocco. The taxi driver got hopelessly lost, arriving ninety minutes late—partially due to having to stop on the busy highway to give the king and his entourage the right-of-way—only to find that the meeting had just started (of course). It was a spotty introduction—samples of natural food products served on plastic plates with no forks, alongside giant bottles of Coca-Cola—but I was intrigued enough to join the Rabat chapter.

Inspired by Leah's visit, we held a Slow Food seminar for other restaurateurs and hotel chefs, also inviting local producers. We had discovered that cooperatives in Morocco had formed around particular products—almonds, argan oil, dates, mint, olive oil, and saffron—and we hoped to assemble a network of buyers in Casablanca. In the Slow Food lingo we were co-producers. Unfortunately, most of the cooperatives lay too far away to participate, but their products had whetted my appetite.

After Leah left, the Slow Food movement drew me in like a moth to a flame. The old saying, "Be careful what you wish for as you just may get it," still lurks over a very special dinner at Rick's Café. The twentieth anniversary of the founding of the Slow Food movement, December 10, 2009, was designated Terra Madre (Mother Earth) Day, with Slow Food chapters and interested parties the world over encouraged to organize events to highlight locally produced specialties.

"This sounds like fun," I said to Issam. "How about we do a special dinner and order ingredients from some of these cooperatives? It's something I'd better do by myself, though. When I see what kind of products I can get, I'll work with the kitchen on a menu."

From Slow Food's resources in Italy and through the chapter in Rabat, I was soon sending e-mails all over the country. When my e-mails went unanswered, I remembered that in Morocco having an e-mail address doesn't mean the person has a computer, so text messaging became our mode of contact. Gathering all the merchandise was a hassle and a joy at the same time. All of the places were in the boonies, and the merchandise traveled by bus. CTM, the bus system in Morocco, is very organized for transporting anything, but it has its quirks.* My first experience with the system took place at the bus station when I went to pick up the couscous. I gave the agent the bill number, and he asked for my I.D. card.

---

* If sending a document, they used to make you buy five pounds of sugar to qualify for shipping so as not to compete with the post office. Now they fill a box with five pounds of rocks.

"There is a problem," he said darkly.

While I mentally translated this as "I want a bribe," I calmly asked in French what the problem was.

"The shipment was sent in the name of 'Kathy.' Your I.D. says 'Kathleen.'"

I gave him my business card, which reads "Kathy Kriger, President." He remained unconvinced, so I explained to him how difficult it was to communicate with the people in the cooperative, especially with names and correct spellings. To give him a sense of superiority I added: "And me as a foreigner speaking such poor French, they did the best they could with the information I gave them."

He considered my statement. "But there is still the responsibility to make things correct."

"Between my bad French and having to negotiate payments and shipment details, I think you need to accept the shortened version of my given name," I said testily.

He finally agreed. When I looked at the bill to see that the *only* name on it was "Caty," I laughed. So much for making things correct.

Cumin powder and seeds were coming by another bus line to an outlying bus station; salt and cumin salt by a bus route not yet defined; dates from the desert, also by bus. Olive oil, almonds, bread, and mint were hopefully coming with suppliers who were attending the dinner. Thankfully, the bus pickups got easier. On the second trip, I only had to show my I.D., no cross examination. On the third and fourth, no sooner had I walked into the depot than the agent went to the back and brought out my box.

One of the nicest surprises was the cheese from a farmer near Essaouira. Most were variations of goat cheese, but two came from cows. These were my favorites—one with a faint Parmesan taste but not as hard, and the other infused with fenugreek seeds. But the names were screwy. There were Sidi Saadi, named after the owner of the Es Saadi hotel in Marrakech, and a great one, Brik Chef Jilali, after a particularly hard-headed chef who worked in the Royal Air Maroc hospitality system. He had promised to make a personalized cheese for Chef Rachid. Fortunately he didn't suggest a Brik Madame Rick.

In the end, we had twenty special products: amazing couscous infused with vegetables, made by the woman's cooperative in Ouezzane in the north near Chefchaouen, where they produced olive oil, cumin, and cumin salt; from the south, argan oil* so pungent that I had to taste it with our shrimp, avocado, and papaya salad to see if it overpowered the vinaigrette, but, no, it made it even better, meaning our local oil was probably cut with cooking oil; *amlouh*, a mix of ground almonds, honey, and argan oil; honey from a cooperative south of Agadir; dates and saffron certified by the French; and of course the cheese.

These days I venture into the kitchen from time to time but only to pass along a compliment from a client, which warms my heart. Just recently, though, I thought I'd come up with a "gotcha" on Rachid. One day in August 2011, during Ramadan, I was going over the petty cash box with Hasnaa, the bookkeeper, reading off the items and taking the receipts.

"Ground *camel* meat?" I gulped.

---

* Argan oil is made from the nuts of the argan tree, which grows in the south of Morocco from Essaouira to Tafraout. Processing the nuts into oil is the work of Berber women's cooperatives. After the nuts are roasted over a steel drum and cracked open, the seeds are ground into a paste that is then kneaded by hand to extract the oil. A "rural legend" exists, no doubt started by the completion in Tafraout, that the Essaouira argan nuts are gathered from the droppings of goats that climb onto the branches and eat the nuts off the tree.

She handed me the receipt, 80 dirhams. That was no doubt a kilo, not very much. It was dated the nineteenth, and Rachid had made me an Essaouira tagine that night. I loved it, but had those delicious meatballs been made from camel meat? I once went through a poor market area in a taxi and shrieked on seeing the point-of-purchase display for a camel meat vendor: a long protruding bloody neck, the head and face still intact.

"Rachid should have at least told me," I said.

Three days of suspense passed while Rachid was taking some time off, but I sought him out first thing when he returned.

"Oh no, madame, I'd never do that," he said. "It was for a special meal I was making for my kitchen crew. The camel meat was a stuffing for this dish that's very traditional in the *bled*. It was a surprise for them during Ramadan."

Confidence more than restored, my mind returned to the reservation list for the night.

Who's coming to Rick's?

TWELVE
Everybody Comes to Rick's

A friend and her party in Casablanca en route to New York were separated when the New York flight was canceled. As the group was herded onto different buses for hotels unknown, someone shouted the line from the film that everybody comes to Rick's. It was the perfect place to meet, and over the years our clients have been as varied and interesting as those in the cinematic version.

One of the first visitors was Aicha Ghattas. Driving through the center of town one day, I spotted her and her daughter Souad, gathered them up in the car, and called ahead to get the tea going. It was the first time she had been back to the grand mansion by the sea—her home for some forty years—since she sold it to me two years earlier.

I thought that all the work that had gone into the place would amaze her, but she showed no reaction to the new front entrance. Gesturing toward the sweeping central stairs, I intended to lead Aicha to the second floor so she could look down at the central marble courtyard while making our way to tea in our Salon Privé. She walked right by them; they hadn't existed when she lived here.

She moved quickly across the courtyard, and that I understood. It held unpleasant memories for her of the tenants who had lived in that space and refused to move when she was trying to sell the house to me. Aicha muttered "Zerktounia" with a tinge of annoyance as she shuffled along.

She ignored the bar and instinctively made her way to the service door, which led her into the kitchen. There she found the first familiar sight: the back stairs that she had climbed thousands of times, to her the only stairs in the house. She seemed to relax.

We went up the back stairs to have tea in our private dining room, which had been Aicha's kitchen. She had served me tea many times in the months before I took possession of the house, and now it was my turn. Her old kitchen now had a fireplace, tadelakt walls, oak floors, and windows, no longer covered with newspaper, offering a panoramic view of the fishing port.

The visit was pleasant enough, and Aicha told me that she was feeling a lot better now that she was comfortably ensconced in her nearby apartment. Oddly, she showed no curiosity about the amazing changes to her old home. She wasn't exactly brimming with nostalgia for the last years she'd spent there. She'd clearly moved on . . . and I'd moved in!

~~~

Rick's Café has become my home, and people therefore eat in my living room. I've always loved giving parties, but I hate cleaning up afterward. Now, every night is a party, and guests often become part of the show. Like any hostess, I try to greet each table, and, using my Management by Walking Around credo, I give personal attention or pick up on potential problems. Waiters who see me treating clients like friends more often give service with a smile and focus less on selling up for no reason. At least that's the idea.

One Sunday night just after we'd opened, we had only four tables of clients. I greeted a French foursome at Table 10—in a corner of the courtyard, next to an intricate Syrian inlaid wood screen that rests against the wall, in front of a niche with a bronze vase filled with birds of paradise—and wished them *bon appétit*. Toward the end of

238

their meal, one of the men asked if I would mind showing him the upstairs. He offered many compliments as I showed him the room where the film was running, pointed out the Iranian and Syrian brass beaded lamps, told him about the fireplaces, and indicated the view down to the courtyard as we walked along the balustrades to the VIP Room, the Salon Privé. As we were coming back to the stairs, he said he had just moved to Casablanca and that he'd lived at one time in San Francisco when the bank for which he worked was setting up a relationship with Wells Fargo. Until then I had been stumbling along in French, but I quickly switched to English.

"Oh, I wish we'd had this part of our conversation when we started the tour, rather than at the end. What bank are you with?"

"BNP/Paribas," he replied.

This must be the replacement for the Frenchman with whom I'd met in May 2003, and who had recently been reassigned to Paris. Struggling not to smile, I said, "Oh, you must be the new president. We have a small account."

That was our second bank, and I couldn't help wonder if things would have been different if he had come to Casablanca a year earlier.

Houssein was cashier then, and I told him to offer a bottle of Beauvallon to the table. As the group was leaving, I escorted them to the door and thanked my new banker friend once again. When I passed by the cashier post, I double-checked with Houssein to make sure he had done as I asked.

"Oh no, I forgot," he said. "But that's more money for us. It's been a slow night."

"No, you have it all wrong," I said. "First, I told you to offer the wine, and the gesture of the offer is worth more than the cost. In this case, that was the new president of our bank. Give me back the cash for the wine right now."

The next morning I wrote Mr. Sibrac a note thanking him for his visit and enclosing the refund for the wine that I had intended to offer him. That afternoon a messenger delivered a handwritten thank-you note saying it was clear that I not only paid attention to detail when it came to decoration but also in serving clients. He was sure Rick's was going to be a success.

Joël Sibrac has been a regular client from that day, and when it was time to buy out the capital risk firm he was the logical person to approach. By that time, we had established ourselves, and, although the transaction was a bit complicated and protracted, we had laid the groundwork that quiet Sunday night back in the spring of 2004.

Of course sometimes personal service, or the effort to give it, goes a little too far. Madison Cox, the noted landscape architect who restored the Majorelle Garden in Marrakech for Yves Saint Laurent and Pierre Bergé, came early to Rick's. Jacques Majorelle originally hailed from Nancy, France, and Marshal Lyautey, the first French colonial administrator of Morocco, had encouraged Majorelle to come. Majorelle built a career painting Moroccan landscapes in the orientalist style as well as Art Deco posters for Moroccan tourism, but his lasting legacy is the twelve-acre garden in Marrakech that bears his name. In 1980, Yves Saint Laurent and Pierre Bergé bought the estate and later opened the gardens to the public. In 2001, Madison Cox supervised a major restoration of the gardens that recaptured the diversity and ingenuity of the original 1924 plantings.

After his first visit, Madison called a week later to make a return reservation and said he was bringing Pierre Bergé. "Oh, and by the way, Pierre owns a company that deals in caviar and other delicacies. He may be bringing some samples."

I was of course excited—but also on pins and needles. Hicham was the chef, which gave me pause. What if Pierre actually brought some caviar, how would we present it? Finding nothing available at our suppliers, I rifled around and found a small silver bowl that could be filled with shaved ice to hold a tin. Now who would serve it? I had no choice.

"Abdallah, have you ever served caviar?" I asked our *maître d'hôtel*.

"Oh, of course, madame, I know how it's done, and you can count on me to take care of Mr. Bergé," he said.

Knowing Abdallah, his remark didn't exactly inspire confidence, and, adding to my panic on the night, Bill Willis called an hour before Pierre and Madison were due to arrive.

"Kathy, I just heard that Pierre Bergé is having dinner at Rick's tonight. You know, Pierre *does* like to eat well. He has a Cordon Bleu chef who travels with him, so I thought you should know that."

"Thanks for the heads up, Bill," I gulped.

When Pierre and Madison arrived, Pierre handed me an insulated sack. "Here's some salmon tartare and some information on the caviar."

Thanking him, I was relieved there was no caviar to deal with, but it was too late to tell Abdallah. Pierre had heard so much about Rick's that he wanted a tour before sitting down to eat, and we took the stairs to the second floor. Before I could stop him, Abdallah was at Pierre's side, whispering something. Pierre looked taken aback, and as I darted over I heard Abdallah say the word "caviar."

"Abdallah, what were you asking him about caviar?" I hissed.

"Well, I just wanted to compare his way of serving it to my style."

"That's not necessary, Abdallah. Anyway, there's no caviar. Just go back downstairs."

They were at Table 9, a choice spot by a corner pillar and palm tree in the central courtyard with a clear view of the bar and piano. I walked over, thinking I might be able to steer their selection.

Caviar Presentation

Preparation time: 20 minutes
Serves 2

After eight years, caviar finally found its place on the Rick's Café menu. In the film, Major Strasser eats it directly out of the tin with a spoon—which would hardly do at today's Rick's! The key is presentation, and the goal is making it last. We buy our Iranian-method caviar from Spain, but even so it's not cheap.

shaved ice

1 (1-ounce) tin caviar

2 tablespoons sour cream

2 tablespoons white onion, chopped

1 tablespoon scallions, chopped

8 blinis

Issam pored over photos and made the rounds of shops in Casablanca's bustling wholesale section, Derb Omar. He found the service described below, but you can substitute with your own metal and glass containers.

On a silver tray, fill a silver bowl with shaved ice, in the center of which goes the tin of caviar. Above the caviar on the tray, place three clear glass bowls, into which go the sour cream, chopped white onions, and chopped scallions. Below the caviar, place a clear glass oval-shaped dish that holds 8 blinis. If you can't find ready-made blinis, Carr's Table Water Crackers, or firm, cooked rounds of new potatoes are good alternatives. Porcelain spoons accompany the presentation for serving.

Note: Two shot glasses filled with vodka from the freezer make for a perfect accompaniment.

"I've been raving to Pierre about the chili con carne," Madison said.

Hicham never seemed to follow my recipe, so there could be a spicing problem. I thought fast. "Tonight we've added chicken curry to the menu. It's my own recipe, along with homemade chutney."

Luckily they both ordered that, ending my worries. We later explored the possibility of importing caviar from Pierre's company, which offered excellent terms, but I was shocked to find the import duty set at 90 percent. Much more sensible to stick with trout eggs from fish raised in the Atlas Mountains and leave the presentation up to the kitchen.

Just as it takes time to train our staff properly, it's also been a real challenge to train some clients. Sometimes it hasn't been worth the effort. The customer isn't *always* right.

When a group of young Casablanca movers and shakers—which I'm inclined to change to divas and fakers—made a reservation for a group of twenty, a la carte, with a birthday cake, I was on my guard.

"Tell them that we don't have any space available that night for twenty people at one table. They'll have to take the two tables in the Blue Room, and there can be no moving tables around," I told the reservationist, who relayed the message.

A zellige-faced fireplace dominates the Blue Room with its wide mantel and surrounding frame in sky-blue tadelakt. A Syrian inlaid wood screen sits at one side of the room, and two brass stenciled lamps with beads provide dramatic lighting. It has a round table for eight people and three tables of four that can be combined to make a table of twelve. In this configuration, the room is beautiful and intimate.

The night of the reservation arrived, and, sitting in my corner at the bar, I could hear furniture being moved upstairs. As I wondered what was going on, one of the members of the group came down.

"We seem to have a little problem upstairs," he said. "It's Latifa's birthday, and we all need to sit together. We moved the tables even though your staff told us not to, but I assured them it was OK with you. I thought you might want to go up and tell them it's all right as they seem to be upset."

"No, it is *not* OK with me," I said. "Go upstairs, and move the tables back to where they were before. You can't just come in and take over the space as if it were your own house."

Birthdays bring out the worst in some spoiled Casablanca socialites. I received an urgent call one afternoon from a client requesting a meeting that day. I agreed, and at the appointed time a young man arrived who said he wanted to make arrangements, but we would wait for Mme. Zaki, his friend who had called. I suggested, while we waited for her, that he tell me about the party. It was to celebrate his wife's birthday . . . in *two* days. It would be for around twenty people with a set menu, but we had to wait for Mme. Zaki, his wife's best friend. An hour late, Mme. Zaki arrived, and we all talked details, fixed the menu, and determined the head count. We asked for an advance, and he gave us around $800.

On the night of the party, more guests came than originally estimated, and although he had specified a fixed number of bottles of Veuve Clicquot the group quickly ran through them.

"Don't worry," he said. "I'll be good for the difference; I just want my friends, and especially my wife, to be happy. Just let me know at the end of the night how much I owe you."

After the cake and the last bottle of champagne, they all got up at once and started to leave. I thanked them, and the maître d' ran after the husband with the bill we'd prepared, showing he owed another $500. He gave the maître d' a wad of bills and said, "If this isn't enough, just give me a call tomorrow. Plus, I want to add 2,000 dirhams more for extra tips."

Sadly, at this point the story sours. He had handed over a paltry sum on the sidewalk, and it became impossible to reach him by phone. I sent e-mails with the total we needed and added in parentheses the 2,000 dirhams for additional tips.

Two months went by.

When Mme. Zaki made a reservation, I sent a final e-mail to the client warning him that I was going to raise the issue of his outstanding payment with her. He answered my e-mail immediately with one of his own, entitled "Manners," chastising me for threatening to report him to Mme. Zaki. Nevertheless, his driver arrived within hours with the money.

I naturally rely on my entrepreneurial experience to deal with clients and problems at Rick's, but on rare occasions I have to dust off my diplomatic skills.

When I was ordering our porcelain, I found an ashtray that looked like a real classic; our palm logo and "Rick's Café" fit perfectly in the center. It was among the samples I showed Bill before placing the final order.

"That's absolutely lovely, my dear," he said, "but it just screams, 'Steal me.'"

"You're right, Bill," I said. "I'll have them add 'Casablanca' below the Rick's Café, double the order, and we can sell some for souvenirs."

We started out with one ashtray on each table and kept an eye on them. On a busy Sunday Jam Session night, Rachid, then the barman, came over to my corner.

"Madame, you've noticed that American couple at Table 7 that have been having such a good time? I just saw the woman take the ashtray from Table 8, where no one is sitting, and put it in her purse."

She wasn't going to get away with it, but how to get it back without making a big scene?

I had an idea.

I asked Rachid for pen and paper and composed the following note to accompany their bill:

Dear Clients,

I hope you have enjoyed your evening at Rick's Café, and we're happy to have you as guests. A small request before you leave—will you please take the ashtray from your handbag and put it back on the neighboring table? Thank you again for your patronage.

Madame Rick

I couldn't look when they asked for their bill, so Rachid gave me the play-by-play like a golf commentator: "The waiter is giving them the bill now. . . . The husband is reading the note. . . . He's laughing and just handed the note to his wife. . . . She looks embarrassed. She's looking over at you. . . . Now she's getting out the ashtray—ooooooh, she's putting it back on the table! . . . Congratulations, Madame!"

The couple paid their bill but decided to have more drinks, and the husband ordered a cigar. That warranted a very big silver Moët & Chandon cigar ashtray for their table, and the man quipped as the waiter presented it: "I hope she doesn't try to put this in her purse."

They were very sweet and apologetic when they came over to thank me at the end of the evening. Fortunately we all had a good laugh over it. They got a bit carried away with the ambience that made them feel they were on the set of *Casablanca*—and for us they definitely added a bit of intrigue to the night's episode!

As Issam says, when people come to Rick's, they leave Casablanca and enter *Casablanca*. And this was really the case when Jimmy Smith, the former owner of Basin Street, together with his son Dodd came in for dinner in April 2007. It was Jimmy's first trip back to Casablanca in over thirty years. Passing Basin Street by taxi on arrival from the airport, Jimmy was so depressed, Dodd told me, that he was ready to ask the driver to take them back. Fortunately Dodd convinced him to stay, and during his evening at Rick's Jimmy seemed to regain some of the feeling he had in the Casablanca of the old days. He saw that the spirit of Basin Street was alive and well in Rick's. Later Jimmy's son wrote an e-mail echoing one of the famous lines in the film *Casablanca* where Bogart says to Bergman that they will always have Paris.

"My Dad thought he had lost Casablanca," Dodd Smith wrote, "but he got it back last night thanks to you."

Sometimes when our guests step into the movie, we get a bit caught up in it ourselves. One evening a young couple was watching me and whispering to each other. When I got up from my seat at the bar, the woman approached me.

"Madame Rick, can you help us? My boyfriend and I are traveling into West Africa. Can you help us with our visa for Senegal?"

She was obviously confusing the movie with real life. I had to tell her that, no, I couldn't get them letters of transit.

Maruja Torres, a journalist for *El País* and an avid fan of the film, took the illusion seriously when she ran into Rick's and asked, "Where are they?"

She was referring to the letters of transit of course, and for just this sort of moment we had a facsimile in the same hiding place that Rick used: the top of the piano.

Exceedingly pleased, she said, "Bring me a bottle of Dom Pérignon," and sat down with us for lunch and conversation.

Another evening, two French women were sitting at Table 43, upstairs next to the balustrade, the best table in the house. You can look across the open space to the lanterns hanging from the cupola, then the beaded chandeliers over the opposite gallery and into the Blue Room. You also have a full view of the downstairs courtyard including the bar and piano. The two women commented on the decor and how much it really did look like the film.

"I've had Casablanca old-timers tell me that it looks like some of the fine restaurants in Casablanca during the epoch of the film," I said. "I want people to think that just maybe this restaurant was here *before* the film."

"It's interesting you say that," said one of them. "We're planning to film a documentary on a Polish man who ran a spy network in North Africa in the years leading up to Operation Torch. The man wrote a book on his experiences, and he mentions looking forward to his visits to Casablanca for the chance to dine well in the city's excellent restaurants."

They asked if I'd be willing to let them do some filming at Rick's, and I enthusiastically agreed. It took some time for them to get funding for *Les ombres de Casablanca*, but they came. I have a cameo walk-through, as the narrator mentions the cosmopolitan dining scene in the city.

Other people in the film business have visited; the scouts for the Casablanca location shooting of *Syriana* often came to Rick's for dinner. They even reserved the whole restaurant for their production launch party. I had my own high expectations that night, but unfortunately the only Clooney present was Rosemary on the soundtrack. Her nephew George didn't show.

～

Playing Madame Rick is never dull, and I often feel like Sam Malone, the bartender in the long-running sitcom *Cheers.* I'm not behind the bar but in my private corner keeping an eye on the action.

My seat lies at the end opposite the cash register and the door to the kitchen, perfectly situated with a diagonal view across the courtyard, the open arches that frame it, and the lantern-lit niche with birds of paradise in a bronze vase behind Table 10. My view takes in the tables and the piano, the lanterns hanging from the cupola, and of course both sides of the bar.

My corner has a little brass lamp with a shade of pleated organza made by the special craftsman in Casablanca who made our lampshades and beaded our lamps. To the side sits an exquisite brass vase from southern Morocco with Hebrew writing circling the rim, reflecting the Jewish and Berber history in that part of the country. The vase contains flowers arranged sometimes by me, but more often these days by Lahcen from the Marché Central. Above the vase hangs a beautiful antique French mirror from my family's living room.

A Japanese chest stands next to my corner; atop that sits Bill's lamp that he used as the model for our table lamps, two iron Orientalist Art Deco sculptures of camels and palms, a dramatic Orientalist camel lamp with a beaded brass shade, and pictures: my father in a white dinner jacket getting ready to play his tuba for a summer park concert; my father as a young man in an Art Nouveau frame; Bill, Slimane, and me at the bar on Bill's visit; and finally the old fashioned–looking family portrait that Issam took for our third anniversary. Among the mementos inside the chest are my mother's cookbook and—hush hush—a letter of transit.

Like *Cheers,* Rick's has its regulars and friends. Some from my earlier diplomatic days drop in from time to time along with a varied Moroccan clientele. One of our regulars tops even me for persistence. I worked with Jamal from the day I arrived in Morocco. He had received a grant from the US Trade and Development Agency funding a feasibility study and business plan for a fish canning factory in Agadir. For a bizarre reason, no doubt connected to the old fishing rights agreement, Morocco imports from Spain cans for processing tuna, mackerel, and sardines. Jamal was working with an American company with a canning process that would use local materials. It all seemed so logical—maybe too logical. During the four years I worked in support of Jamal's project, and even with some pre-contract signings with the government, the canning plant never materialized.

A year or two after we opened, I came down one night and saw Jamal at the bar.

"Tell me, Jamal, how is it going? Surely you've opened the plant by now."

"Well, no, not really. But I have a chance to do another plant canning soft drinks."

"What happened to the fish?"

"I'm still working on it, but, you know, here in Morocco these things take time."

True enough. Jamal has been coming in for five years now, and as they say in the *Cheers* theme song, everybody knows his name. Neither project has had a groundbreaking ceremony. Either there's a problem with land, or they have to wait for an industrial park to be built—the current excuse—or there are problems with city authorities. Nothing seems to happen.

"Why haven't these projects, which would be so positive for Morocco, been approved yet?" I asked him the last time he came in.

"It has to do with my father. Before he died, he made me promise not to pay bribes."

We exchanged looks of sad understanding. Clearly Jamal wasn't going to give up. Equally determined to launch his project and keep his pledge to his father, Jamal's stoic acceptance of his fate reminded me of a Japanese phrase often used to express a cruel turn of luck: *Shikata ga nai*. It can't be helped.

Rick's Café officially hit the map, in terms of tourism, when suddenly we were receiving Japanese groups. I took special pride in welcoming Japanese customers at the bar. Our first regular was Fujiwara-san, the local representative of Itochu, one of the big trading companies. We talked a bit in French, English, and Japanese, and he loved that I had lived in the Sendagi neighborhood of Tokyo, in an area called Shitamachi, the lower town. Getting out a folk-art map of the old district and pointing out sites always made me nostalgic for happy times in Tokyo. Doing so became a ritual as Fujiwara-san brought people from the Japanese Embassy, friends from Tokyo, and finally one night another of our Japanese clients, Yoshizawa-san, the head of Mitsui in Morocco.

Together, in classic Japanese drinking style, they ordered various combinations: Jack Daniel's, followed by a Casablanca beer, then maybe a vodka, back to Jack Daniel's, all the while chatting and calling me "Ka-shi-san."

One night Yoshizawa-san was talking about karaoke and asked if he could sing.

"Absolutely not. *Karaoke dame desu*," I said. No karaoke allowed— but I let him murmur along when Issam played "Night and Day." He looked wonderfully proud when I said he sounded like Mel Torme.

While we love and enjoy the tourists and ex-pats, it's a source of real pride that we have attracted a good number of fine Moroccan clients. It's fascinating to look at our most loyal clients and see what a diverse group they are. They are all individuals, not ones to follow the pack, and each has found something here special for him or her.

Mohamed Chaibi, one of the Usual Suspects and a prominent businessman, heads the Hassan II Golf Association, which sponsors an annual golf tournament that has become part of the European Tour. As busy and involved as he is, Mohamed often drops in for lunch with his close friend, Prosper, a real Casablanca old-timer. Part of Casablanca's Jewish community, Prosper has a sister in Philadelphia and other family in Israel, but he is happy to have stayed in Morocco and loves reminiscing. He needs no encouragement to share stories about the old days, particularly during World War II and Operation Torch. The American involvement and presence during that time gave great courage to the Moroccans and no doubt seeded ideas leading to the independence movement, which resulted in the end of the Protectorate in 1956.

As in the movie, Rick's is a neutral zone where you can leave troubles—or unpleasant memories—outside. In that capacity, it has served me well in restoring friendships frayed during the time I was creating it.

One Saturday night a few weeks after opening, I saw on the books a reservation for the deputy director general of our bank. I was in tears the last time we met. Now I could thank him and clear the air if necessary. He and his family clearly were enjoying themselves that night, during a time that Issam was making "We've been there" postcards for special clients. I took a photo of the family, and Issam printed out the card, which had a longer caption. At the bottom, his card read: "We've been there . . . and we own it!" Ali roared with laughter. He has since retired from the bank and looks a lot more relaxed. We've even shared a laugh over his famous remark to me: "Mme. Kriger, this is no cause for tears. This is finance!"

Some years after opening, a former head of Citibank Morocco was passing through Casablanca and made a reservation. Imagine my surprise and loss for words when I saw Ahmed, my former investor, and his wife in their party. They had avoided coming to Rick's. I greeted them warmly and could sense their reserve. I led the group upstairs to the round table in the Blue Room. It was a busy night with Issam playing beautiful music, the place looking its best. As they came downstairs to say goodbye and thank me, Ahmed came over and said, "Bravo, Kathy, you did it." Since then, they've come in often, and I hold my happy memories of Ahmed to the time prior to getting the idea to open Rick's. I hope he does the same.

Not all the cameos were wanted, though. One summer, a party of three sat at the center table in the courtyard. I had greeted them all when they sat down, but one man, dressed all in white, seemed to be looking at me a bit too intently. Their starter was ready to be served, and as I walked toward their table I realized, aghast, who the man in white was: the former director general of the capital risk firm who had tried so hard to derail my project and, failing that, had saddled me with an incompetent accountant.

"*Bon appétit*," I said through clenched teeth.

"*Comment va tu?*" he said—How ya doing?—using the terribly inappropriate familiar form.

My stomach tightened as I stared him down and said, "*Mieux*."
Better.

━

Sunday Jam Sessions have always been popular with Casablanca residents, and in that more informal atmosphere anything can happen.

One Sunday night a poignant story unfolded quietly, almost casually, at the bar during an otherwise boisterous evening.

Two Americans about my age took the last two stools at the bar next to me and we started talking. Craig and Brenda had been stationed at the US Naval Air Station in Kenitra over thirty-five years ago. Craig had recently retired to Marrakech, and Brenda and two other friends had come to Morocco for a reunion. They booked a table for dinner and Mohamed, a Moroccan friend, soon joined them. Before they went upstairs to eat they shared their story.

Craig asked if I was familiar with the 1972 coup attempt, the plot by the military to shoot down King Hassan II's plane. Yes, I knew the story, especially about the skillful pilot whose defensive maneuvering of the royal Boeing 727—fired upon by Moroccan F-5 fighter jets— saved the king's life. Craig filled in other details, including the tension over high-level corruption that remained, particularly in the Moroccan military, after an earlier and also unsuccessful coup attempt in 1971.

The king's minister of defense and interior, General Oufkir, was deemed responsible for the 1972 plot and died that evening either by suicide or murder. Half of the young military officers involved perished in the skirmishing that took place after the the king landed safely in Rabat. The family of General Oufkir and surviving pilots and other participants were rounded up and incarcerated in the notorious prison at Tazmamart, where they remained for nineteen years in deplorable isolation.

At Kenitra, Brenda threw regular parties, and American and Moroccan military and civilians became fast friends. They were all young, idealistic, and frustrated with the Vietnam war, the political divisions, and the human suffering. The Americans talked frankly to their Moroccan friends, and both sides expressed mutual frustration with the status quo in their respective countries.

At Kenitra, after the 1972 coup attempt, Craig, Brenda, and their group reeled after learning that some of their best Moroccan friends had taken part in the coup and had disappeared from sight, sent to Tazmamart. Haunted by what had happened, the Americans wondered if their political discussions had had any influence on the decision to participate in this rebellion against what they saw as a corrupt autocracy.

Soon after Craig retired to Marrakech, he came across *Operation Boraq F5, L'attaque du Boeing Royal,* written by Ahmed El Ouafi—one of his old friends from the base in Kenitra. He bought the book and read it nonstop, fascinated to learn the inside story of such a dramatic moment in Morocco's history. It also hit stirringly close to home as it recounted his friends' incarceration in Tazmamart and release in 1991. He contacted El Ouafi, who shared the phone numbers of two others, and when Brenda and other friends arrived they made plans to meet once again.

A day earlier, they met up with Casablanca resident Mohamed Al Zemmouri for the first time since 1972, inviting him to Rick's. As their story unfolded, their strong bonds of friendship and all the emotions felt on both sides, spanning more than thirty-five years, deeply touched me. Mohamed was charming, modest, and, as Brenda said, had "great skin." It was one advantage for spending nineteen years in the dark, he joked.

I invited them to join me back at the bar after their dinner. When they did, Craig added that El Ouafi's book explained that Mohamed and the other officers had followed their superior's orders to arm the F-5s and had no idea of the plot. They talked more of their days in Kenitra, and we all marveled how Mohamed evinced no bitterness and seemed so unscathed by what he'd endured.

"You really don't look sixty," I observed.

"It's what I have to show for nineteen years in a freezer," he replied darkly.

Al Zemmouri's is the ultimate "We've been there" story, the man robbed of nineteen years of his life but still retaining a strong love for his country.

Because I've lived outside America since 1985, I've always had to explain the love I feel for my country. "Just because I'm an expatriate doesn't mean I'm not patriotic," I like to say. The distance gives me a better understanding of the big picture and also how some US policies appear to a global audience. One of my objectives in leaving government to open Rick's Café was to engage in my own version of round table diplomacy.

Happily, I'm no longer "addressee unknown" at the Consulate and Embassy, and when Ambassador Sam Kaplan and his wife, Sylvia, arrived in Morocco, lunch at Rick's was one of their first stops.

The Kaplans later starred in a vignette that showcased the best of America and Morocco simultaneously. They reserved Table 1, a round table in an alcove in front of a black marble and zellige fireplace just at the entrance. A green Syrian blown-glass and brass lamp hangs from the ceiling, and on either side of the fireplace stand brass table lamps with stenciled or beaded shades. The dinner welcomed Sylvia's sister Beverly and three friends from Minneapolis.

I joined them at the table, and Sylvia commented that the place looked busy. Barbara, one of Sylvia's friends, particularly noted one of our regular bar customers, Hadj. With his portly frame, dressed either in all black or all white, cigar in hand, Hadj cuts quite a figure. Always standing and accompanied by an entourage usually including his wife and son, Hadj is our version of Norm, the regular who held down one of the corner seats at Cheers.

I drew Ambassador Kaplan's attention to a family of four sitting at the center table. Accompanied by their two young children, the man was wearing a white suit and fedora, his wife in a slinky silver cocktail dress.

"The young man is serving in Afghanistan," I said, "and the wife and kids are in Denver. He has two weeks' R&R, and they met up here at Rick's to celebrate their fourteenth wedding anniversary."

The story moved everyone at the table, so much so that Ambassador Kaplan wanted to meet them. I introduced the ambassador, who shook hands all around and thanked the man for his service, his wife and children beaming with pride.

No sooner had I'd returned to my corner than Barbara headed over to Hadj and his group with camera in hand. Wanting to avoid any embarrassment—to him or her—I dashed over.

"Barbara, let me take a photo of you with our friends."

She was relieved, and Hadj was beyond happy for the attention— so much so that he had a bottle of Moët & Chandon sent to their table. The gracious gesture floored Ambassador Kaplan, who thanked Hadj and gave him his card.

The Kaplans and friends settled down to dinner but once more responded to a request from the military family. The wife, Cat, asked if the ambassador would mind posing for a photo. Happy to oblige, Ambassador Kaplan not only posed for the photo but gave them the rest of the champagne.

⌒

I never tire of the nightly scene at Rick's, a constant source of pride and entertainment. Not a day goes by that I don't think about the minor miracle of putting together all the pieces that brought Rick's Café to life. I can't help but believe that destiny really did take a hand.

Two women sipping champagne at the bar one evening said something that brought tears to my eyes: "We work for Time Warner, and I can tell you, the brothers would be proud."

In the movie, Casablanca lay either at the end of the road or at the beginning of a new life. For me, it has been the latter. When I look back at some of the most frustrating or humiliating moments, it seems as if I've followed an Arab proverb that I love: "What is past is gone, what is hoped for is absent, for you is the hour in which you are."

There's nothing I would rather be doing. Each night, Rick's, like its cinematic namesake, welcomes a cast of characters to step into a bygone era and play their own parts in *Casablanca*.

As time goes by, the legend continues.

EPILOGUE
Casablanca and the Arab Spring

Rick's Café is an oasis of calm and nostalgia. Unfortunately, when you step out of *Casablanca* and into Casablanca, reality hits you in the face. The problems Driss Benhima and I discussed in spring of 2001 still exist and over the years have worsened.

Corruption remains rampant, whether it's the police changing a turn sign during Ramadan to shake down unsuspecting motorists on their way to the Marché Central or the sorry situation in the national hospitals where the sick must pay bribes in order to receive treatment. As minister of health, Yasmina Baddou launched a campaign to reform the system, but some politicians and members of the entrenched old guard of the medical community used the media to attack her and her family.

The Art Deco center of downtown Casablanca, dominated by the decaying Hotel Lincoln that posed as bombed-out Beirut in location shots for the film *Spy Games*, still waits for civic attention and rehabilitation. Traffic is worse than ever, and, as streets are torn up to make way for the tramway, more taxi licenses are issued to placate the taxi unions, line bureaucrats' pockets, and ensure continuing gridlock.

Expectations rose in the fall of 2003 when Casablanca changed its administrative structure and fellow representatives elected the mayor, who received real power and authority. There was a lot to be done. However, faced with daunting social and economic problems, pressure from special interests and no clear vision, the mayor fell back to his field of expertise: developing real estate with no regard for community or continuity. Residents of a neighborhood woke one

Monday morning to the sound of bulldozers clearing their local park. The property had slipped back into private hands without even the knowledge of the commune officials. Preservationists seethed after discovering that a venerated Art Deco building in line for landmark status had been demolished over a weekend. The *Al Bayane* newspaper likened one City Council meeting in 2010 to a gathering of wheeler-dealer real estate developers and their hangers-on.

There are two Casablancas—one the old Casablanca that I love: Boulevard Mohammed V with the Marché Central, the crumbling façade of the Hotel Lincoln, and blocks of Art Nouveau and Art Deco structures that desperately need preservation. These bits of history wait as construction for the tramway has all but closed down blocks of the commercial area from the Marché Central all the way to the Place des Nations Unies. Shops lining both sides of the street, which have been in business for decades, are falling into desperate straits with no compensation for lost sales.

The other Casablanca, which could be anywhere, is a new, monotonous shopping strip loaded with franchise stores near the Twin Center. The mayor's critics rail against contracts allocated without proper bids and against budget excesses as the area has undergone a beautification project that has widened sidewalks and planted trees in the median. There's no concern paid to the suffering stores on Mohammed V, but here care is taken to ensure parking and access to the shops.

Ten years after Driss Benhima challenged me to find a house in the Medina, restore it, and create Rick's Café that would entice other investors, not one new project has been introduced in the Old City, though change may be on the way. In August 2010, King Mohammed VI established and funded the Committee to Restore and Rehabilitate the Ancienne Medina. New social, cultural, and tourism projects are finally being discussed. I was honored to be nominated to the Committee. I am informally their eyes and ears of what is—and what is not—happening.

The Committee faces the challenge of trying to reconcile members comfortable with the old, close-knit, quick-fix, crony-based system with those who have more high-minded objectives in looking at new approaches using tourism and cultural projects as vehicles for social development. Change will not come easily in the Medina, ignored for decades, where all the problems of Casablanca seem to be magnified.

A resident as well as a member of the Committee, I saw firsthand the lack of communication with the local population, who stoically accepted noise, dirt, and disruption in their lives. They kept to themselves and avoided involvement in the changing scene around them. As tensions were building in Casablanca, the winds of the Arab Spring inevitably wafted over Morocco.

Marches began under the banner of the February 20 Movement, a loose organization consisting of a wide array of factions and interest groups in an effort to build numbers. They lacked a core theme, a central message, but they weren't calling for abolition of the monarchy. And they were also missing a direct opponent. There was no Ben Ali, no Mubarak-type dictator. While the local authorities were uncertain how to react, the illegal operators of street carts seized the initiative. Suddenly street carts proliferated all over Morocco, taking over sidewalks and parking strips, their owners sure that no one wanted another Mohamed Bouazizi on their hands.* Protests ebbed and flowed over succeeding Sundays. Political authorities seemed

---

* The Tunisian street vendor who set himself on fire on December 17, 2010, in protest of official mistreatment and corruption, igniting the Arab Spring.

ill-prepared in dealing with them, but King Mohammed VI cleverly preempted the Movement.

In the early 1990s, the Algerian government blocked a runoff election which an Islamist hard line party was sure to win, sparking a decadelong state of emergency. King Hassan II read the metaphorical tea leaves and strategically decided to implement changes in the education, economic, and political systems to put Morocco on the path to development. The reforms didn't come quickly and were imperfect, but it set the country on a gradual path leading only in one direction.

The first democratic elections in 1998—in which a former exiled opposition leader from the Union Socialiste des Forces Populaires (USFP), Abderrahmane Youssoufi, returned to form a coalition government—were remarkable in that they even took place. Over the years, the moderate Islamist Party of Justice and Development (PJD) had been participating in elections, and in the process had been somewhat demystified. The palace still exerted heavy influence in selecting key ministers, and some of the old rivalries and jealousies within and between parties presented—and still are—strong impediments to attracting citizens to undertake their civic responsibilities.

After the death of Hassan II in July 1999 and the accession of Mohammed VI, tremendous solidarity and optimism developed. The people still feel a solidarity with the monarchy, but a malaise has settled in among a populace resigned to political bickering, corruption, opportunism, and cronyism that pervades daily life.

King Mohammed's speech on March 9, 2011, threw down the gauntlet to the political parties and challenged the people to play their part. Standing next to him was his eight-year-old son, Hassan, heir to the throne. The symbolism of the Alaouite dynasty's four hundred years of continuity was lost on no one.

The king established a committee for constitutional reform, and once their work was complete a new constitution was submitted to a national referendum. Among the changes proposed were limitations on the monarch's role in selecting ministers, a prime minister from the party with a plurality, and an independent judiciary. An overwhelming turnout passed the referendum with a wide margin. Organizers of the February 20 Movement were invited to send representatives to participate in the work of the Committee for Constitutional Reform, but they declined. Their calls for boycotts of the referendum and subsequent elections had little effect.

During the king's visit to the Ancienne Medina in August 2011, he presented temporary housing certificates to fifteen Medina residents, representing a larger group of citizens being displaced while workmen repaired and reinforced the buildings in which they lived, which were in danger of collapsing. They all wore starched, clean djellabas, proud as, one by one, the king received them. It was a touching ceremony, and, from the kind look in the king's eyes and his rapport with the Medina residents, it was clear to me that the monarchy is the stabilizing force in Morocco, the one constant in the people's lives, for the poor and elderly the only thing they understand. Outside the cities, in poor, rural areas where people live day to day, the monarchy is seen as the sole provider. Given their ambivalence toward government, the whole notion of voting in rural areas and congested urban bidonvilles routinely devolved into receiving money in exchange for voting for a certain party.

The election scheduled for November 25 wasn't going to sweep the nation. It was one thing to vote yes for changes in the Constitution, another to find a political party to articulate to the voters why this election would be different. The PJD committed to run a full slate of candidates and tailored their message to fighting corruption, offering job training, and good governance. The younger members of the Istiqlal and USFP, parties from the governing coalition, were expected to do well, but the parties themselves, weighed down by old leadership at the top, mounted traditional campaigns. Speculation escalated about an alliance of parties—a coalition formed seemingly "just for winning," called the G8—led by Minister of Finance Mezouar of the Rassemblement National des Independents, and the Party of Authenticity and Modernity. Banking on their ties to the monarchy, they aimed their message at the top tier of business and elites, oblivious that discontent wasn't confined exclusively to the young marchers.

When the campaign opened on November 15, I didn't see signs plastered everywhere.

"It's because they've outlawed vote-buying," came the reply.

Trucks blared messages not for political parties but for a circus.

Then one Saturday afternoon, I heard chanting in the street. People were marching in orderly fashion up the Boulevard.

"Who's marching?" I asked Rachida, our receptionist.

She looked out the window. "The Justice Party." The PJD.

They were young and old, male and female, veiled and unveiled, bearded and shaven, mostly dressed in western style. I was impressed.

Before the election, people were fed up with a city overrun by greedy opportunists. There was a real desire to end graft and favoritism and to reinstate responsible governance. One friend told me that his parents, principled Casablanca elites in their eighties, were voting for the PJD because they were sick of the corruption. A member of the Ancienne Medina Committee, upset at the lack of respect shown for sacred monuments in the Medina, said he was voting PJD. One of our bar customers from a prominent family, said, "I'm embarrassed to say this, but I'm voting Friday for the first time in my life. I'm going to the left. I don't mind paying more taxes. We have to make some gestures that will help the people. We're closing our factory at 12:30 p.m. on Friday, and I'm telling all the employees to vote because this time things are going to change."

This time, things did change.

The overwhelming success of the PJD didn't surprise me. Their message seized the common refrain: wipe out corruption, improve education and job training for youth, and establish public responsibility. It was a decisive result, and now they have their chance to bring about the changes that they promised with enough concerned citizens from all walks of life willing to help.

The strength of any country is its people. There are some amazingly brilliant, clever, creative, dedicated, honest, patriotic, and talented Moroccans in all strata of society. The next few years will challenge them and others like them to take the lead in inspiring people to realize that they have a stake in building a responsible and democratic society.

What better place to start than in Casablanca? That Casablanca had to get so bad for the population to react should remind everyone concerned never to let it happen again. If anyone needs a reminder of the spirit of the real Casablanca, wander over to the grand old mansion in the Ancienne Medina with the elaborate carved wooden doors.

Faint sounds of music and laughter drift from inside. The doors open to another world, a pianist playing a song of the 1940s above the hum of voices and the clatter of glasses. Arches divide the space, and hanging lamps and stenciled lanterns cast dramatic shadows on white walls. Inlaid wooden screens and clusters of palms give tables privacy for dining as customers escape the present and step back in time. Rick's Café hosts a cosmopolitan crowd of Moroccans, Americans,

Europeans, Japanese, Koreans, and Chinese who all blend together to create today's Casablanca.

Unlike Rick, I didn't set out for something more interesting in Brazzaville. I stayed—much to the chagrin of some who appear in this book. I'm still here, perched in my corner seat at the bar, waiting expectantly and hopefully to see how the people writing the real story of Casablanca are going to decide not the ending but the beginning.

The End

Animation
Serge and Co. from Atlantic Beach, Khalid from
Garage Neptune, Maximillion Cooper of Gumball 3000,
Casablanca Table Movers

Stunts
Abdallah Ghattas, Allal, Chef Abdou, Ghazouli, Brahim

Service and Catering
Chef Rachid
An ensemble cast who perform their roles as waiters
and cooks and are key to the spirit of Rick's Café

Marché Central
Mustapha Légumes, Mustapha Fruits, Zohra Oysters,
Khouiled the porter, and Lahcen the florist

Set Decoration
Designer Extraordinaire . . . Bill Willis
Assistant Set Designer, Draftsman . . . Slimane
Architect . . . Hakim Benjelloun

Set Construction Engineering
Mr. Refas, hole digging, structure;
Hassan Chlieh, civil engineering;
Mr. Berrada, technical

CONTRACTORS

Pierre, heavy construction; Abdullah, heating/cooling
and plumbing; Abdesalam, the "Butcher of Bourgogne," wood
and metal; unapproved subcontractor of flooring and tile.
In addition, contractors for electricity, plaster, painting,
telephone and sound as well as Houssein, *chef du chantier.*

FINANCING

The Usual Suspects

Ahmed

BANK #1

HEADQUARTERS

Abdelaziz El Alami, retired president;
Khalid Oudghiri, president;
Ali, deputy director general;
Mr. El Kettani, deputy director general in charge
of investment; Nabil, investment officer

BRANCH

Mouna

BANK #2

President and Investment Director in 2003
Joel Sibrac, successor to president

CAPITAL RISK FIRM

Mr. Bakkali, Deputy Director General,
Director General #1 and #2

FINANCIAL STRATEGIST/ACCOUNTANT
Mehdi El Attar

TRANSPORTATION
Salah, Mr. Mourabit, Aicha, Youssef

OUTTAKES/NOT READY FOR PRIME TIME

ACCOUNTANTS
Mr. Belkabir, CompteCo

COOKS
Abdou, Hicham, El Baz, Houcine, Youssef, Imad, Jamal

BARMAN
Darryn

TRANSPORTATION
Aicha, Youssef

Acknowledgments

More than six years ago a bar customer asked me, "Can you write?" He was in publishing in New York and said, "Just looking at this place, I can tell you must have quite a story."

I knew I had a tale to tell, but I was also still juggling all the traps and curveballs that you've finished reading about—and I needed someone to help me find my voice and structure my story. Three years later, I touched base with a friend from my years in Tokyo, Cathie Gandel, and asked if she wanted to collaborate with me on a book recounting my adventures creating and running Rick's. I gave her a tome of a narrative as well as hundreds of e-mails that I'd sent friends over the years that better expressed my personality, indefatigable optimism, and sense of humor. Cathie wove all this together into a structure that worked, and we fed off each other's ideas and enthusiasm. During two visits to Casablanca, Cathie saw Rick's in action, even witnessing some of the scenes recounted in these pages. She also became a part of our Rick's family. This book wouldn't exist without Cathie's help, and I am profusely grateful.

Marvine Howe, author of *Morocco: The Islamist Awakening and Other Challenges*, was finishing her book as I embarked on my project and encouraged me to get the story out. My best friend, Susan Stroemple Williams, one of the early Usual Suspects, has sympathetically listened to rants and read drafts over the last six years as I struggled to find the right collaborator to help me bring this off.

I again acknowledge the psychological—not to mention financial—importance of the Usual Suspects in taking a chance on a bungling American woman and the critical support of then-wali Driss

Benhima, who's still looking over my shoulder. Mohamed Chaibi has my undying gratitude for the role he played in the exit of the capital risk firm and his continued support and friendship. I am grateful to my former husband and Kyle's father, Bob Ewing, for undertaking more than his share of Kyle's last two years of university tuition, for the lovely housewarming gift of the Syrian green blown-glass and brass lamp from him and his wife, Nancy, for my Marrakech house that now hangs over Table 1, and for becoming a Usual Suspect.

It's impossible to measure the love, comfort, and devotion I felt in the year that Kyle and Sarah spent in Casablanca, transforming a terrible period into one of precious memories. There is always room for more words to express my feelings of friendship, trust, and respect for Issam and all he does every day to keep the legend alive and a smile on my face.

Bringing the legend to life—and keeping it alive—involved a variety of actors playing major roles and others equally influential backstage. My thanks to Yasmina Baddou, Hakim Benjelloun, Saad Berrechid, Jason Brantley, Pierre Bergé, Madison Cox, Mourad Cherif, Aziz Dadas, Mehdi El Attar, Mohamed Fouzi, Emilio de la Guardia, Mohamed Hassad, Saad Hassar, Monika Henreid, Said Lamrani, Rachid Marrakchi, Elisabeth and Von Millard, Said Mouhid, Omar Naciri, Khalid Oudghiri, Khalid Safir, Nadia Salah, Carol and Lew Simons, Mahir Tammam, and Mohamed Tangi.

I again salute the inspired work of the late Bill Willis in helping create a Rick's Café that far exceeded all our expectations: Bill, I miss you and think of you every day.

Finally to the late Dr. Abderrahim Harouchi and his wife, Claude, my deep gratitude for your friendship, loyalty, and your inspiration in the early days to make Rick's a Sunday-night gathering place.

Special thanks to our agent, Jill Marr of the Sandra Dijkstra Agency, and our editor, James Jayo of Lyons Press.

My story is true, the events forever riveted to my brain because I was so surprised that the script wasn't unfolding as it does in the movies. Only in a few cases have I changed names for the sake of the characters' privacy.